WHITE DI
BLACK G

ALSO AVAILABLE FROM BLOOMSBURY:

Discourse and Ideology
Craig Martin

Race and New Religious Movements in the USA
Edited by Emily Suzanne Clark and Brad Stoddard

Stereotyping Religion
Edited by Brad Stoddard and Craig Martin

WHITE DEVILS, BLACK GODS

Race, Masculinity, and Religious Codependency

Christopher M. Driscoll

BLOOMSBURY ACADEMIC
LONDON • NEW YORK • OXFORD • NEW DELHI • SYDNEY

BLOOMSBURY ACADEMIC
Bloomsbury Publishing Plc
50 Bedford Square, London, WC1B 3DP, UK
1385 Broadway, New York, NY 10018, USA
29 Earlsfort Terrace, Dublin 2, Ireland

BLOOMSBURY, BLOOMSBURY ACADEMIC and the Diana logo are
trademarks of Bloomsbury Publishing Plc

First published in Great Britain 2023

Copyright © Christopher M. Driscoll, 2023

Christopher M. Driscoll has asserted his right under the Copyright,
Designs and Patents Act, 1988, to be identified as Author of this work.

For legal purposes the Acknowledgments on p. viii constitute an
extension of this copyright page.

Cover design: Jess Stevens
Cover image © Aliaksandr Litviniuk

All rights reserved. No part of this publication may be reproduced or transmitted
in any form or by any means, electronic or mechanical, including photocopying,
recording, or any information storage or retrieval system, without prior permission
in writing from the publishers.

Bloomsbury Publishing Plc does not have any control over, or responsibility for,
any third-party websites referred to or in this book. All internet addresses given
in this book were correct at the time of going to press. The author and publisher
regret any inconvenience caused if addresses have changed or sites have
ceased to exist, but can accept no responsibility for any such changes.

A catalogue record for this book is available from the British Library.

Library of Congress Control Number: 2022934948

ISBN: HB: 978-1-3501-7592-1
       PB: 978-1-3501-7593-8
       ePDF: 978-1-3501-7595-2
       eBook: 978-1-3501-7594-5

Typeset by Integra Software Services Pvt. Ltd.
Printed and bound in Great Britain

To find out more about our authors and books visit www.bloomsbury.com
and sign up for our newsletters

In memory of
Charles M. Driscoll
(September 17, 1949 – July 28, 2001)

CONTENTS

Acknowledgments viii

Introduction: White Devils? 1

1 "We Made It" 19
2 Hell 29
3 Theophany 41
4 I Am That I Am 57
5 Troglodytes 67
6 Authenticity 75
7 Neuroses 85
8 Codependent 99
9 Shadow Work 111
10 Shame 121
11 Abuse 133
12 Emotional Intelligence 151
13 Step Work 161

Conclusion: Discernment 179

Questions for Discussion 195
Notes 196
Bibliography 208
Index 213

ACKNOWLEDGMENTS

White Devils, Black Gods came together with support from the following folks: Sharon Welch, Jason Jeffries, Roy Speckhardt, Kristin Wintermute, and Maggie Ardiente; David Kruger, Daniel White Hodge, and Charles M. Stang; Anthony B. Pinn, Stacey Floyd-Thomas, Juan Floyd-Thomas, and David Nelson; and my colleagues at Lehigh University. I would also like to thank everyone I met at Courdea in Philadelphia, both clients and healthcare workers including Tony Lapp, Darrell Carson, Natasha Watson, John Franks, and Daniel Cantor. Dr. Cantor introduced me to the ACA program and voyaged with me as I rediscovered myself. His impact on my life cannot be measured. I also want to thank the participants of ACA meetings in the greater Philadelphia area, especially the Trinity Tuesday night fellowship. I also owe a huge debt of gratitude to the Gods and Earths that make up the Nation of the Five Percent. To the Gods I met at Allah School in Mecca and elsewhere, all praise is due! To Natural Being Allah, thank you for building with me. Thanks to Lalle Pursglove, Lucy Carroll, and Lily McMahon at Bloomsbury for making this book possible, and to Oana-Alexandra Chirilă for very helpful feedback at various stages of writing. There are no words to express my gratitude to Monica R. Miller for the time we shared together, part of which is now commemorated in this book. I also want to thank Rob, Michael, David, Chris, John, Jonathan, Linda, Kelly, Elle, and Vayda Blue. Lastly, thanks to my mother Barbara Driscoll and sister Kelli Driscoll Crews for allowing me to share some of our family business. May it help us and others who find this book.

INTRODUCTION: WHITE DEVILS?

Since I'm known to be a student of the Five Percent, people know that I was taught that the white man is the Devil. But I believe people misunderstand the practical application of that wisdom. It relates to what Jesus said about the flesh being weak. Yes, I believe the white man has a nature he must contend with, and historically, that nature has been aggressive, violent, conquering, and prone to devilishment. But to me, there's a simple explanation for that. If you have a birth record of six thousand years on a planet that's trillions of years old, with people who've been here for millions of years longer than you, you're a baby. You just need to grow up.[1]

RZA

Their God justifies every fucking thing they do.[2]

RAS KASS

Perhaps for many years our relationship with God might be termed codependent because we deal with God in the magical way that is characteristic of children. An important fruit of contemplative prayer is to be purified of our childish ideas about God. As our idea of God expands, there is no word, no way, no gesture, that can articulate it anymore. Hence, we fall into silence, the place we should have been in the first place.[3]

THOMAS KEATING

Let me begin with a philosophical axiom I teach to my students: Our experiences with other people, different from ourselves, define us as human. However, the *kind* of human we become is determined not in the Kumbaya moments when we get along with all these other people, but in how we respond when these other people tell us "No!" This "No" may appear to us through competing claims to knowledge, an ethical prohibition, personal criticism, critiquing a social convention we regard as important, or any number of instances where the experiences of others (and the expectations and motivations they carry because of those experiences) conflict with the experiences, expectations, and motivations that we carry into each moment of interaction with them.

Several examples of the kinds of "Nos!" I have in mind appear in the epigraphs above. Rap artist RZA (founding member of the Wu-Tang Clan) says "No" by characterizing white men as "babies" who lack human maturity. RZA offers the analogy of babies to soften another "No" heard over the years in various circles having to do with white men being devils. According to these beliefs, the white man is not the hard-working, morally upright free subject that we—as white men—often fashion ourselves as. Rather, we are the embodiment of evil. We are devils, according to some strands of black esoteric wisdom as well as some segments of black popular culture. Ras Kass, another hip hop artist, makes a related but distinct intervention into white masculine presumptions about ourselves when he charges that "their God justifies every fucking thing they do." Particularly, this "No" is directed toward the white man who believes in God, while it also critiques the *way* that God has functioned for so many of us for so long, as a great cosmic excuse mechanism. For many white men believers, our use of God as an excuse for bad behavior is connected to the sense of childish innocence RZA describes. Like the angry adult child of a dysfunctional parent, we blame God for our (ongoing) bad behavior so that we do not have to take responsibility for our actions and attitudes. Lastly, Christian mystic Thomas Keating offers yet another "No" framed as a kind of gnostic awareness of God's utter mystery. Rather than waxing theological on that mystery, however, he offers an admonition to the believer: As our idea of God expands, God will not leave believers acting as these codependent children—lashing out or wallowing in self-pity—rather, God will enact in believers an opportunity for deep silence. In that silence, the voice of God might be heard anew. Getting back to the axiom I offer my students, no matter whether we are black, brown, white, yellow, red; straight, gay; female, male, non-binary, etc., the quality of our humanity is decided by how we respond to our experiences of people telling us "No!" *White Devils, Black Gods: Race, Masculinity, and Religious Codependency* captures and explains the "Nos!" offered here by RZA, Ras Kass, Keating, and others, and begins a process of deeply listening to the knowledge, wisdom, and understanding of those who have sought to tell white men "No" through the trope of the "white devil." Do I argue in these pages that white men are devils? No. But I wanted to understand why others would regard us as the embodiment of evil, and I hoped that such understanding might offer an opportunity for healing and maturation of the sort RZA suggests is lacking among so many white men. Becoming comfortable with negative feedback was the first step in my journey toward understanding who I am as a white man.

Robin Wall Kimmerer's 2013 text *Braiding Sweetgrass: Indigenous Wisdom, Scientific Knowledge, and the Teachings of Plants* describes the importance of negative feedback in terms of natural science:

> Stable, balanced systems are typified by negative feedback loops, in which a change in one component incites an opposite change in another, so they balance each other out. When hunger causes increased eating, eating causes decreased hunger; satiety is possible. Negative feedback is a form of reciprocity, a coupling of forces that create balance and sustainability.[4]

Hearing a person or group tell us "No!" is an opportunity to cultivate change within ourselves that will promote "balance and sustainability" in our ecosystem. In Kimmerer's terms, telling another person "No!" is a form of reciprocity, akin to one human telling another human what they need for there to be health and balance between them.

Both historically and today, some of us respond to the kinds of "Nos!" exemplified by RZA and Ras Kass by ignoring the specific issues they address and instead turn the people telling us "No!" into problems. Rather than allowing ourselves to change when we receive negative feedback, we dig our heals into the ground and begin to treat all those other people as problems. Refusing to accept responsibility for our role or involvement in the acute issues, the people bringing these issues to our attention become problems for us. In these moments, we transform cultural disagreement, the weight of history, and competing worldviews into problems to be ignored or denied, and anyone reminding us of these things become our problems instead. So prevalent was this sensibility among white men in US history that this basic experience came to define what it meant to be black in America. In 1903, noted sociologist W.E.B. DuBois came to define blackness as the experience of existing as a problem for others.[5] The sociologist came to capture the nuance of this "problem-status" with his now-famous notion of "double-consciousness," writing that

> It is a peculiar sensation, this double-consciousness, this sense of always looking at one's self through the eyes of others, of measuring one's soul by the tape of a world that looks on in amused contempt and pity. One ever feels his two-ness,—an American, a Negro; two souls, two thoughts, two unreconciled strivings; two warring ideals in one dark body, whose dogged strength alone keeps it from being torn asunder.[6]

DuBois captures the experience of having all your negative feedback toward others ignored rather than addressed. Blending Kimmerer's and Dubois's insights, blackness can be thought of as the experience of promoting health within a community or society or nation (through the sharing of negative feedback), and then being blamed for causing the illnesses and imbalances within the community or society or nation.

DuBois also offered a way of understanding whiteness and its relationship to blackness. The two identities were bonded at a deep, deep level, born of shared experiences of confrontation. For instance, DuBois suggests that in moments when the black man "begins to dispute" various assumptions of superiority or entitlement held by white men, "the descent into hell is easy."[7] DuBois elaborates his allusion to hell, by effectively describing the moments when white "devils" are made, moments when otherwise ordinary humans are faced with people or ideas that run contrary to their own sense of self-understanding:

> On the pale, white faces which the great billows whirl upward to my tower I see again and again, often and still more often, a writing of human hatred, a deep and passionate hatred, vast by the very vagueness of its expressions. Down through the green waters, on the bottom of the world, where men move to and fro, I have seen a man—an educated gentleman—grow livid with anger because a little, silent, black woman was sitting by herself in a Pullman car. He was a white man. I have seen a great, grown man curse a little child, who had wandered into the wrong waiting-room, searching for its mother: "Here, you damned black ..." He was white. In Central Park I have seen the upper lip of a quiet, peaceful man curl back in a tigerish snarl of rage because black folk rode by in a motor car. He was a white man. We have seen, you and I, city after city drunk and furious with ungovernable lust of blood; mad with murder, destroying, killing, and cursing; torturing human victims because somebody accused of crime happened to be of the same color as the mob's innocent victims and because that color was not white! We have seen,—Merciful God! in these wild days and in the name of Civilization, Justice, and Motherhood,—what have we not seen, right here in America, of orgy, cruelty, barbarism, and murder done to men and women of Negro descent.[8]

Following from DuBois's description, perhaps, a "white" person is someone whose capacity to live in a healthy human ecosystem is offset by our difficulty living with different humans. Pressing further the description offered by DuBois, it is almost as if these white men transform into monsters in these moments of cultural contact, a kind of demonic possession takes over an otherwise placid, well-meaning white person who begins to take on the qualities of a devil. Perhaps, a "white" person can be defined as anyone who turns the person saying "No" into a problem (instead of dealing with the problem, itself, whether that problem is enslavement, police brutality, racism, misogyny, patriarchy, homophobia, etc.). Perhaps, a "white man" is someone who has turned women and people of color into problems for all the "Nos!" that they've spoken to us and that their very existence evokes in our minds. *White Devils, Black Gods* offers a way of answering how and why this transformation takes place, and ultimately offers a strategy for mitigating these demonic and/or childish fits and outbursts. But the mythical trope of the devil is not the only way to make sense of these moments, and for what it's worth to you as reader, white men are not the only humans who have ever struggled to adapt to negative feedback.

Similar in scope to how the idea of the white devil functions in this book, Kimmerer offers a usefully distinct allegory in her discussion of the Windigo myths of the Anishinaabe Native American peoples. "The Windigo," according to Kimmerer, "is a human being who has become a cannibal monster," never able to "enter the spirit world but will suffer the eternal pain of need, its essence a hunger that will never be sated … its mind a torture of unmet want."[9] "Born of our fears and our failings," Kimmerer writes, the "Windigo is the name for that within us which cares more for its own survival than for anything else."[10] Become us, or be destroyed is the logic of the Windigo. The Anishinaabe peoples would use stories of the Windigo to teach at least two central ideas. First, that greed and "thinking only of oneself" are "self-destructive" for a community and should be avoided.[11] Second, that every human—not just the Anishinaabe ones or the white ones—has "two faces—the light and the dark side of life."[12] In other words, the Anishinaabe understood that overcoming the evils brought by the Windigo required a mature understanding that the feelings and motivations that lead to self-centered, self-destructive behaviors are within all of us as humans. Hence, I do not teach my students that *how* they respond to the "Nos!" they hear determines *if* they will be regarded as human or not (by self or others). Rather, how we respond to negative feedback determines the *quality* of our human experiences. Each of us can potentially transform ourselves into monsters. Keeping sight of the horrors we are capable of *as human* is how we offset the likelihood that we will become monsters. Similarly, learning all about how we've been devils in the eyes of others might equip us to hold those devils at bay in our individual lives and our shared future.

The Windigo creation stories, for Kimmerer, "offer a glimpse into the worldview of a people, of how they understand themselves, their place in the world, and the ideals to which they aspire."[13] In learning about the Windigo, we learn about the Anishinaabe people. In turn, we learn about ourselves. I begin with this brief reference to the Windigo to make it clear that the issue of how we treat one another as human, especially those who tell us "No!", is a *human* issue. All of us, regardless of race, ethnicity, gender, geography, time period, and other factors, are capable of acting toward others with balance, reciprocity, and gratitude. And all of us are also capable of treating others with immense evil and disregard. On this score, we are all human. But historical circumstance and proximity to some groups over others sometimes give the impression that some of us are more likely to cause harm than others. The tendency of so many Western white men to treat other people as problems, in recent history, has caused some to speculate that maybe we are not fully human. Yes, humans have problems, but only a special kind of human turns other humans (with problems) into problems. This possibly "special" kind of human is where the language of "devil" is both dangerous but useful. Moving away from the Windigo and toward the subject of this book—devils—shifts the cultural frame away from several indigenous peoples and toward one of the central mythical motifs believed in by billions of people the planet over, especially those billions of humans connected to Western modes of monotheism, the belief in one supreme God who demands our adoration in one form or another. What the Windigo teaches us about how the Anishinaabe people "understand themselves, their place in the world" and their ideals has a parallel in western notions of the devil.

Over the nineteenth and twentieth centuries, various indigenous discourses emerged that characterize white men as demons or devils. This notion of the white devil became particularly prominent among certain black esoteric traditions that emerged in the United States during the twentieth century, most notably the Nation of Islam (NOI), a religio-racial[14] movement started by an enigmatic, charismatic figure named W.D. Fard Muhammad who taught that white men were devils. Another of these black esoteric traditions is called the Nation of Gods and Earths (NGE), also referred to as the "Five Percenters" or the "Five Percent" (as mentioned by RZA above). Started by a former NOI minister and Korean war veteran named Clarence Edward Smith—known to his followers as "Father Allah"—with Smith's leadership, the NGE transformed the NOI's Islamic teachings into a humanistic life philosophy organized around self-improvement, science, and numerology. The idea of "God" is transformed from some vague reference to a mystery figure and reimagined as a reference to the black man. Black men *are* Gods, and the monotheistic God is a ruse meant to deceive and deny this basic fact. Those who believe in the mystery God are therefore implicated in the deception. While the NGE would jettison many of the doctrinal and disciplinary codes of conduct associated with the NOI, the new group continued to propagate the claim that white men were devils. The first several chapters of *White Devils, Black Gods* go into much more detail about what these groups believe, about how their beliefs diverge from one another, and how the details matter for white people. The NGE came to have a profound impact on many in Harlem and throughout the United States, working to empower young black men that the larger (white) society had forgotten. Thanks to the NGE's no-nonsense attitude toward social conventions and their use of lyrical wordplay and many other factors, the NGE came to profoundly impact what became hip hop culture. It is not a coincidence that rap artists commemorate the start of a book engaging the Nation of Gods and Earths. The NGE is woven into the fabric of hip hop culture.

By the 1960s, spurred by growing NOI membership, as well as the national popularity of the NOI's most famous former member, Malcolm X, prominent white officials of the day showed interest in the goings-on of the NOI and the NGE. These groups came to be of interest to J. Edgar Hoover and the FBI, the NYPD, and, for a time, New York City Hall. Official FBI records, as well as academic and popular cultural resources, suggest that many white men in positions of prominence and leadership used the claim that white men were devils as a barometer for deeming these black esoteric traditions threats to public safety. To this day, many state prison systems regard the NGE as a gang and the Southern Poverty Law Center continues to spuriously label the Nation of Islam as a hate group.[15]

Paradoxically, the notion that white men are devils is simultaneously feared and disregarded. In addition to those who regard these groups as threats, many more white folks have tended to simply dismiss or demean these groups and their members for holding such seemingly hurtful views about white people. In my own experiences talking with other white people about the idea of the white devil, whether sympathetic to black suffering or not, white people tend to dismiss the notion as the result of black pain or ignorance. Most white folks respond to the charge with pity or indifference, while many others respond like Hoover with fear, anger, and paranoia. By the 1970s, the characterization of white men as devils had entered Western popular culture to such an extent that today many within the west are familiar with the reference. However, the notion of the white devil has received relatively little critical attention or thoughtful response from those folks characterized as devils—namely Western white men. Very few white public officials, scholars, journalists, or otherwise commentators have taken the claim seriously as a means of self-awareness and critical reflection on who we have been as white men.

White Devils, Black Gods: Race, Masculinity, and Religious Codependency is an interdisciplinary survey of the significance of the trope of the "white devil" for understanding and responding to the contemporary context of fraught tensions related to white masculinity. Themes and ideas taken from psychology, hermeneutics, history of religions, and even self-help are here woven together to present an intersectional, humanistic alternative narrative that reveals white men anew (to ourselves) by taking seriously how we have been perceived by certain black esoteric traditions. In addition to this survey, the book weds innovative application of autoethnography with clinical psychology to argue that wrestling with our responsibility to the trope of the white devil enables white men to come into greater "Knowledge of Self," a lack of which finds many white men marked by an under-the-skin self-hatred that destroys our ability to be in healthy relationships with women, people of color, or even ourselves.

Blurring the line between ethnographic study, theological polemic, and psychologist's couch, *White Devils, Black Gods* argues that white men have come to look like "devils" because of longstanding patterns of religious codependency concealed (and revealed) through various defense mechanisms at work within our social and interpersonal experiences with others. By "religious codependency," I refer to common shared cultural traditions, sacred texts, and other learned beliefs and behaviors that inflexibly prioritize the needs and desires of a specific community (or certain members within, or representatives of, that community) ahead of the wellbeing of any individual member or of outsiders. I understand codependency to be a personality disorder marked by tendencies to procure self-esteem through the preoccupation with other people's (or Gods') feelings and actions, taking responsibility for other people's (or Gods') feelings at the cost of one's own feelings, leading to poor boundary maintenance and problems with emotional regulation.[16] In referring to *religious* codependency, I am extending this clinical understanding of individual codependency to social group dynamics. Whiteness, masculinity, and monotheism converge when considered in terms of codependency. In fact, codependency offers another frame for understanding DuBois's description of whiteness, and helps to underscore why DuBois would turn to religion for describing the patterns at work in and through race. Blackness, the experience of existing as a problem, is created through a white codependent overreliance on enslaved Africans and their children. But the story extends far beyond (or before) this racial dynamic. As religious and social groups come to preoccupy themselves with a religious object like God, insiders develop atrophied senses of autonomy and selfhood, finding their sense of self in adherence to God and leading to antagonism toward both insiders and outsiders deemed a potential threat to God. This dynamic cultivates within members a savior-complex where the member or group pathologically preoccupies itself with the problems of others in constant denial of self-awareness. As a result, monotheism has cultivated in many white men a near wholesale failure to allow negative feedback (from anyone but the codependent object) to create change or growth for ourselves or for the collective health of the group. Dale S. Ryan and Jeff VanVonderen characterize the basic features of religious codependency in this way:

> Suppose for a moment that God has poor boundaries. Or that God spends his days in a frenzy, trying to get us to make the right choices. Or that God's mood is completely dependent on the choices we make: happy when we make good choices, but sad when we make bad choices. Or suppose that God is full of resentments because he is always the one who has to solve the world's problems. Or suppose that God is manipulative, trying to get things to work his way by using indirect and dishonest means. If we serve a Higher Power with any of these characteristics, we are probably in for a very troubled relationship. It is possible to serve a codependent God, but it is physically, emotionally, and spiritually exhausting.[17]

Ryan and VanVonderen characterize this codependent relationship with God as one of many possible theological postures—what we call "doctrines of God"—available to a practicing Christian or theist. However, as I argue in these pages, religious codependency is not unique to certain Christian theological postures.[18] As is demonstrated by the archives available as the history of religions, the source and prototype of this religious codependency is biblical monotheism, implicating nearly *all* Western expressions of Judaism, Christianity, and Islam as potentially prone to religious codependency. *White Devils, Black Gods* follows the work of Egyptologist Jan Assmann and what he calls a "Mosaic distinction," which marks aspects of these Patriarchal monotheistic religions as deeply flawed and prone to violence, fundamentalism, and unhealthy modes of social interaction.[19] Unlike Ryan and VanVonderen, I am not convinced that "healthy" expressions of monotheism are possible. Some may be less harmful than others, but to the extent monotheism requires accepting the belief that any of us as individuals are less important than God, even and especially in times of hardship, this book wrestles with the possibility that monotheism is inherently pathological. Philosopher Peter Sloterdijk suggests that through the notion of covenant, these monotheistic traditions essentially produce a "political phobocracy," becoming

> a new form of fear control with primarily inward effects … In this constitution, the general religious aversion to numinous things and the vengeance of the gods takes a special form: the fear of a covenant breach and its consequences … the believers find themselves confronted with the self-contradictory command to have unconditional faith in God's mercy because otherwise God will mercilessly exterminate them. This can only result in a habitus in which trust is reshaped by the fear of fear.[20]

This "fear of fear" ensures that religious formation becomes an extended practice of walking on eggshells around others *because of belief in God*, cultivating in believers a religious codependency that then shapes their outlook and expectations about the world, in general. Other expressions of religious codependency surely exist beyond monotheism, but insofar as monotheistic traditions follow the notion that there is but one God and that God is of supreme value, these traditions foster religious codependency at the level of culture (as well as ideology and psychology). Importantly, one does not have to be a practicing believer for this dynamic to impact their thinking, being, and doing. The Western world has been so deeply shaped by biblical monotheism that all Westerners today are impacted by this codependency even if they have adopted non-western traditions or rejected monotheism altogether through atheism, various forms of spirituality, or religious indifference. Religious codependency, in these ways, is a contemporary acute phenomenon expressing itself in history and worthy of our awareness while it is also a comprehensive model for theorizing a social world so deeply influenced by biblical monotheism across Western history. In effort to come out of denial about our religious codependency, *White Devils, Black Gods* provides space to consider the relationship between perceptions of self (i.e., who we are), emotional regulation, and our behavior toward others (i.e., how we act). Ultimately, I argue that white men wrestling with our status as "devil" provides an important path toward no longer acting in such devilish ways, offering insights for more healthfully sharing in intersubjective exchange with other people.

The tendencies to turn other people into problems and our difficulties with self-identification can both be thought of as personality traits in keeping with those traits often associated with the mythical figure of the devil. But what, exactly, is a devil? In the history of religions, devils are spiritual entities who experience an identity crisis as a crisis of faith. The Devil sought to be the one thing that it wasn't—God. Here, "God" represents both awareness of Knowledge of Self as well as orientation toward other selves. Devils are angels who struggle with self-love and pretend to be Gods, entities who are not content with the "natural" order of things. Devils resent that they are not God, and they set about to become God, and in their effort at denial of self, they cause greater harm toward self and others than they would have had they simply accepted their subsidiary status under God. As a result of these problems with self-love, devils inflict harm—both willfully and willingly—on those around them. When we turn every other person into a problem for ourselves, we transform social life into hell on Earth—such is the point made by DuBois in his description of the possession that takes hold on white men when others offer us negative feedback.

Humans become "devils" when we reject the divine agency of others. This is not a theological statement predicated on my "belief" so much as my use of theological language to remark on the natural order of the cosmos. In the study of religion, we call this "ontology"—the study of being. Following a blueprint set by the NGE in their reimagining of Islamic language, turning to the theological language of "God" and "devil" enables a conversation that simultaneously attends to the challenge of recognizing the nature of the universe as we've inherited it (i.e., our proper "ontology"), and accepting our place inside that universe (i.e., affirming that proper ontology). Following the wisdom offered by Keating, RZA, and Ras Kass, our inability to courageously hear the "Nos!" of other people as well as our traditional cultural relationship with the idea of God speak to a childlike arrested emotional development at work within some of us. Many white men appear unable to attend to the nuances of and emotional bandwidth necessary for personal and social maturation. Quite literally, Western American culture has taught white men to hold our emotions at a distance from ourselves. As a result, many of us are capable of little more than childish tantrums and outbursts in moments when we face negative feedback. Growing up involves coming to terms with the impact of religious formation on our behaviors and self-image. Keating, Ras Kass, and RZA all seem aware that a kind of reckoning is needed so white men might no longer maintain a codependent relationship toward a mystery God. The idea of the "devil" is the figurative "rock bottom" drawing us into an opportunity for growth within ourselves. When we recognize ourselves as having been devils in the eyes of others, there we have decided to practice self-love and trust in the natural order of the universe and take responsibility for our place in it.

According to these black esoteric traditions, Yakub was a mad scientist who lived thousands of years ago, who is responsible for creating the white race. This creation is part of the timeline rap artist RZA references, when speaking of white people as the youngest on the planet. Later chapters go into depth about who Yakub was, and how white people were "made" through a grafting process. In that process, we may or may not have ended up with certain character traits that predispose us to devilish behavior. Scholar of religion and white convert to black esoteric wisdom, Michael Muhammad Knight frames the utility of thinking about the white devil this way: "While debunking any genetic basis for the white devil, I found a more challenging truth. Even if there was no Yakub, and even if race is not the key to understanding every injustice throughout the whole of human history, recognizing whiteness as Satanic gave me something that I could use."[21] Like Knight concludes, the historical veracity of the story of Yakub is not necessary for the story to offer something useful. Following much of the work Knight has done on this topic already, but pivoting from it in significant ways, *White Devils, Black Gods* uses the trope of the white devil as a path for taking responsibility for ourselves as white men. The book offers an historical, theological, and philosophical account of the "white devil" as it appears in these black esoteric traditions, particularly as these traditions are expressed through the contemporary cultural expression of hip hop. In this way, the book provides a concise introduction to the topic of the white devil. The book also describes and analyzes the contemporary social crisis of white masculine identity in a way that does more than problematize white men but rather, seeks to both understand the sources of our inhumanity and begin a process of recovering our full(er) humanity.

Toward these goals, *White Devils, Black Gods* also offers a constructive response to some of the problems associated with a low self-image operative among white men, particularly through application of a twelve-step recovery program known as Adult Children of Alcoholics (ACA). ACA is designed to address the codependent behavior that characterizes adults who were raised in alcoholic or dysfunctional homes during childhood. I argue that the ACA recovery program offers many tools useful for coming into emotional maturity. Whilst RZA and Ras Kass help to diagnose white men's childish codependency, and Keating helps to orient ourselves toward that black wisdom, ACA offers pragmatic strategies for our maturation. Such an intervention could seem counterintuitive to some readers, so hear me out. It may seem morally appropriate for white men to work toward a low(er) self-image today because many of us have maintained a bloated sense of self-worth for so long. Rather, some humility is in order for white men. But we should not confuse self-hatred expressed as narcissism for genuine self-acceptance and self-love. We must, as white men, find a way to lament and rehabilitate the self-sick sensibilities we have inherited from our families and our culture precisely because folks with low self-images and senses of self-worth have a propensity to do (more) harm toward *self and others* than otherwise healthy, emotionally mature selves. While this is certainly not work everyone is obligated to do across all lines of social difference, the harm white men do to others is intimately connected to the harm once done to white men, and it is vital that our raced and gendered analyses and conversations begin to account for unprocessed trauma within white men.

***

White Devils, Black Gods interweaves academic theory, (auto)ethnography, memoir-styled narrative, and personal vulnerability into a method of inquiry. Autoethnography grounds my comparative analyses, while history and clinical psychological theory work together to help me draw specific conclusions about myself (as a white man), and about white men in general. The book takes seriously the claim that the "black man is God," operating according to what I call "ethnographic vitalism," an effort to "believe" in the folk theories of the people. This vitalism is a method, a kind of method-acting akin to the theatre actor who does not break character throughout the filming of a motion picture. Vitalism is the philosophical idea that a force of creation exists and undergirds the development of life, a spirit indwelt in each of us as a feature of our circumstance as alive. Generally, this vitalism lends itself to dualist thinking, as if a spirit or a spirit world exists on a plane otherwise than the one we live day to day, and that such a spirit world is the suprareality. My use of vitalism tries to avoid this dualism and instead methodologically believes that we white people are not in a binary antagonism with black and brown people, but that we were *made* by them. If the Nation of Gods and Earths maintain that Knowledge of Self involves recognition that "The original man is the Asiatic Black man; the Maker; the Owner; the Cream of the planet Earth—Father of Civilization, God of the Universe," then *my* Knowledge of Self must accept that I am the "Colored Man the Caucasian (white man). Or, Yakub's grafted Devil—the Skunk of the planet Earth."[22] As part of the same human family, we are indebted to biological and evolutionary processes. But somewhere along that creation timeline, older humans intervened in these natural processes and created "us," white people. This vitalist perspective explains why white people have no autochthonous homeland, why the archaeological and genetic record dates us relatively recently, and why we may have intergenerationally transmitted, unprocessed trauma impacting our emotional maturity and perhaps even a biochemical predisposition toward "devilishment." Importantly, white men are not "devils" because our racialized opposite, Black men, are regarded as Gods. Rather, this vitalism trusts the exegetical wisdom provided by Gods which understands white men look like devils because of our historical behavior.

Undergirding my ethnographic vitalism is the work of anthropologist John L. Jackson, Jr., whose *Harlemworld*—as a methodological principle—maintains a "specific conflation of identity and behavior as a potentially useful way of hewing antiessentialist social identities."[23] Jackson finds something of value in thinking about the narratives maintained by everyday folk about the relationship between race and behavior. Of course, as Jackson is quick to point out, racial behavioral rules are made to be broken. The very act of maintaining them at an ethnographic level enables the dismantling of the associations. My entertaining the notion that white men might be devils makes use of what Jackson calls "folk amalgamations of race and behavior,"[24] turning "the arbitrariness of [assumptions about] racialized behavior" into opportunities for "critique and contradiction."[25] Taking folk positions seriously allows us "to rethink" our own "assumptions about racial differences." *White Devils, Black Gods* is an intentional effort to intellectually trouble and socially destabilize some of our assumed-yet-often-denied and ignored assumptions about white men. According to Jackson,

> Once the claim is made that the discreteness of racial groups can be seen in the things its members do and that racial difference is mirrored in behavioral difference, the lid falls from a Pandora's box of falsifiable claims and counterclaims. Anytime a social group is categorized as such with respect to how that group supposedly behaves, this very move opens up space for exceptions to be made and stereotyped behaviors disproved.[26]

Throughout this book, I tack between a quasi-disinterested description of the trope of the white devil in the discourses of certain black esoteric traditions as I understand them, and the decidedly normative ethnographic and ethical intervention that is my effort to recover myself from the charge of being a white devil. Ultimately, readers already skeptical of the generalizability of ethnographic claims will not be convinced by the methodological vitalism I make use of here. And I make no inductive assumptions that the stories offered in the chapters that follow will be applicable across all the social and cultural spaces we have collectively come to associate with (and as) white men. That said, enough of us (as white people, and white men, especially) are impacted by religious codependency that I am confident the interventions I offer in these pages will be acutely beneficial for many white men even if not all of the book's claims are applicable to *all* white men.

Another basic theoretical foundation upon which *White Devils, Black Gods* rests is the notion that hurting people hurt people—unmetabolized trauma continues to cause pain for ourselves and others. Psychotherapist Resmaa Menakem's groundbreaking 2017 text *My Grandmother's Hands: Racialized Trauma and the Pathway to Mending Our Hearts and Bodies* makes the audacious and insightful claim that much of racial harm is connected to unresolved trauma stored in our bodies. So often, many of us assume a conscious and willful racism, general negligence and indifference, or implicit bias are at work shaping the disparate social circumstances felt across race. The tacit assumption is that if only some or most of us would change our minds, then we could solve these problems. We foster a cognitive, mental bias toward social issues, in general, assuming that changing our minds will change the world. But our bodies shape our behaviors and our thinking, too. In a remarkably refreshing intervention into conventional discussions of racial tensions, Menakem argues that much of our contemporary responses to these issues are shaped by unconscious, unprocessed trauma stored in our bodies. Whether we are talking about police shootings of unarmed black men, unjust surveillance by "Karens" in grocery stores, or explicitly racist or sexist behaviors, we have yet to fully account for the impact of past trauma stored in our bodies, which today shapes our interactions in these (and myriad other) moments of cultural contact. Trauma, for Menakem, "is the body's protective response to an event—or a series of events—that it perceives as potentially dangerous. This perception may be accurate, inaccurate, or entirely imaginary."[27] As Menakem's remarks make clear, the mere *perception* of danger is enough to induce a trauma response. "We can have a trauma response to anything we perceive as a threat," Menakem continues, emphasizing that the location of these threats is not always concrete, but can include "not only [perceived threats] to our physical safety, but to what we do, say, think, care about, believe in, or yearn for."[28] The history of anti-black violence (e.g., enslavement, lynching, Jim and Jane Crow, and contemporary police shootings) has traumatized black and brown folks, as well as white folks. The deep wounds from these events are not only stored in history and in our minds, but they are also stored in our bodies as trauma. When left unprocessed, this trauma is transmitted across family and cultural generations. The traumatic patterns that emerge from these experiences produce what Menakem characterizes as "traumatic retention."[29] When left unaddressed, these wounds risk overdetermining our behaviors and shaping the "look" of both individuals and groups:

> When this happens repeatedly over time, the trauma response can look like part of the person's personality. As years and decades pass, reflexive traumatic responses can lose context. A person may forget that something happened to him or her—and then internalize the trauma responses. These responses are typically viewed by others, and often by the person, as a personality defect. When this same strategy gets internalized and passed down over generations within a particular group, it can start to look like culture.[30]

Menakem borrows Eduardo Duran's notion of "soul wound" to characterize this intergenerational trauma. Such soul wounds can result from (1) "families in which one family member abuses or mistreats another,"[31] (2) "unsafe or abusive systems, structures, institutions, and/or cultural norms," and (3) "Through our genes. Recent work in human genetics suggests that trauma is passed on in our DNA expression, through the biochemistry of the human egg, sperm, and womb."[32] This framework has implications for understanding white men. Could we understand toxic masculinity or what Menakem calls "white-body-supremacy" as a result of intergenerationally transmitted, unprocessed trauma? I follow Menakem's notion of the intergenerational transmission of trauma as it helps to understand both where codependency comes from and how it is transmitted within families and communities. Codependency is intergenerationally transmitted, and it impacts (and is impacted by) these "soul wounds." As a result, at times in this book I write of a spiritual transformation necessary for white men. By this, I do not mean to offer an empty theological gesture but to hold together a sense of the harm that we have done as white men, with the harm done to us historically, by other men (often, and almost always under the auspices of religion). To the extent "religion" has fostered codependency among white men that then plays out through harmful behavior toward self and others, "spiritual" in this book connotes an openness to the exchange of energy between ourselves, other selves, and all that is in the multiverse. It may seem counterproductive to think about white men as having been victims of white supremacy or of our having been wounded by patriarchy. After all, when it comes to these perennial social issues, white men are perpetrators, not victims. But Menakem makes a bold and necessary claim:

> If you're a white American, your body has probably inherited a different legacy of trauma that affects *white* bodies—and, at times, may rekindle old flight, flee, or freeze responses. This trauma goes back centuries—at least as far back as the Middle Ages—and has been passed down from one white body to another for dozens of generations.[33]

One tragic irony of white supremacy and the religious codependency that fosters and sustains it is not that we treat other people differently than we treat white men. In a certain important sense, a look at history suggests we treat everyone else as we have come to expect to be treated by other white people—with deep suspicion and the constant threat of violence. As implied by Menakem, the people escaping religious persecution from Europe also reinforced the religious legitimation of persecution when they arrived at African and American shores. Leading their actions and ideas from the standpoint of past pain, our unprocessed trauma dictated our behavior and thinking in early and ongoing moments of cultural contact.

Trauma is not only intergenerational, but also intersectional. The neat, tidy categories we place the sources of our trauma into, for instance "racism," "religious persecution," "domestic abuse," or "alcoholism," are also deeply connected to each other, as they overlap (as a Venn diagram) and enmesh themselves among all of the literal biochemical and figurative, psychological "spaces" where we store our trauma. For a white man (such as myself) to do the soul-searching work of learning how to be a better white person or a better man, it will require a comprehensive evaluation of the various sources of my trauma. For instance, in this book I tell the story of my own sexual abuse at the hands of a pastor's son.

This story may seem disconnected from racial issues but is deeply relevant to understanding the behaviors and thought patterns that shape my interactions within and across competing lines of social difference. When we assess the moods, motivations, and actions of white men during moments of racial (or other sorts of) stress associated with cultural contact, are we accounting for the aggrieved little children and the wounded souls that shape our personalities and our behaviors in those situations? Are we accounting for our past victimization when we make split-second and/or deliberate decisions to victimize other people? *White Devils, Black Gods* provides an inchoate model for such accounting to begin, offering an opportunity to experience what Menakem refers to as "clean pain." Clean pain, Menakem writes, "is the pain that mends and can build your capacity for growth."[34] This is the pain associated with coming out of denial and beginning a process of healing. Stated thematically, this is the pain of recognizing that many of us as white men have been living in a hell of our own making. We are not responsible for the sins of our fathers or our perpetrators, but we are responsible for ourselves and to others that we not project our unprocessed trauma onto them. Recognition of this latter point is where so many of us fall short so often. Clean pain is the pain endured when escaping from hell. The analogy toward childishness discussed by RZA and Keating comes up in Menakem's analysis, as well:

> For generations, white-body supremacy allowed many white Americans to avoid developing the full range of necessary skills for navigating adulthood. Instead of building resilience, and accepting the full pain and grief and disappointment of human existence, they outsourced some of that pain, grief, and disappointment to dark-skinned bodies. They also hired (or forced) dark bodies to protect them. At the same time, many white Americans tried to protect themselves by retreating to all-white or mostly white enclaves.
>
> Paradoxically, these efforts made many white Americans more vulnerable to trauma and caused them to feel more fragile and threatened, in the same way that overprotecting a child encourages him or her to become a helpless, frightened adult. This is the ultimate irony of white-body supremacy: in the name of protecting and serving white Americans, it has done immense harm to them.[35]

Like children, we do not deserve the harm done to us. And we do not deserve to experience the "clean pain" that Menakem says "hurts like hell,"[36] even if it is "clean." Also like children, we exert considerable energy denying and avoiding pain, as if something about believing that our circumstances were unfair was enough to change those circumstances. Menakem refers to this "avoidance, blame, and denial" as "dirty pain," characterized by responding to social circumstances from the standpoint of unprocessed trauma, "from their most wounded parts, becom[ing] cruel or violent, or physically or emotionally run[ning] away."[37] Part of emotional maturation involves no longer wasting our time and energy wishing that the world or our circumstances were different than they are, and this means making the decision over what kind of pain we will experience. The discourse on the white devil offers a choice-point for white men: will we experience this knowledge of ourselves as devils as "dirty pain," growing defensive, violent, or running away? Or will we allow the vision of ourselves as devils to become an opportunity for experiencing clean pain? Like hell, clean pain hurts. But in a courageous confrontation with who we have been, we are offered now the possibility "to grow through our difficulties, develop nuanced skills, and mend our trauma."[38] Menakem promises that,

> In this process, the body metabolizes clean pain. The body can then settle; more room for growth is created in the nervous system; and the self becomes freer and more capable, because it now has access to energy that was previously protected, bound, and constricted.[39]

***

In the chapters that follow, I argue that the mystery, agential God of the Mosaic traditions is the source of a longstanding religious codependency that predisposes many white men toward devilish behavior. The Devil misunderstands the nature of the universe, and so perceives himself as in competition with others. When we look unflinchingly at ourselves through the eyes of many others, this "devil" is who we see. Turning the problems humans face into a problem with the humans around us, we white men have effectively isolated ourselves from our humanity because we have isolated ourselves from the humanity of others. The chapters that follow tell the story of the white devil as discussed in certain black esoteric traditions and embodied in the life circumstances, thoughts, and behaviors of many white men. The chapters tack back and forth between discussion of these traditions and reflexive analysis of what these traditions demand of white men. Early chapters focus on the traditions that give rise to the idea of the white devil. Latter chapters shift attention toward offering concrete, practical interventions into the behaviors and thinking of white men, myself included.

For most of my life, I allowed the emotional pain I experienced from the idea of God to get in the way of my emotional capacity to forge rewarding relationships with other people and the cosmos. The constructive component of this book consists in ongoing polemic against the Abrahamic mystery God of the Patriarchal religions and an embrace of the idea of God as one of many names for sheer, intersubjective exchange with others. In place of the deadbeat God of monotheism is the wisdom of Gods in the flesh, black Gods, found in our ancient history as much as on contemporary street corners and inside recording studios. From these black Gods comes the wisdom that "God" is another name for the transmission of energy. Engagement with these Gods gives way to a renewed understanding of and willingness to think of the word "God" as a term expressing the cosmic order of the universe and the experiences available to us all when that cosmic order is cultivated and celebrated rather than fought against. Our capacity to be in relationship with this God of energetic exchange is predicated on and provided by the metabolization of our stored trauma, which can only happen through a hard look at who we have been to ourselves and to others.

1 "WE MADE IT"

"I'm sorry, Miss Drizzy, for so much art-talk, silly me, rapping bout shit that I really bought,"[1] I overheard from a blacked-out Mercedes that was stuck in traffic in Time Square. It was the spring of 2014, and these lyrics were from the hottest rap song of the moment. As I waited for my then-wife to get out of Sephora, where she was buying her "Medium/Dark" foundation powder, I meditated on the lyrics coming from the late-model E-Class Benz. Amongst many fans of hip hop culture, the Jay Electronica and Jay-Z "We Made It: Remix" is remembered as a diss of Drake, who one month earlier in a *Rolling Stone* interview complained about all the art references Jay-Z makes in his music. In a retrospective of Jay-Z and Drake's relationship, *Billboard* writer Mark Elibert claims the track was the first time "both parties sent shots to each other."[2] To be sure, the song *is* disrespectful toward Drake, referring to him as a woman. Masculinity binds men in brotherhood, and sometimes, we men—all of us—commemorate that bond through criticisms of each other that come at women's expense. But the track was more than a diss.

The song is also replete with references to religion, jam-packed with theological grammar, and appeals to myths and religious institutions. These religious features of the song spoke to me because I am a professor of religion. When, in the track, Jay Electronica raps about all the "lost and forgotten black angels" who have waited for the new song, it is not a generic appeal to all black folks. He is referring to the "Lost Found" Nation of Islam and those connected to the teachings of W.D. Fard Muhammad, the enigmatic leader of what would become several distinct black esoteric traditions. Lyrics like "the Son of WD" are subjugated, unorthodox, and unrecognizable if one does not have the ears to really listen. Rather than a shout out to his biological father, Jay Electronica is referring to Fard, and situating himself (and his art) within the traditions created by Fard.

Not many people realize this, but hip hop is religious. I mean this in a few different ways. First, it literally looks like the early moments of a religion taking shape. Charismatic rappers and DJs are everywhere, and each one makes something artistic and meaningful of where they are from. References in rap songs to "ATL" or "H-Town" may as well be the biblical writer Paul referencing the people of Galatia or Corinth. In these ways, hip hop looks like religion. Beyond this "look," thanks to thinkers like Paul Tillich, Gordon Kaufman, James Cone, and Anthony Pinn, I understand religion as an effort to express the fullness of one's being. One of the most famous theologians of the twentieth century, Paul Tillich came to see that all of religion was an expression of culture. Based on this, Tillich came to understand religion as the places in culture where we find and celebrate our "ultimate concern." "God," for Tillich, is a term for describing the ground of our being, that aspect of culture that means the most to us in a world where we must find meaning for our lives.[3] Tillich's turn to culture for understanding religion set in motion a shift in how we study religion today. Today, many recognize that one of the things religion does is reveal to each of us a heightened or an exaggerated version of the self we wish to be. Hip hop, for the last forty-five years, has been a space where this sort of religious revealing takes place. White, black, brown, whoever the audience of the art, fans and producers alike continue to turn to hip hop because of this revealing. Hip hop persists as a cultural product, in no small part, because of its impact on how we feel about ourselves. So often, it orients our current selves toward who we hope to become. Simultaneously, it provides us a map for self-creation and self-definition, and it also offers an escape from ourselves so we're not as likely to succumb to our (temporary) failures. In all these ways, I understand hip hop to be a religion. Indeed, in many ways it is *my* religion, and has been since the white Christianity I was brought up with proved a failure.

The relationship between religion and rap is more explicit than what my abstract cultural sense of religion, noted above, might suggest. More was happening in "We Made It: Remix" than simply rappers beefing like early Christian church fathers. Hip hop is also deeply connected to very specific, literal religious traditions that not too many people know about, and of those who do know about these black esoteric traditions, fewer still know much about them. The Jay Electronica and Jay-Z song was tapping into these traditions. Jay Electronica's verse is filled with references to the Nation of Islam and the Nation of Gods and Earths, two related but distinct traditions emerging out of what we (scholars) refer to as black Islamic traditions. References to "the greatest story ever told," to being "the Farrakhan of rap," and to getting it "from the wheel," reflect on the positive impact of the Nation of Islam on Electronica's formation of self-hood and self-understanding. Wrapping up his verse with the Islamic Shahada—which testifies that there is no God but God, and Muhammad is his messenger—Electronica blends various features of black American Islam, noting the unity of black Islams, and arriving at recognition of the *reality* of God.

To the extent we might imagine Jay Electronica's verse a theological treatise on the sovereignty of a black God, Jay-Z's verse provides nearly a full-blown doctrine of what that God looks like. But not everyone heard the message. For one instance, in a write-up about the song, Billboard writer Erika Ramirez noted Jay Electronica's many "religious references" but only discussed Jay-Z's jabs at Drake, either ignoring or being ignorant of the many religious references in Jay-Z's verse. Lines like "Y'all hella jealous of my melatonin. I could black out at any given moment" give way to all-out apotheosis: "I'm God—G—the seventh letter made," referring to himself *as* God, and to him "all praises due," an inversion of the usual object of such veneration, away from what these traditions call a "mystery God" and toward the God within oneself. These are not references to a cosmic sky God, but to a God in the flesh, what Jay-Z emphasizes when claiming finally that he is "the true and livin'" [God], and he's "ready to chase Yakub back into caves."

Few could blame average listeners and casual fans of hip hop for not knowing about all these esoteric references. Philosopher of religion Biko Mandela Gray refers to blackness as the esoteric secret of the Western world.[4] Traditions like the NOI and NGE trade in knowledge of *that* secret, in part through significations and double entendre meant to conceal various aspects of these traditions. These traditions, as well as many rap songs discussing these traditions, are veiled on purpose, and hidden in plain sight behind hip hop's well-known braggadocio, where figures like Kanye West, Eminem, and many more make use of the idea of God to describe their artistic prowess. Jay-Z and Jay Electronica were doing something more. Their song taps into these traditions that are deeply important to many people, even if most people do not understand them. I knew about them, but perhaps, being a white boy meant I wasn't supposed to know some of this material. Or was I?

I am not simply a scholar of religion, I am a *white* scholar trained in African American religion, and I study the relationship between race, religion, and culture—including hip hop culture. From the comfort of my eight-minute commutes between my house and my office at the university, the "We Made It: Remix" had blared loudly. The song had been my personal anthem for months before that day in Time Square, and it was maybe even the "insider" voyeuristic feeling that *I should not be listening to these references* that likely had the song at the top of my playlist. It is composed of a dope beat and a brilliant hook, set off with samples from the posterchild of white masculine ignorance, the portly, curly haired major league failure, Kenny Powers. It evoked and called out in me a sense of confidence and "swagger" common from hip hop. From the warmth of my heated, leather car seat I played the track repeatedly, as I prepared to teach mostly affluent, mostly white college students. I knew what all the references to Yakub and devils meant and channeled those meanings into my consumption of the song. I didn't feel so much convicted but compelled to champion the concerns heard on the track. But I experienced something of a confrontation (within myself) that day in Time Square, between me and the two black men in the blacked-out Mercedes. For me, the song had been my secret, under wraps. In that moment in the city, I felt about it how, well, lots of white boys feel when we are blasting rap music at an intersection and a black person pulls up next to us. *Do we turn down the music? Do we roll down the windows to show them that we're cool? Do we slink down in shame and feel convicted as if they just heard us singing the n-word?*

Back in Time Square, the Mercedes had been stopped at the traffic light long enough that I listened to the entire radio-edited song. Curse words had been censored, but to my astonishment, the more dangerous religious vocabulary had not. I practically knew every word of the song, and everything that could be exegeted from it. I wore it like armor, as I went to school to teach the stuff of religion, race, and culture. My life was an exercise in woke whiteness, and this song was my little guilty pleasure. But it was not "mine" anymore. Something about the possible popularization of this content struck a nerve with me. In the city that day, my mind opened, and my mouth closed with nothing to say, frozen. At one level, I was happy and proud that this song was receiving the recognition that I thought it deserved. But at another level, that very recognition terrified me. I was awestruck by the normalization of such seemingly radical, racialized views. My professional training had given me the knowledge to know what "We Made It" was all about, but it had not provided me with the tools necessary for truly understanding the implications of the song's popularity.

In the study of religion, we have this idea of an experience with the sacred being characterized by mystery, terror, and fascination. We call it the *mysterium tremendum et fascinans*, a Latinized way of talking about an experience of the divine or of the holy, filled with a radical awareness of unanswered questions, a yearning to know more, and a caustic dread that holy ground is dangerous ground for humans. For the people who have them, these experiences evoke an immediate sense of both the beauty and splendor of life as well as the tragic ugliness of it and a sense of awe mixed with deep anxiety. That day in Time Square was one of these experiences for me, though it would not be my last. As you'll read, I have grown somewhat accustomed to experiences of Gods in the flesh, Gods on the mic, Gods threatening from the literal and figurative heart of white America—New York City—that they are about to "chase Yakub back into caves." Run-of-the-mill fans of hip hop do not know what these references mean. Many black folks don't know what these references mean, either, even though they are aspects of *Black* religion. "We Made It: Remix" was a diss track alright, but Drake was the least of its concern. Underneath the Drizzle was a full-scale ideological assault on the white Western world. I was as excited at the possibilities conveyed by the song (and the song played in Time Square), as I was terrified that it might mean finding myself on the hot seat.

***

In the minds of most white Americans, the Nation of Islam (NOI) is probably best known for its role in transforming the life and activism of Malcolm X, for organizing the 1995 Million Man March, and for its long-time leader Minister

Louis Farrakhan's often flagrant, incendiary comments about white people (and white Jews, in particular). Today, the Nation of Islam claims tens of thousands of active members who worship in distinct mosques across the country. Due to its substantial outreach efforts—which include emphases on incarcerated populations, youth, and all sorts of dispossessed folks—the NOI's influence in black America extends far beyond those listed on its membership rosters.

Central to the teachings of the NOI is the notion of Knowledge of Self. According to the Honorable Elijah Muhammad, the NOI leader who was a student of Fard's and systematized much of the original teachings, Knowledge of Self begins with recognition that the "Christian mystery God" is a lie, that God exists in the physical person of Fard Muhammad, who the Nation of Islam regards as the prophesied Mahdi—a political savior who would come at the end of the white world, and that the black man is the original man of the earth, progenitor of all the world's people. Little is known about Fard, and his origins are hotly debated and widely speculated. Most agree that Fard taught black men (and women) "the knowledge of ourselves, of God and the devil, of the measurement of the earth, of other planets, and of the civilization of some of the planets other than earth."[5] Much of Fard's teaching includes recovered knowledge of a past where black people are recognized as the original people of the earth, as well as a robust cosmology that includes an explanation about contemporary black oppression—the original people disobeyed God, and consequentially, have been forced to endure a six thousand year rule by devils created by a mad scientist named Yakub, for the purpose of tormenting the original peoples of the planet. As the Mahdi, Fard's arrival signals the end of this six-thousand-year reign, making even more significant the need for black people to learn the proper place of the black man (and woman) in the world order, atop it. According to Malcolm X, this "'true knowledge' … was that history had been 'whitened' in the white man's history books, and that the black man had been 'brainwashed for hundreds of years.' Original Man was black, in the continent called Africa where the human race had emerged on the planet Earth."[6] Suffice it to say that the idea of Knowledge of Self has historical, mythical, scientific, and psychological dimensions. It amounts to the full conversion of a person, synergy and balance between the id, ego, and the superego, between who one is and who one aspires to be. To "have" Knowledge of Self is to express oneself as actualized and fulfilled by using the facts and recovered knowledge taught by Fard and systematized by Elijah Muhammad. In these ways, Knowledge of Self is the beginning of a journey and also the destination of a journey.

In the late 1960s, a young NOI minister in New York City originally named Clarence Smith Jowars or Clarence Edward Smith—known in the NOI as Clarence 13X or to his followers as "Father Allah"—broke away from the NOI over (primarily) a theological disagreement of vital importance to adherents. Was the black man connected to God through his blackness, or did this connection to God through race mean that the black man was God in the flesh? Clarence 13X affirmed the latter possibility, and subsequently taught that proper Knowledge of Self meant each black man was God in the flesh—sovereign. This would become a core precept of the Nation of Gods and Earths (NGE), also known as the 5 percent Nation or the Five Percenters, originally formed through Father Allah's street corner philosophizing with black youth in Harlem. Personal sovereignty would come to be a priority for Father Allah. His rationale: If each black man is God, then the NOI cannot tell him or any other black man what to do. To this day, FBI documents reveal that bureau agents thought references to the "5 percent" referred to the percentage of black Muslims who continued to drink, smoke, and gamble. As NOI ministers suggested that young black men submit to the will of Allah, Father Allah was telling the youth that they only need appeal within themselves. They were God, if only they would "do the math" and tap into that potential.

Recognizing oneself as God had certain additional implications for understanding the teachings of Fard and Elijah Muhammad. If each black man was God, then they were on equal footing to Elijah Muhammad and to Fard. As a result, many of the dietary and moral restrictions imposed by the Nation of Islam were no longer necessary features of finding Knowledge of Self as a God. The choice of how to dress or eat, whether to drink or smoke weed, or any variety of "stylistic" choices would be determined by each God, unto himself. You might imagine how this doctrinal looseness will inevitably appeal to and overlap with the "do for self" ethos so common in hip hop culture. In lieu of the exceedingly disciplined moral structure offered by the NOI, Father Allah taught a system of numerology and wordplay referred to as the 120 Lessons, the Supreme Mathematics, and the Supreme Alphabet. Within the NGE, black men achieve the status of God only after mastery of the 120 Lessons (including comprehensive memorization of every lesson). Within the numerological system, these Gods are also referred to theologically as the 5 percenters of the earth, the poor righteous teachers who have Knowledge of Self. The rest of the world is divided according to 85 percent who are deaf, dumb, and blind, lacking Knowledge of Self and often lacking in awareness that the final 10 percent of the world are evil devils, bloodsuckers of the poor, who have as their cosmic task ensuring that the 85 percent remain blind, deaf, and dumb.

Throughout *White Devils, Black Gods*, I refer to the teachings of the NOI and the NGE in ways that sometimes flatten the major (and minor) distinctions between them. When necessary, I will telegraph those differences. One place they disagree is on this point over whether only Fard is God, or does the story Fard taught demonstrate the natural divinity of black men. Another important difference is that the NGE do not regard themselves as a "religion" but a humanistic life philosophy, a "culture," predicated on *science*, as opposed to faith. Additionally, the NOI understands itself as part of the global Ummah, the brotherhood of believing Muslims throughout the world (even though the exact relationship is complicated). The NGE, on the other hand, make use of the vocabulary offered by

Islam, but reframe many key concepts as signifiers of human capacity. "Allah" refers to "Arm. Leg. Leg. Arm. Head" and Islam can mean "I Self Lord am/and Master," these backronyms emphasizing the embodied theologies and the importance of black skin, flesh, and being to Knowledge of Self. Despite these vital differences, both agree that proper Knowledge of Self includes not only recognition of one (or more) black man as God, but also attention to white men as a race of devils. In general, we white men are the 10 percent.

In this book, when I refer to "we" I am referring to white men. When I mean to include men of other races, I will say so. When I mean to include white women, I will say that, too. So, where do "we" come from, we white devils? According to the teachings of the NOI and the NGE, white people are about 6000 years old. Around 6600 years ago, about 70 percent of the world's population was satisfied with the order of things, and about 30 percent were dissatisfied. A precocious, gifted black youth with an extremely inquisitive mind decided his lot in life would be to sow discord among the satisfied through "mischief" and a special science he called "tricknology." While playing with some magnets, the young boy came to understand the scientific principle of "like repelling like, and attracting unalike." His name was Yakub, and he would grow to be a powerful scientist and would apply this principle to human populations. Withdrawing to the island of Pelan, called the Island of Patmos in the Bible, Yakub and his followers set about a 600-year grafting process. Through population regulation, what in scientific literature is called "strong" or "positive" selection, Yakub forced lighter skinned people to mate with other lighter skinned people. Lighter babies would be kept; darker babies would be killed swiftly. After 200 years, the brown race was made. The red and yellow races were formed simultaneously across the next 200 years. Finally, after the last 200 years, the white race came into our being. After this much grafting, the white race was an amalgamation of recessive human traits meaning that we were, at best, the least human of the lot. At worst, we were not human at all. It is thought that all of this took place c. 4600 BCE–3800 BCE. After some time, around 3200 BCE, the white race moved from the island to the mainland. This would include modern-day Turkey, and perhaps Iran and Iraq. After only a short time, people realized that this white race was unfit for civilization. And so, we were tied up and walked from the arid lands of the Middle East to Europe, into the lands of today's Macedonia, the Balkans, and the Caucus Mountains. In the caves of Europe, we lived for 2000 years, subsisting as savage cave dwellers with our dogs our best companions. Then, around 1100 BCE, the man referred to in the Bible as Moses led us out of the caves and taught us how to terrorize the world's populations. Chronologically, perhaps this narrative correlates to the historic battle of Troy (at least one or some of them) and to what some have called the Late Bronze Age Collapse and the Mediterranean (or Greek) Dark Ages. Presumably, we were the invading forces that led to civilizational collapse across the region—some might speculate we were the Sea People who summarily terrorized all the established city-states of the Eastern Mediterranean during this period. If the story sounds too fanciful to be true, keep reading.

***

In the teachings of the NOI and the NGE, Yakub is the black scientist that gives birth to the white race. But in popular parlance, Yakub has come to refer to we white devils in general. And so, from the center of Time Square, Jay-Z was telling me and the rest of the white world that he wanted to chase us back into those caves in Europe. He was signaling to us that our reign over the world had for others been a story of terror and torment, and that the evils of tricknology were coming to an end. In the eloquence offered by Jay, he would be showing up to the "Last Supper" in some brand-new Air Jordan sneakers. I stood on a square block of concrete convinced that a particular truth was taking hold across the nation and maybe the West, in general, exemplified by the syncopated proclamations offered by the two Jays. "We Made It" was proclaiming that the white man's rule was ending. And this truth would be increasingly hard to swallow for some of us as Americans—especially those of us with the devilish traits brought into existence by the mad black scientist, Yakub.

Knowledge of Self makes sense to me; the need for an origin for the sake of social identification, the ego's need for a model external to oneself, and the comprehensive explanation of black suffering and white social ascendance (this, in the study of religion we call a "theodicy" or "anthropodicy" to get technical). As a fan of hip hop, and a student of black religion, all of this made sense. But as a white man, I had some reservations. Did suggestions about the end of the white world scare me, and if so, why? How could I square the two sides of *my* identity? Who, exactly, had "made it?" For reasons that will become clear soon enough, I was in desperate need of Knowledge of Self. Somewhere in my life journey, I either lost it or never had it to begin with. And so, like so many white folks constantly guilty of appropriating black culture, this black wisdom was appealing to me, and I wanted it. Only there was a catch. If I accepted the veracity of the black man's Knowledge of Self, I had to also accept that—at some level, in some way—if black men were God, I was a white devil.

How we see and understand ourselves and the world is intimately related to who we are—what our eyes and ears can see and hear. I am a fan of "We Made It," and sing it often (still). I know every word by heart. But from under the LED canvases of Time Square, I came to realize that if I had any integrity at all—as a scholar of religion, as a fan of hip hop, or as a human being, I had to square with the knowledge, wisdom, and understanding offered by the story of Yakub for my (own) white masculine self. Coming into Knowledge of Self had been key to Jay-Z and Jay Electronica's personal victories, and surely tens of thousands of black Muslims would not profess as much if the notion of Knowledge of Self did not concretely impact their lives and the lives of so many black and brown folks. Selfishly, I wanted what they had, but it came with this humbling catch: I could accept it but only at a severe cost to my ego. However I felt about myself, an entire religious worldview had sprung up across the last few hundred years (thousands depending on whether we believe the worldview or not) that situated me (and folks like me) as devils. I had to internalize the meanings associated with the story of Yakub with my knowledge, wisdom, and understanding of myself and my white male counterparts. This book is my effort to do just that. If the black man is God, what does that mean for white men? Even if black men are not Gods, some aspects of our white behavior over the last centuries have seen to it that others see white men as the embodiment of evil. This awareness struck at the core of my being—at that being Tillich talked about as the "being" at the root of our religious understanding. I found meaning in hip hop. The "white" world had not provided it. I found it in hip hop. And now, under those lights of the city, I was convicted by song and sense of self, alike. I had to know how I fit into the story of white devils. I had to know how white devils would fit into the story of myself and my life. Would the knowledge of myself as a devil provide new avenues for understanding my role as teacher, brother, son, and partner? Or, would it simply recast hatred into self-hatred? Could I escape the shadow cast by a devilish past—our collective white masculine past? This book chronicles my attempt to do and think and be something different … to the extent that is possible. What follows is a story of salvation sought but not deserved, and an exposé of the devil inside of myself and the devils who are my compatriots as white men.

2 HELL

For many people, church is a place of peace and hope—where people come to find and connect with God. Many believers in God feel closer to God when inside of mosques, synagogues, and churches. Sure, many folks—especially white folks—will talk of finding God in nature, but if they are referring to the Judeo-Christian mystery God, these institutional spaces are where they learn about *that* God. But for many unlucky people, we find more than God while at church. I first found God at Kings Highway Christian Church in Shreveport, Louisiana. But I also found the devil.

I grew up in the church. It was a mainline Church, the Christian Church (Disciples of Christ). The denomination is known for being fairly progressive on social and theological issues. Their primary unifying doctrine stipulates an idea often attributed to St. Augustine: "In essentials, unity; In non-essentials, liberty; and in all things, charity." From a very early age, I was able to believe essentially what I wanted about God and religion without fear of getting kicked out of the church. At the same time, the church was in the deep south. Shreveport is the parish seat of Caddo Parish—which had the nickname "Bloody Caddo" during the Reconstruction period because it was one of few places in the United States where white folks literally made a sport of hunting black people. The church where I grew up was a *theologically* progressive space set within a deeply socially conservative space with an incredibly racist, violent history. Like many white churches in the Bible belt, we only had one black member. The other black folks I knew from that church all worked there.

In the 1980s, the corner of the church property was a spot where the Ku-Klux-Klan would hold small-scale rallies. Mind you, they weren't picketing *our* church. Neither was our church affiliated with the rallies, as far as I know. I don't recall the pastor ever saying much (or anything) about those rallies, but I do remember one Sunday the church service ended and my father walked over to talk to the Klansmen. I still don't know what they talked about. He didn't take me with him.

But he still went. I must have been five years old. The church property, adjacent to two well-traveled streets in the town (Line Avenue and Kings Highway), was deemed safe by the Klan members. But only one black person in town thought it was safe enough to join us in worship.

The social and geographic contexts of the church were complicated, and tragic, but for me at the time, they didn't shake a stick at the chaos inside my own family. My father was an alcoholic. He was a lot more than that; but never less than that. His alcoholism contributed to pervasive family dysfunction. I grew up seeing my mother exert a considerable amount of time and energy in the church. The church was her escape—a codependent psychological safe haven. Who could blame her? It was her way of getting away from our toxic home environment. And from birth until about age seventeen, I would go with her. We were church people, broken, and hoping against hope that the church offered an avenue to address that brokenness. To this day, both my mother and sister are pastors within the Disciples of Christ denomination. My sister went to seminary and is an ordained pastor, while my mother eventually—through continuing education classes—became comissioned as a pastor. Our flight away from family dysfunction turned into our family business, religion. Before these careers, church offered us community. Church wasn't necessarily "good" or "bad," (although we fawned that it was good); it simply *was*. It was the water we swam in. And in that water, there were devils.

Across 1992–93, between the ages of ten and eleven, I learned all about sexuality from my pastor's son. His name was Chris, too. He was several years older than me, and well on the other side of puberty. I wasn't. I didn't know what masturbation was. I certainly didn't know anything more than that. But I knew what he was showing me felt good when I did it to myself. And I knew that it was wrong. He showed me how to masturbate at my family home. He showed me how to do it at his house. Chris showed me how to do it in my grandparents' townhouse. He even masturbated in front of me at church on at least one occasion. How many people can say they learned how to masturbate at church? I can.

The abuse I experienced is not unique. I'm not alone. One 2004 Catholic Church study found that more than 10,000 boys had been abused by approximately 4000 Catholic Priests.[1] But sexual abuse within church communities isn't only a Catholic problem. Recent reports from the *Houston Chronicle* found that across a twenty-year period, more than 350 Southern Baptist Church leaders "left behind more than 700 victims, many of them shunned by their churches, left to themselves to rebuild their lives."[2] My abuser was not a Catholic Priest, and my church was not Southern Baptist. Yet these numbers make me wonder where Chris learned everything he taught me.

Sexual trauma is perverse and insidious. As commonly occurs for victims of childhood sexual abuse, I became despondent, aggressive, and mean-spirited, and my behavior worsened. One Sunday, I exploded violently at church. We had a recreation room in the church where all the kids would congregate between Sunday

School and "Big Church." It had a pool table in it. I was in there with some girls who were my friends—I may have "liked" one of them, I don't remember. Chris came into the room and started joking with the girls. At the time, the girls tended to tease me (like girls that age are wont to do to the boys around them). They said something to Chris that embarrassed me, and my body filled up with rage. I ran to the pool table, picked up a ball, and hurled it at him. Of course, nobody in the room (or the church) knew he had been abusing me. In that moment, I looked like the asshole, and I didn't care. I picked up another ball and chucked it at him. The girls and other folks ran out from around the proximity of Chris, while the balls kept flying his way. At first, they thought I was bluffing and many in the room responded with different versions of "lighten up." But I didn't. By the fourth ball, they knew something was wrong. I knew I couldn't stop. I threw those billiard balls as hard as I could, chasing Chris out of the room and down the hall. I didn't stop until adults out in the hall started screaming and jumped in my line of fire.

Our name meant "Christ—bearer" but to me he was a devil. And although he's been dead for the last several years, he'll always be a devil to me.

The day of my explosion, I cried throughout the church service, seething in anger and unable to express myself because the worship of God came first. After we got home, my mother sat me down and I lied to her so that I could tell her the truth. I told her all about the playboy magazines he had shown me, his constant exhibitionism, and him convincing me to touch him, only I concocted a story that he had succeeded in all this grooming and abuse by violently threatened me and my family if I ever told anyone about what he had been doing. My shame was too great. I didn't realize it was still abuse even if I was ambivalent about it or liked parts of it. I didn't know that my being a child made a world of difference. I just knew what my white Christian parents had taught me: that sex was bad and not to be discussed, and that homosexuality was a huge sin in the eyes of God. I knew all this long before Chris taught me how to masturbate. I already knew how to hate others and hate myself. I had learned it in church. When I had finished telling my mom about the abuse, she and I made a pact to not tell my father, agreeing that he drank too much to handle this information in a healthy way. I was only eleven years old.

The Christianity I was raised with had not prepared me for these experiences, but it had predisposed me toward them. It made suffering a virtue, and selflessness an even higher virtue alongside the judgment of others. With my mother as the model, we escaped our family dysfunction by finding solace in longstanding, deep, institutional dysfunction. In short, we were taught to allow others to cause problems for us and to solve other people's problems at the expense of solving our own. God would take care of the rest and reward us for any suffering along the way. This is called "redemptive suffering" theology and it is bullshit. The suffering we experience doesn't make us better; it makes us more fucked up than we would have been had the suffering not occurred. I'm not talking about the process of building muscle or suffering the result of practice to improve at an activity. I'm talking about all the suffering we endure that is then repackaged to us—thanks to white Christianity—as a blessing from God: That there are "reasons" why bad things happen, and that these reasons always point in the direction of personal growth. This idea was far more devilish than what I had experienced from Chris. The Christians peddling this codependent theological nonsense were devils, too. More than that, *these* devils didn't even have a game plan to follow when one or more of them were proved to be dangerous for the community. That day of the altercation, after I told my mom, she had immediately driven over to the associate pastor's home (Chris' parents) and confronted them. She confronted Chris, in fact. And from what my mother has always told me, he confessed to everything in front of his parents. His confession—whether it happened or not—has always given me comfort. It has made me feel less dirty, more heterosexual, if I am being honest. I wonder if this was her lie to me that sought to preserve a bigger truth for her: my innocence?

Days later, Chris' confession didn't matter to our senior minister who didn't seem to know what to do when we told him about the abuse. Why wouldn't the pastor simply kick the kid (and/or his parents) out of the church? After studying theology for decades now, I know this is because the church is for the dispossessed, the marginalized—and sometimes that means the criminal, the "sinner." Popularly, a common quip is that the best definition of a "Christian" is a sinner. Such an idea couldn't be truer. But on this point, I still feel now just as I felt back then as a child: what an awful idea and a dangerous institution, white American Christianity. To translate it, this means that Christianity—or at least the white American version of it—holds itself and the unity of the church higher in esteem than the value of a child. Baked into white, American Christianity is the assumption that the world is fucked up, and the notion of the church as a space for addressing that trauma. But what's missed by most people who do not read the "theological" fine print is that you'll have to cavort with sinners of all sorts: pedophiles, rapists, liars, and killers. It isn't ironic that so many church leaders abuse children; Christianity is welcoming to them whether they are pastors, priests, or their children. Essentially, white Christianity was a social experiment in the mitigation of guilt for devilish behavior and the normalization of abuse. To this day, I don't know what did more harm to me: my sexual abuser or the community that provided the context for the abuse to occur, made me feel so awful about experiencing it, and told me that there was nothing they could do about it (when I took them at their word that the behavior was, in fact, abhorrent). My family's attempt to escape the hell of our family dysfunction only produced more of it for me. At home or at church, I was living in hell.

***

One of the tensions related to ongoing cultural conversations about racial or gender discrimination has to do with the degree to which black folks are treated differently than white folks by white folks. But from my childhood perspective, this assumption begs the question: who the hell would want to be treated the way that white folks treat our own? Celebrated womanist theologian Delores Williams coined the term "demonarchy" to situate the spiritual stakes of the gendered, racial, and economic oppression black women face.[3] Particularly, Williams uses it as a corrective to the normative whiteness at the heart of patriarchy. Demonarchy, on the other hand, refers to

> the demonic governance of black women's lives by white male and white female ruled systems using racism, violence, violation, retardation, and death as instruments of social control. Distinguished from individual violent acts stemming from psychological abnormalities on the part of the perpetrator, demonarchy is a traditional and collective expression of white government in relation to black women. It belongs to the realm of normalcy.[4]

Demonarchy is also a good term to describe the church setting I was raised in. Something about my sexual abuse provides a window for me to see why black folks did not feel comfortable in my white church. It seems to me that much of the unresolved racial tension in the United States and globally involves the way black women have long refused to be treated in such devilish ways. Too many white men and women are too comfortable acting like and being treated like devils. Demonarchy captures the insidiousness of abuse rampant within many white Christian communities, including where my abuse occurred. As has long been the case among clergy and other would-be leaders regarding speaking up to other white women and men in the face of racism, church leadership thought it more appropriate to protect the whole at the expense of victims of elements within that whole. My pastor thought it appropriate that my sexual abuser remain in the community of the church. His mother, today, holds the highest honor at the church, the title of Elder. Elders are who members call when they need help. For years, I believed this white lie that ecumenism—the greater church community—mattered above all else. I held it as a theological (or, demonarchical) virtue, in fact. One Christmas service when I was about twenty-two years old, I even participated in communion with my sexual abuser. That Christmas, he and I did not interact directly, but the knowledge of his continued participation with that church—and my own growing anger at the delusions of Christianity that transform such circumstances into virtues—became the mustard seed through which I arrived at atheism. I can only imagine how many other people share similar stories. Soon after that Christmas, I finally stopped feeling personally guilty for noting or addressing the hypocrisy of the Christians around me or of the white mystery God who loved to see us suffer. But even as a child, I couldn't make sense of the moral messiness of white Christian spaces. I didn't have the training or vocabulary to articulate this messiness as a child. But I felt it in church. Man, I felt it. The people teaching me to love my enemy were putting me and many others in danger within the community, while at the same time, these white Christians were not welcoming to people who did not look like me. Somehow, sexual predators were allowed to be part of our church family, but black folks were not.

Martin Luther King, Jr. is remembered as having said that the "eleven o'clock hour on Sunday is the most segregated time in America," and that largely remains true across the country. My white church was no exception. Reasons for this separation are varied and complicated, and have to do with different motivations, be they white racial separation for sake of racial "purity" and the preventing of the enslaved from being baptized in the brotherhood of Christ; Or, black racial separation for the sake of communal health and wholeness in the face of anti-black racism. White churches are segregated because white people don't want black folks there. And, black churches are segregated because white people don't want to be there.

White people have always meant something to me, but white churches have not. I smelled the hypocrisy of white people and places long before I had the language to articulate it. From an early age, I knew that white spaces were not "my" spaces. Very early on, I found solace in something categorically different. Whether we're talking about the early campy, family-friendly albums of Kris Kross and DJ Jazzy Jeff & the Fresh Prince, or ultimately the gangsta rap of Too Short and UGK, hip hop gave me a sense of somebodiness. It covered the ground that the church could not. As a child, I found strength and courage, a sense of honesty and of self in hip hop culture. Growing up in the deep south I was surrounded by black folks, but I was talking about something more specific than cross-racial familiarity. Hip hop told a particular truth to my white existential self about alienation and the forging of community on one's own terms. As the white Christ, and the white God, and the white Church hung me up on figurative crosses, black art, culture, religion, and ultimately black people were there to take me down from them.

All churches, but white churches in particular, like to talk about grace. Grace is a theological idea that means receiving something for nothing (from God). God's love is the classic example of grace; God's salvation is another common example. Noted German theologian Dietrich Bonhoeffer spoke about grace in terms of "costly" and "cheap" varieties. Too many Christians, Bonhoeffer cautioned, accept their grace as "cheap" when God's grace is deeply costly. In fact, he famously said that "When Christ calls a man, he bids him pick up his cross and die."[5] This is "costly grace." I had come to realize that all white grace was cheap, and for reasons related to racism and slavery, black grace—whether from the church or from hip hop—had a costly component. It had been hard fought. The history of black suffering at the hands of white supremacists did not immediately resonate with me. I was on the other "team," so to speak. But the suffering, itself, I understood. I knew about a life lived through the prism cast by the ugly and tragic things humans sometimes do to other humans.

Hip hop was my grace, giving me something for nothing. It "loved me into wholeness" to paraphrase a popular Christian quip. I would spend my time in white churches fascinated by the deep unanswerable questions I could pose to Sunday School leaders, pressing them on their ideas about God and religion that they adhered to. Then, in "Big Church" as we called it, I would spend my time jotting down notes about sermons and peeping glances at girls' exposed thighs as their dresses rode up on the pew seats. I was eclectic and promiscuous when it came to understanding the material presented in those church spaces. I was always "thirsty" for understanding; I always left still thirsty. Hip hop was a 40 oz. St. Ides on an August afternoon.

As soon as white church let out, I'd check back in with my real spiritual leaders, black Gods on the mic. In grade school, I'd find my Walkman; in middle school, my portable CD player that skipped if you walked too vigorously with it; in high school, blast "back, front, back, and side to side/never let hoe ass niggas ride" from my Jeep Cherokee as I left the church parking lot. And I wouldn't experience any dissonance until black folks saw me showing out. My white pastors would finish their sermons on notes about redemption and hard work; my black pastors—Bun B, Pimp C, MJG, Eightball, Mr. King George, TRU, and the Geto Boys—preached about hard work, too, especially about how nothing in life is handed to us, and to be something in this world, you had to act. To this day, basically, I still know every word of the entire catalogs of No Limit Records and Cash Money Records. These were my hymns, my sermons, and my sacred texts. Hip hop told the truth about the grittiness of life, what my teacher Anthony B. Pinn calls the "texture" of human life.[6] Rappers weren't concerned to make a virtue of suffering, but instead cashed in (and out) on human suffering. They encouraged listeners to make a virtue of themselves. Hip hop doesn't suffer itself a fool. It talks openly about the struggles of life in a racist world, but it doesn't blame a lack of success on those hardships. It offers a do-for-self philosophy of life at odds with the suffering servant motifs propagated by white Christianity. As I left for college, my taste in rap grew in lyrical sophistication and political sensibility, but I never stopped prioritizing hip hop as the space where I would make meaning for myself in the void left by my white church family.

Until twenty-two or so, I was a believer in God and a follower of Christ. I would go to church and hear stories that mattered to me. I really believed them. Over the years of my adolescence, and more systematically as I began formal education in religious studies, I began to recognize the moral hypocrisy of white Christianity. I started to feel neglected by God and the white people around me who loved God. Alcoholic fathers leave sons feeling neglected and abandoned. So do dysfunctional Gods and churches. In clinical psychology, particularly as it concerns responding to domestic abuse, there is a commonly taught idea that "love is not enough." Love is a powerful force, but many of us love and feel responsible for people that abuse us. My relationship with God was abusive. God did more harm than good, bringing more pain to my life than joy. And like many abusive relationships, it took a while to leave the church, but in the end, I did thanks to the strength hip hop provided.

I had lived in the white church. I had deep connections to that church. Yet, hip hop truly became my church. Rappers were telling me things about myself and the world that the church was not. I was able to see and feel its messages. It was helping me to articulate the grittiness of life. I believed rappers but not pastors. And I still do. From a very early age, I had this traumatic experience occur in the church. And neither I nor my abuser was allowed to leave that space. And I can only imagine—and I mean this sincerely—that the only person who may have felt more alienated and alone than I did was my abuser. Rappers can be called a lot of things, but I was confident they would not have tolerated the same toxicity. They may participate in their own abuses, but they know better than to get punked by someone else without going down swinging. Rather than swinging, Christianity told me that the best of the lot ends up naked on crosses—wearing a crown of thorns. Fuck that.

Rap songs became my homilies. Rappers were my pastors. And they took me to the right hand of Gods that don't hide in the sky or behind church walls. To the extent church is a space where people are edified, taught how to behave and how to feel about oneself, my white church left me feeling small, impotent, incomplete, and apathetic. Rappers, on the other hand, talk about overcoming the world's obstacles. Do many of them do so in ways that are complicated and that often reinforce social issues like patriarchy and misogyny? Of course. But the church is no better on these issues. For some of us, it is worse. No rapper ever tried to sexually assault me, but some have tried to assault women I have loved. Church people, on the other hand, have tried (and some, succeeded) in assaulting me and women I have loved. From my standpoint, hip hop is the lesser of the dangers and it offers the greater of what's to enjoy.

Hip hop saved me from the devils in my church. Across thirty years of white-boy fandom, I had done intellectual jumping jacks to make space for the importance of hip hop to my life, to my orientation toward the world. But as I developed as a thinker and a scholar, my interests in hip hop *as a religion* shifted toward learning more about the esoteric lessons found within a relatively small-scale, but influential, segment of the hip hop universe: the Nation of Gods and Earths (NGE). Hip hop was and remains my religion. There was a life philosophy inside of hip hop that didn't require waxing philosophic on hip hop in general. My first exposure to the teachings of the Five Percenters made it clear to me: I didn't need to find figurative Jesus in hip hop when God was already on the mic.

***

Anger management classes are humbling. I learned this at Philadelphia-based Courdea, a program designed to address domestic and intimate partner abuse. Founded in 1984 as an initiative of Family Services of Philadelphia, Courdea's mission is to intervene in domestic abuse and retrain men who have abused so that they might maintain healthy relationships with their families.[7] Over the years, Courdea eventually privatized and began taking insurance. As a result, it now provides both individual and group-based therapies to a variety of different cultural and socio-economic demographics. It also caters to court-mandated anger and domestic violence clientele. In the fall of 2018, I enrolled in their program.

I will not tell you what I have put my ex-wife, former girlfriends, mentors, sister, or mother through over the years. Those are their stories to tell. It will suffice to mention that services at Courdea begin with an initial intake evaluation. Before my evaluation was over, my intake facilitator (and later, therapist) Daniel Cantor, Ph.D. was confident that Courdea could help me. Immediately, he scheduled me for weekly individual and group therapy sessions. I was required to commit to at least ten group sessions (I have since participated in over fifty), weekly individual sessions with Dr. Cantor, and to active participation in local Adult Children of Alcoholics (ACA) twelve-step meetings. The latter was a condition of Dr. Cantor taking me on as one of his clients, and as you will read, ACA came to have an incredibly powerful impact on my Knowledge of Self.

Dr. Cantor explained to me that at Courdea, men embark on a kind of psychical surgery of the self. By "self," I mean *my* self. Actually, my *self*, not a generic "self." It is a type of surgery that takes place through talk therapy, and the naming, locating, and deconstructing of different concepts and beliefs that allow for a reorganization of other beliefs and concepts. This reorganization of beliefs and concepts then helps to improve behavior and promotes a health(ier) self-image, one strong enough to do less harm (to self and others) than a hurting, painful, aggrieved self. In our time together, Dr. Cantor would constantly refer to a moving river as a metaphor for understanding myself. In reflecting on who I have been as a white man—or an identity at all—I am a relatively autonomous rational feeling being floating through a river of culture and society and ideas and energy. The riverbed filled with rocks and strainers and old cars and trees all shape my sense of and any expression of my identity in every moment. This all gives contour to the flow of self. Self, understanding it as the energy of awareness that gives us our animation, transforms based on our location in the river. This notion of the self, existing in and as the stuff of a cultural and cosmological river, helps in coming to terms with the ways that my *self* is available for reevaluation and transmutation. My self is never static. It also helps in seeing the parameters of what sorts of changes in myself are possible in the short and long term. At this point, I can choose what sorts of features of self I want my *self* to express. I don't have to act like a white devil. I can be whoever I want to be, insofar as I understand that it isn't only me involved in that process. These sorts of transmutations involve no longer fighting the river's current but coming to terms with it. Rather than feeling constantly at risk of drowning, we can reposition our feet downstream and begin to let the river do most of the work of identity formation. In doing so, we then grow empowered to steer our *selves* in the direction we choose. The shift in thinking encouraged by Dr. Cantor relates to the Greek maxim to "know thyself," only the truth now is recognizing that "thyself" has never actually been a singular construction. Through emotions, and how we process them, we are inextricably linked to everyone else.

The purpose of *White Devils, Black Gods* is to argue that through an embrace of this "Knowledge of Self"—who we are and where we have come from—white men might be better equipped to short-circuit and take responsibility for our devilish behavior, to the extent that such efforts are possible. Based on my experiences, both personal and specifically in my participation in anger management classes, and my day job as a researcher of race and religion, I came to the thesis put forth in this book: a problem with self-hatred is at root of much of white masculine anger and our contemporary (but also historical) difficulty regulating our emotions is at the heart of behavioral patterns that have led some folks to call us devils. In our childlike arrested emotional and cultural development, many of us as white men have treated others horribly.

Although neither Courdea nor ACA meetings focused on race, I couldn't help but consider how race was part of my story of self. Courdea offers two levels of group meeting, beginner and advanced. Most of the beginner meetings were very racially diverse, and Dr. Cantor and I were often the only white men participating. Mind you, he was the facilitator. This feeling of difference left me reflecting on the way that the patterns of toxic masculinity and its relationship to codependency that I was learning how to recognize might also operate at the level of race. When I moved to the "advanced" group, racial difference was exacerbated. All the participants in the upper-level group were white, and one of the facilitators was a black woman. Moreover, across the several distinct ACA fellowships I participated in, they were (and remain) predominately white affairs. They looked and felt a lot like the white church spaces I grew up in. At one level, this might say something about the privilege of white people having the means and time and energy to engage in, to "pay for," this psychical surgery. At another level, it is as easy to conclude that we white men (and many women) were the ones who needed the most work (and help) dealing with our anger and emotional dysregulation.

White or black, all of us in anger management teetered between blaming our circumstances for our behavior or blaming our genetics. Before learning to take responsibility for ourselves, our parents were initially to blame (at some level), but whether it was their behavior and social circumstances that transformed us into abusers or the genes we inherited from them was a complicated issue. The tension between the characterological and the contextual often emerges whilst engaged in consideration of "big" ontological questions, questions about the nature of being, as such. For instance, is everyone equally predisposed toward devilish behavior? Had my dad a choice in his drinking or neglectful behavior? Could my sexual abuser Chris control himself or was his behavior hardwired into his physiology? Was there something about white men that predisposed us toward abusive behavior? Are we "devils" because of how we act toward one another or are we devils biologically and therefore, we behave devilishly toward one another?

There are levels of abuse. Some abusive behavior is more severe and detrimental than other behaviors, for instance, my yelling could hurt differently than another man's blocking behavior. Despite the variety of abuses and the range of their severity, most of the clients at Courdea shared certain psychological patterns. The members of our groups were perpetrators, in terms of our own behaviors and belief structures and ill-conceived concepts connected to what a man should or shouldn't be or act like—the norms that governed masculine identity construction. We had underdeveloped egos that played out in terms of codependency, seeking to control the women around us. The efforts at control played out behaviorally, as various abuses ranging from neglect all the way to intense physical violence. And relatedly, various losses-of-control were experienced by men when our bloated sense of self-importance was questioned. Despite the differences over who (or what) we blamed for our behavior or whether we drew causal links between certain races and behaviors, and regardless of the range of behaviors, our abuses tended to share the same motivating features: emotional dysregulation and immaturity, and codependence strategies that objectified women in an ill-fated effort that our control of them would work as a replacement for our arrested emotional development and our atrophied egos. Across all our differences, we were humbled and ashamed and bonded by the harm we had caused others.

To accept responsibility for abusive behavior (or our status as victims of it) requires accepting that there are certain psychological patterns either hardwired into our wetware or that serve as ardently strong software, and that these scenarios produce character traits that shape the "look" of our personalities. My parents' character traits produced an environment that developed my brain to respond in certain ways to sensory stimuli. I grew to be very good at keeping myself protected from dangerous situations, but at the expense of knowing when—or having the courage—to be vulnerable when vulnerability would prove advantageous. I grew adept at destroying difference and ambiguity while I remained as a child when handling the ambiguity that I could not destroy. I grew up to become an Adult Child, unsure of myself and in constant need of external validation.

Hell always has a zip code—mine was 71105. Taking responsibility for ourselves requires recognizing that devils are made by virtue of location—social context; "nurture." Hell is the abuse that our perpetrators have done to us, but it is also the agony of knowing that we cannot escape what our unprocessed trauma shapes us to become. Despite the genetic factors we inherit or the life experiences of our parents, where and how we grow up molds us in the image of our parents, and their parents before them. This tragic awareness is also an opportunity for intervention. Knowing we were made over time and moulded by misguidance, neglect, or some other abusive experience, we can begin addressing our character defects, and through intersubjective engagement with others, we can learn how to escape hell.

3 THEOPHANY

In the history of religions, the word "theophany" describes an experience or encounter with God. In the Hebrew Bible, Moses has several of these experiences. The book of Exodus tells the story of Moses tending the flock of his father-in-law, Jethro. Incidentally, tending flock is a classic euphemism for civic or social duties of leadership. The Bible *might* be talking about people when it describes "flock." Moses is said to take the flock to the "west" side of the wilderness, coming to Mount Horeb or Mount Sinai, two different names for the "mountain of God." Here, Moses saw a burning bush. Well, it was on fire, but it wasn't burning. We're told the bush was not "consumed." When Moses goes in for a closer look, he hears the voice of God. God tells him to not come any closer to the bush, and to take off his shoes, as he was walking on holy ground. In Exodus 3:6, God says that "I am the God of your father, the God of Abraham, the God of Isaac, and the God of Jacob." This shout out to his ancestors frightened Moses enough that he decided not to look directly at God. Based on Moses' precedent, many still maintain that folks having theophanies would do well not to make direct eye contact with Gods. God then charges Moses with delivery of God's people from Egyptian bondage. Moses' task was to go to Egypt, and with the help of this nameless God liberate the Israelite slaves so that they might meet up with the Canaanites, Hittites, Jebusites, and others in the "land of milk and honey." It is here in the Bible that Moses asks the name of this mystery God, to which God replies: "I am that I am." Before translation into English, God's name is revealed with the Hebrew consonants "Y H W Y." This then is transliterated into "Yahweh" (pronounced: Ya—Way), and comes to be called the "tetragrammaton," a description of the mystery God who literally expresses itself iconographically—that is, through language. The ambiguity of God's response, matched with the power of the theophany, saw to it that in traditional Judaism it is forbidden to speak or write the name of God. Answering the question of God's identity with more of a statement than an answer, the mystery God is just that, mysterious. And it is this "mystery God" that Moses takes to Egypt, and through its powers convinces Pharaoh to free the slaves (after a series of plagues). A lot happens during theophanies.

Noted Protestant theologian and reformer John Calvin believed that Mount Horeb and Mount Sinai were the same place, with Horeb the name of the mountain when ascending from the West and Sinai the name from the East.[1] We do not know a geographic location for Horeb—where God names Godself—nor do we know if they are the same mountain or different mountains. In Exodus 19, another theophany occurs atop Mount Sinai. There, YHWY makes his covenant with the newly free Israelites who are now living in the "wilderness" of Sinai. Mount Sinai is an actual mountain today, although we cannot be sure if that mountain we call "Sinai" today is *the* mountain from the story. This hasn't stopped Jews, Christians, and Muslims over the centuries from treating the place as if it were surely the mountain depicted in scripture. Today, Mount Sinai is thought (by many) to be near the town of Saint Catherine, Egypt in the Sinai Peninsula, the area of Northeast Egypt bracketed by the Gulf of Suez on its Western shores and the Gulf of Aqaba on the East. Billions of adherents believe that somewhere in this "wilderness" region exists the mountain where God made a covenant with the Israelites, and a bit later, gave Moses the Ten Commandments, too. Demanding that the Israelites keep their promise with God, God, in turn, promises that everywhere the Israelites maintain the codes of conduct and ritual laid out by YHWY, that land they would possess.

***

The most powerful theophany I have experienced occurred on July 21, 2016, at the home of the Nation of Gods and Earths, known as the Allah School in Mecca, two weeks after my first marriage. Monica and I were married in a small-scale family affair, that included a ceremony at City Hall in Manhattan, followed by a small gathering on the North Fork of Long Island. In the presence of our families and one of my best friends, David—who served as my Best Man—we got married, simultaneously breaking the rules of both white supremacy and black nationalism. With the wedding festivities concluded, David, Monica, and I went to visit the storefront school on the 2200 block of Adam Clayton Powell, Jr. Blvd in the heart of Harlem.

Walking up to the school is intimidating for many. On sunny days, you'll find several Gods posted up out front, sitting in shoddy chairs or standing in a semi-circle sometimes shooting the shit with one another or just posted up in a defensive posture. They are quite an imposing sight. Congregating in front of the door and working as a kind of buffer between the inside and outside worlds, these Gods are the biochemical version of the stone visage at the Great Temple of Ramesses II at Abu Simbel. In short, these Gods are striking. The three of us did not give off a similar vibe—a size zero tattooed black woman and former model with two doe-eyed white boys, one from the American South, and the other with diasporic roots in the American South, but who was born and raised in Basel, Switzerland. Undeterred by their show of both blackness and masculinity, we said awkward hellos and nodded, walking past them and into the front office. Once inside, a large portrait of Father Allah hung over the desk. A young man greeted us. We told him we were researchers of hip hop and of the NGE, and noted that one of us—David—had traveled all the way from Switzerland to make this pilgrimage. In unison, the four of us laughed at the seeming absurdity of it all. Largely because of the absurdity of our presence, we were all able to breathe a small sigh of relief when the young man offered to give us a tour. Presumably, the young man assumed that not even the FBI—who has a long history of surveilling the group—would send in such a convoluted trio. Soon, the young man was showing us around the building.

I was expecting more of a church setting, but what we found resembled some strange combination of Elks Lodge and underfunded youth recreation center. Photos of young black men with their arms blocked in squares and standing or crouching in "prison poses" adorned the walls of every room, as did old issues of "The Five Percenter," the group's newsletter and magazine. The school looks a lot like a typical urban rec center, with different rooms dedicated to different activities. Each room billowed with history, and the young man was eager to talk about *one* part of that history: three white Gods. What at first we thought was a general introduction to the space was more particular; we had all been thinking about racial particularity without mentioning it once. He showed us the "first white God," Azrael, who was a friend of Father Allah, having met while both were hospitalized at Matteawan State Hospital for the Criminally Insane. Then, he pointed to another photo of a group of black guys probably thirty-deep with one white boy salted into the scene. This was the only other "real white God," we were told. He then darted out of the room and down the hall, again, beckoning us to follow him. Pointing to a third photo, he pronounces that *there* is the third white God, an "honorary" God, the former mayor of New York City, John Lindsay. We learned that the Allah School in Mecca had been obtained, effectively gifted, to the NGE by Mayor Lindsay who saw some utility in a black organization focused on uplifting the youth. In the late 1960s, Lindsay had calculated that working with the NGE made more sense than alienating them from the administration. Lindsay enabled the group to sign one of those 100-year, one dollar type leases with the City of New York. And so, thanks to Lindsay, the group will have a home in Mecca (Harlem) until at least the 2060s. To this day, Lindsay is regarded as an honorary God.

As the young guy brought us back to the front, we came across another God who was standing between us and the exit door. Older and with darker skin than the young guy, he didn't pay us any mind, at first. He focused his attention to the guy who'd shown us around. The older God started questioning the young man over various aspects of the lessons. He was quite critical, harsh even, to the young guy. The questioning left us all nervous and brought us back to the racialized world in which we all lived. After a couple of minutes, we soon realized that the young guy was not actually a "God." He was a student of the lessons but had not mastered them. We quickly deduced that the older man—who we at the same time realized must be a God—was upset that the would-be God had taken it upon himself to show the three of us around the school. Who were we to expect such a tour, and who was he to provide it? Ostensibly, we didn't belong there at all, or we had not earned the right to be there, yet. After chastising him with Socratic questioning that forced the young guy to always answer incorrectly, the God trained his attention on David and me. Monica was a bit of a spectator during this turn of events. She was an expert on both hip hop and the NGE, but the intersectional cloud of hypermasculinity and racial anxieties hovering around us made it hard for us to see her and easy for her to see us. The experience reminded me that within the NGE, black men are Gods and women are "Earths," at best—"secondary, but most necessary" as it is put by God and rapper Lord Jamar.[2] Or it could have been that race was signaling to the God that Monica was safe, and that David and I were potential threats. I could not make full sense of it then, or now. No matter if race or gender was more to blame, David and I found ourselves alone on Mount Horeb, in the presence of a patriarchal God, and exposed by our whiteness made up of equal parts arrogance and curiosity.

The God told us a bit about who he was—he had been (re)born by one of Allah's first born—the teachings of Father Allah had rescued him from a hard life of hustling. He told us of his past misdeeds and about how coming to Knowledge of Self was his path toward getting out of precarious circumstances. He included stories of hustling and violence, as important to be told for its impact on his redemption narrative as to also remind us of what this ~~man~~ God could do. He looked squarely at David and me, and said, "Look, you're welcome here, but the thing you need to understand is that you're in the presence of a God." Bear in mind that David's Swiss geographical and vernacular context of race is different than mine, yet via hip hop, we shared an experience of God's proclamation to BOTH of us about who he was and who we were. While I comported myself to the occasion—as best one can know how to act during a theophany—internally, I was a ball of dangerous kinetic energy. Whatever was inside of me—the whitest part of me, so to speak—responded caustically to his naming himself a God. I didn't want to believe it. I wanted it to be absurd. I wanted to file this information away into the folder in my mind that stores all the other times I feel self-righteous in the face of black self-determination. That's a big folder for white people. I just didn't believe that this God was, in fact, a God. Instead, I chose at that moment to let go. I "leaned in" to believing in the impossible. I decided to embark on a journey that I knew would be difficult, would gain ridicule from many of my stuffy, "objective" colleagues, but that would potentially be life changing for me. Hip hop had long been my religion. This was the next logical, ironical, and paradoxical step—submitting to the knowledge that the black man was God.

I could not have predicted this turn of events when I was being abused by my pastor's son. I would not have imagined to supplicate myself to black divinity, years earlier when I found my dad's decomposing body after he drank himself to death. The white world and white Christianity had not prepared me for this black theophany, much less, the salvation it would end up providing me. Yet I understood then that my mandate as both an unlikely race-traitor and a scholar of religion was to *believe* in the truth espoused by this God. I decided to accept that this man, speaking to us with a hard-earned grittiness and a deep theological confidence that rarely go together, was, who he said he was, a God. It wasn't an analogy. It wasn't a metaphor. This knowledge became my ethnographic and existential truth. I would alter my thinking, my behavior, and my being to make room for this truth: the black man was God. *This* black man was God. This theophany came to be the organizing principle of my research for the next few years, reordering my life in the process. The experience at the school was one of the most powerful in my life, offering an opportunity to reimagine my relationship to all that exists in the universe. But there was a catch.

Practically speaking, there is absolutely nothing noteworthy about a white boy rendering God in the image of the black man. In a sense, black men (and women) have been our Gods already and for far too long. Whether it is white reliance on black bodies for economic advantage, wet nurses, or the seemingly sacrificial murders of black men by lynch mobs or police (who in their death bring a kind of sacrificial offering to the altar of white concerns to feel safe and sure of ourselves), white men have been relying on black men in (God-like ways) for a very long time. My theophany wasn't novel. And my knowledge of the mundanity of what I regarded as innovative forced me to think more deeply about my toxic codependent reliance on blackness and my damnable need to feel so innocent.

I came to a growing awareness that if I was to take seriously *their* claims to Knowledge of Self, I had to come to terms with *my* Knowledge of Self. I could not simply follow black wisdom or ask to join their group. I had to turn inward and examine who I was. The seed of this awareness was planted that day in Mecca (i.e., Harlem). As the God reiterated that we were in the presence of divinity, awkward words left from my lips, a liturgy learned from hip hop: "all praise due," "all praise due." David and I nodded in genuine, if still under-analyzed, supplication to this God. At some level, we were coming into our own Knowledge of Self. In his telling us who he was, he acknowledged that he knew we were lost, and in need of Knowledge of Self. My recognition of his Knowledge of Self was pointing us toward our Knowledge of Self. If he was the true and living God, then it meant I had to accept the claim that I was a grafted, white devil. In a way, I was experiencing a conversion. At a cognitive level, I left the school that day convicted in this new plan for myself. I would believe in these Gods and pray to help my moments of unbelief. At a deep level, I was changed, coming out of denial of who I was because I had finally stopped denying who the black man was.

Changing one's mind is not the same thing as changing one's behavior. My conversion was only partially complete. It would take a series of family crises, to which I responded with dangerous anxiety, depression, and anger, for me to finally begin the long process of changing my behavior. This book is a product of those experiences. Essentially, I came to be convicted that my behavior toward others was often devilish—not merely because of my aggressive and abusive behavior, but because unprocessed trauma from my childhood inhibited my abilities to be in relationship with others. Past trauma I experienced as a child taught me to isolate and not trust others, yet it also made me emotionally dependent on external validation. The survival traits that had gotten me to where I was in life had come at a cost. As I grew in awareness of who I really was, I slowly started to address long-standing behavioral patterns that had been doing harm to myself and others for many years.

***

For years, I have considered myself a protest atheist—someone who thinks that belief in the monotheistic God of the patriarchal, Abrahamic religions, YHWY, is a bad idea on moral grounds. Mine is a *moral* atheism. Yet atheism has always been a clunky term for describing me. I had always "believed" in God, and despite my humanism and atheism today, I've never stopped believing in God(s). My childhood neglect and family dysfunction shaped what became a full-blown hatred of God, what has been called misotheism. Misotheism is the *hatred* of God. That was me. Misotheism can be thought of alongside misogyny. A misogynist is someone who hates women. A misotheist is someone who hates God, a hateful believer. Similar meanings, with different referents. My childhood experiences feeling abandoned by God turned into an outright hatred of this white mystery God and utter disdain and mistrust of all white church-related perspectives. I have never been what we call an epistemological atheist—someone who doesn't believe in the possibility of God existing. It isn't that I care whether God exists or not; God is an idea, and as a teacher of religion, I make use of both possibilities. In terms of what we as humans can know about God, I am agnostic and always have been. If someone tells you they are sure the mystery God exists, or that they are sure the mystery God does not exist, know this: both are lying to you. But for me, personally, if God does exist, we need to do what he did to me—abandon him.

Theologian James Cone, whose work deeply influences mine, in the 1960s started to talk (and eventually, write) about the inherent blackness of God. He wrote that "Because blacks have come to know themselves as *black*, and because that blackness is the cause of their own love of themselves and hatred of whiteness, the blackness of God is the key to our knowledge of God."[3] By this, he meant that God was on the side of the oppressed, and since the black condition in the United States was one of constant oppression, then to be on the right side of God was to be on the right side of blackness in the freedom struggle. Little did I know how far—how deeply embodied—this initial understanding of "ontological blackness" would take my thinking as I came to believe in black men as Gods.

Another powerful influence on my thinking is the German philosopher and staunch antisemite Ludwig Feuerbach. In the middle of the nineteenth century, Feuerbach argued that the Judeo-Christian God was a cosmic projection of human ideals and aspirations, concluding that "theology is anthropology."[4] All claims made to or about God could be reduced to human affairs and interests. Essentially, he was making a humanist point, namely that what we said about God said far more about ourselves. Based on this Feuerbachian point, it seems clear that Cone was prioritizing black liberation ahead of all-else. His black God was a pragmatic, useful God and his naming of the white God was in reference to white people who had used the mystery God to enslave and oppress black folks, historically. Feuerbach's theory that God is a cosmic projection helps to understand what is happening when black esoteric traditions claim the black man is God and that they do not believe in any mystery God. In short, when members of the Nation of Islam speak about the perils of the white man's mystery God, the qualifier "mystery" suggests white people are lacking in Knowledge of Self. Our God is a mystery because who we are is a mystery. Rather than address that mystery, we have preoccupied ourselves with other people, and sought to take their identities as our own (in various ways). In all this taking, the mystery God has meant misery for black and brown people, historically. Quite literally, in the naming of God as an abstract, ethnic-less metaphysical entity, it enabled white people to offer a narrative of universal applicability to indigenous peoples across the globe. White people would then rely on that shared religious belief in the mystery God to exploit those indigenous communities. Monotheism, in this way, relies on mystery to feign inclusiveness. Relatedly, when members of the Nation of Gods and Earths remark on their status as God, they are not making a theological pronouncement so much as an anthropological one. In the person of the black man, the very distinction between theology and anthropology is blurred.

The history of religions as well as theories of identity emerging from social anthropology may substantiate certain claims to divinity made by Five Percenters. I offer here an interpretation made possible by taking seriously claims to black divinity. If we track backwards in history, cross-referencing the Western mythical record against the Western historical and archaeological records, we have a good idea of where the idea of God comes from. In super-archaic history, it comes from two places, producing two different "kinds" of Gods, that are then unified in Ancient Egypt in the form of Pharaoh. At least 200,000 years ago, *Homo sapiens sapiens* stepped onto the archaeological scene. Their form of subsistence included hunting and gathering. They came to subsist in small groups, we think, as a practical issue of safety. Against the inhospitable wilderness, there was strength in numbers. But as humans in groups tend to do, some of the people started getting onto the nerves of others in the group. For the sake of this illustration, imagine this is only happening for one group, but it is likely that this pattern was happening in different places and times among different groups of humans. Nevertheless, the conflict in the first group eventually leads to violence, and that violence leads to the first murder in human history. In response to this murder, some members of the one group punish the murderer and his/her family through banishment. Another group then organizes around the banished family. The process continues. Over tens and even hundreds of thousands of years, this basic social structure leads to a world populated by bands of nomadic hunter-gatherers. Let's call each group a "tribe." These tribes were almost always nomadic, but they tended to stay in the same regions. Nomadic, here, means they were moving, but it does not mean they were intentionally moving from one place to another. More like birds, they were probably moving in a kind of cycle, following their food or the seasons. Across these millennia, different groups came to associate themselves with features of the regions where they roamed. If one tribe was always in the presence of beavers, they came to think of themselves as a beaver tribe. When another tribe was always around lions, they became the lion tribe. They did not have to be animals, however. Some tribes could have been the "big mountain" or "fast creek" tribe. The point is that they took their identities from their geographic location. The objects inspiring the names of each tribe, we call a "totem."

As tribes come to organize themselves around their totems, the totems come to take on a transcendent quality, mattering more than any one member of the tribe. Each totem becomes the most important aspect of social life in the tribe. In fact, the world comes to be thought of in a dichotomy by members of the tribe. There are things in the world that work to reinforce the totem. Scholars of religion come to call these things that reinforce totems, "sacred" things—things set apart from ordinary people and society. The things in the world that potentially take away from the totem, or that threaten it, scholars come to call "profane." These things could include outsiders wanting to harm the group, or insiders wanting to harm the totem. In either case, tribes would deal with profane people and objects through banishment or destruction. Supposing that many of the world's tribes operated according to this totemic principle, we can imagine that this totemism provided a kind of homeostatic existence for the tribes. They would sometimes fight internally or against other tribes, but so long as the totems were respected, most tribes and their members remained relatively safe and content.

This relative social equilibrium began to change with the advent of agriculture, around 10–12,000 years ago (when it started depends on where we look). Agriculture brought a variety of pressures and changes to the general totemic social structure, leading ultimately to the development of city-states where people began living together in much larger groups than the tribal settings. Living in cities and subsisting on agriculture allowed for the division of labor, which produced art and culture on a scale previously unseen in the archaeological or historical record. Classically, the Western world identifies four "first" civilizations, including the Egyptian, Minoan, Mesopotamian, and Indus Valley Civilizations. Today, we know very little about the Indus Valley or Minoan civilizations. We know a great deal, however, about ancient Egypt and Mesopotamia, including about their religious beliefs and practices. In both Egypt and Mesopotamia, we see the introduction of the idea of Gods to society. The sacred/profane binary division already organized totemic life, and in Egypt and Mesopotamia, Gods will both confirm and complicate that binary structure.

In Egypt, the first Pharoah Menes comes to unify two confederations of tribes. These were groups consisting of several different tribes that had banded together as a sedentary agricultural lifestyle proved advantageous for one reason or another. Classically, we remember these confederations of tribes as Upper and Lower Egypt. Upper Egypt came to be represented by the most powerful totem among the various tribal totems within that confederation. Power could be procured through belief in the deity, effectively meaning power was held and used by worship of the totem, itself. Or, perhaps, power may have rested with the military commander and was represented by whatever totem that military commander associated themselves with. Either way, totemism was transforming into polytheism, the simultaneous introduction of disparate totems into a singular geographic location, that constitute the first pantheon. Various archaeological evidence shows that Upper Egypt experienced various totems (a scorpion, then a bull and back to a scorpion, for example) before the totem shifts to the name of a person, Menes (aka Narmer). In the developing city-state, the power once held by the totem came to rest in the form of a political and military ruler, Menes. Lower Egypt went through a similar process of unification under various totemic symbols. The falcon is remembered today as Horus. The crocodile is another totem that shows up in 5000–3000 BCE in Lower Egypt. These totems are attested in the iconography of what we call the "proto dynastic" rulers of Lower Egypt.

Around 3100 BCE, Menes unifies Upper and Lower Egypt. The effect of this unification is that the symbolic and political importance of these totems—better still to think of them now as Gods—gets relocated into individual human persons who we come to know as "Pharoahs." Different ethnic communities continued to maintain allegiance to, and worship of, their respective totems, yet the symbolic and material worlds came together in the body of Pharoah. In the person of Menes and subsequent Pharoahs, the western world is introduced to the idea of an anthropomorphic and agential God. These first Western Gods had human qualities because they were made in the image of Pharoah. The first truly powerful God in the world is a man, probably a black man but undoubtedly a black or brown man. This is the thread of the story most pertinent to my broader focus, but a slight detour helps flesh out the other origin story for the idea of God in the western world.

Around the same time that Upper and Lower Egypt are unifying, another couple of confederations are slowly unifying as well in Mesopotamia, between the Tigris and the Euphrates rivers in what is today Syria and Iraq. These are the Sumerian and Akkadian civilizations. The Akkadian peoples initially followed a totemic social structure very similar to the Egyptians. As a result, the Akkadian pantheon of Gods came to look very similar to the Egyptian pantheon. However, the Sumerians are different. They did not organize themselves totemically. In fact, we do not really know where they came from because we struggle to track them in the archaeological record. This has led to what some scholars call the "Sumerian Problem." We do not know where they came from or how their mythology developed, although we do know a lot about their mythology. The Sumerians gave the Western world the first symbolic representation of God, the dingir ✳. The Sumerians worshipped a sky God called An, believing that as a people, they emerged from workers, or "angels" of this sky God, called the Anunnaki. The Anunnaki have come to be a part of contemporary popular culture because some have suggested that the Sumerian origin story is the origin story of all of humanity. According to this line of argument, we humans all came from some ancient alien race whose angels, the Anunnaki, created us as a slave race. We do not have evidence to support these claims. But what we can conclude is just as fascinating. In the Sumerian effort to document and archive their origin story—that is, to write it down—they gave us another Western origin account for the idea of God, that of an abstract or symbolic authority. The dingir is the first written symbol marking this abstract understanding of God.

From what we know of these Egyptian and Mesopotamian cultures, we can develop a portrait of our past that suggests God, for Westerners, is about 5000 years old, and is expressed in two ways, first in the person of pharaoh, and second, through symbolic representation. The history of God as it matters for our conversation picks up more forcefully in Egypt, as Egypt shows up in the biblical record, as well. As many scholars contend, what we come to understand as "monotheism"—the worship of one God and the prohibition of belief in any other Gods—first appears in Egypt under Amenhotep IV circa 1340 BCE, who began worshipping a singular God to the exclusion of the rest of the pantheon. He attempted a brief political and religious revolution, which included changing his name to Akhenaten, in homage to the high God Aten. However, this revolution was short-lived and upon his death, Egypt went back to understanding Pharoah as the literal and figurative seat of power. What we generally regard as Biblical monotheism emerges again connected to Egypt, but this time in the form of the Exodus of the Israelites from Egypt under the protection of the God YHWY. Initially, and as is attested in the Hebrew Bible, YHWY is one of many deities in a pantheon of deities, each associated with various tribes, who eventually come together in different city-states and social contexts. What sets the Judeo-Christian tradition in motion, however, is what German Egyptologist Jan Assmann has called the "Mosaic distinction."[5] Perhaps inspired by the former high God Aten, or not, ancient Israelite religion came to organize itself in terms of this distinction. Assmann characterizes it as an effort to distinguish between "true and false religions."⁶ The Mosaic distinction follows a simple, if exclusionary, and dangerous logic, not found in the history of religions prior to this period (except, perhaps, with Amenhotep IV). Mosaic religion will (a) draw a distinction, (b) call the drawn distinction the first distinction, and (c) call the space in which it is drawn the space severed or cloven by the distinction.⁷ Prior to this revolution in religion, "religions always had a common ground."⁸ Despite different "cultures, languages, and customs" found across the Near East, the different polytheistic pantheons "functioned as a means of intercultural translatability … The different peoples worshipped different Gods, but nobody contested the reality of foreign Gods and the legitimacy of foreign forms of worship."⁹ For adherents, this Mosaic distinction bifurcated the world into opposing factions of good and evil, with Moses and the Israelites understood as "good" and all things related not only to Egypt but also other ethnic totems and deities understood as bad and evil. It also had the effect of dislocating YHWY from any geographic location—symbolically presented as the Israelites lost in the wilderness. In the naming of a high God superior to all other Gods and in labeling the rest of the pantheon false Gods, monotheism effectively severed the cultural specificity available to the community of worshippers. In effect, YHWY is a totem that has no corresponding homeland, an "empty" God—hence, a mystery. Believers in YHWY will be in a perpetual state of homelessness, necessarily, because Moses, at the end of the day, is an Egyptian. Assmann notes that

> By drawing this distinction, "Moses" cut the umbilical cord which connected his people and his religious ideas to their cultural and natural context. The Egypt of the Bible symbolizes what is rejected, discarded, and abandoned. Egypt is not just a historical context; it is inscribed in the fundamental semantics of monotheism … Egypt is the womb from which the chosen people emerged, but the umbilical cord was cut once and for all by the Mosaic distinction.¹⁰

Thinking about the Abrahamic religions in terms of Moses, rather than Abraham, helps to emphasize the essentially antagonistic nature of what emerges as biblical monotheism. There is no way to distinguish monotheism from this antagonism, because in its constant effort to fill the totemic void left by having severed the umbilical cord to Egypt, it does not fulfill the functional role that Gods initially filled in the socio-historical record. YHWY can only ever then exist as an ongoing cosmological confrontation with all other claims to divinity. In this way, YHWY is essentially "white" to the extent it is "transparent," to use the idea put forth by historian of religion Charles Long. Long defines first "opacity" as a posture toward others that recognizes "the specific meaning and value of another culture and/or language."¹¹ "Transparency" involves the denial of cultural specificity and therefore, the humanity of that specific culture. Monotheism produces this denial *within* its adherents, effectively denying the community of believers from knowledge of what makes them special or unique. In terms of both the concrete antagonism toward Egypt, and in terms of the effective emptiness of the totem YHWY, monotheism comes to look like the white man's religion. Of course, such claims run the risk of being read as antisemitic, in no small part because such arguments have been used toward antisemitic ends, historically. Nevertheless, one can hardly deny the implications of the overall portrait presented by Assmann, regarding the deeply violent underpinnings of monotheistic religion. In his 2013 book *In the Shadow of Mount Sinai*, Philosopher Peter Sloterdijk bolsters and nuances Assmann's criticism of monotheism, suggesting

> that it is not the single or plural nature of conceptions of God among collectives or individuals that plays the decisive part in releasing acts of violence. Rather, what determines a disposition towards the use of violence is the form and intensity of the absorption of faith practisers by the system of norms to which they subordinate their existence.[12]

Blending the insights from Assmann, Sloterdijk, and Long suggests that the problem of monotheism involves the transparent identity it leaves for believers, not in any specific theological claim about oneness. Monotheism is "white" by virtue of the norm of dislocatedness and disorientation produced from the fissure existing between communities and their God. In short, monotheism prevents Knowledge of Self. An empty identity is then believed in with such fervor as a way to offset the psychological deficit at work for the believer. Despite potentially faithful belief, believers never receive the one thing needed—identity. Violence then offers a recourse. Sloterdijk continues, noting that

> It is impossible to image the overall finding of the Sinai schema without the cultically explicated duty to be cruel, which was meant to be demonstrated by the execution of severe commands from God to human leaders. Thus, Moses orders the warriors to exterminate the Midianites completely when they exact vengeance for the seduction. He is angered by the news that the Israelite army killed only all the men, taking the women and children prisoner. In his zeal, fueled by awareness of the covenant, Moses insists on killing all boys and grown women too, sparing only the virgin girls: 'save for yourselves every girl who has never slept with a man' (Numbers 31:18). In the subsequent Israelite conquest, the Jewish armies are given the task of preventatively exterminating the local populations of Amorites, Canaanites, Perizzites, Hivites and Jebusites so that they cannot even tempt the still impressionable covenant people 'to follow all the detestable things they do in worshipping their gods.'[13]

Only under the threat of violence is monotheism able to account for its basic failure to address the question of identity. The violence is not intrinsic to the people committing the atrocities, nor is it directly connected to a theological belief system. It is connected to the failure of this particular system to address the missing identity of the community and the deeply violent anxiety arising from this transparency, this lack of Knowledge of Self. Perhaps, YHWY does not provide an adequate answer to the question of who he is because YHWY does not know who he is any more than he knows who the Israelites are. Why? Because the Israelites are Egyptian, and because all Gods connect to geography and topography. Through that location to land and place, Gods provide a functional ethnic identity.

Both literally and symbolically, God is originally a black or "opaque" idea.[14] God has an ethnic origin and is the symbolic object originally functioning to reinforce ethnic identity. Soon enough across the dynasties, the specific personhood of God—for some people—got detached and dislocated from a specific person with a specific geography (e.g., Pharaohs) and was overtaken by the idea of an abstracted, omnipresent, omnipotent God. But in origin, God is a black idea and God is a black person. The degree to which this information is historically verifiable is complicated, and really involves what the person is hoping to accomplish with claims toward evidence one way or another. But what we can say with a fair degree of certainty is that in our mythical record (I mean to include scripture here) we know the origins of the idea of God have roots in a black and brown Near East community of Northeast Africa, and that the idea of the God that exists across time and space and shows favor with one community to forsake all others arises in the Hebrew Torah, or the first five books of the Christian Bible.

Intersectionality has become something of a buzzword in recent years, and rightfully so. The term conveys the overlapping, enmeshed nature of our social identities. But not enough thinkers recognize that how and what we believe in is as much a part of any intersectional matrix as is our gender or our race or our income-level. Maybe all white men have something of hatred in us, and race and religion are just two ways it expresses itself. I could have a "healthy" relationship with this white God but hate black folks. Or, I could hate women intensely, yet have a "healthy" relationship with both the mystery God and men of color. I could not help but see (and feel) a relationship between these different salient identities, as if we're playing a game of cosmic wack-a-mole. I stamp out my hatred of one group over here, or one object over there, only for another group or object to pop up somewhere else. In thinking about who I represent socially—the white man, we could say that I have an historical relationship to the black man that is antithetical, based on antipathy and derision. Indeed, the description of my hatred of this monotheistic mystery God would be a good model for describing the white man's past (and perhaps, present) hatred of the black man. The notion of misotheism helps to understand human racial dynamics and it helps emphasize the Feuerbachian point that theology is nothing more than the projection of human social concerns onto a cosmic screen. What we have always and ever said about God has always and forever referred back to humans. It makes logical, biblical, historical, anthropological, and some would even say physiological sense, that the person of God would arrive in the form of a black man. I have a personal hatred of this monotheistic, Judeo-Christian Mystery God and I have an historical and collective responsibility to bear the sins of my fathers who hated the black man who had once been God. In circular fashion, historically the white man has hated the black man. And in the Bible, God promises to be a weapon for the Israelites against the black and brown Egyptians. At the very least, I must clarify which God, or Gods, I hate. Cone offers hermeneutical wisdom, writing that "Oppressed and oppressors cannot possibly mean the same thing when they speak of God. The God of the oppressed is a God of revolution who breaks the chains of slavery. The oppressors' God is a God of slavery and must be destroyed along with the oppressors."[15] From one perspective, we are left to attend to the reality of the origin of the idea of God in the black man. From another angle, the white man has long hated the black man. Whether we are talking about God, or certain human groups in terms of blackness or whiteness, the object we all fight over when we fight about religion is social identity—ours and "theirs."

I didn't arrive at misotheism as a means of responding to the racism in the church, although some might have that impression from reading my first book, *White Lies*. Rather, I arrived at misotheism because of the sexual trauma I endured at church and the neglect experienced at home. Seeking to escape the mystery God I hated, I sought solace among black people, first in hip hop and later, black religious and philosophical communities. While I retained certain levels of white and male and straight privilege, I shared with many black folks a sense of the tragic side of life. I deeply appreciated the black capacity to "tell the truth and shame the devil." It didn't make sense to me that God could exist and be content to exist alongside all the suffering humans. And it did not make sense that the mystery God YHWY who was so implicated in the oppression of black and brown folks, and women, was worthy of worship. But misotheism was not a panacea. I didn't escape social issues when I fled into the arms of misotheism. Through my embrace of misotheism, I merely shifted my hatred away from black folks and/or all women and toward the mystery God. This was a better option, but did little to address the hatred, itself, a hatred arising from not knowing who I really was. Like so many from my white heritage, the famous white atheist philosopher David Hume taught me the violent perils of induction fallacies and offered a way to respond to the pain of my sexual abuse as it concerned God, but Hume was also a staunch racist. White folks tend to compartmentalize very well—"well, his capacities as a philosopher are not connected to his racism." We fail to ask if maybe there is a relationship between my white Church allowing a predator to stay within its midst and that community's whiteness. Are there some black folks that would allow something similar to happen in their churches? The quick answer is yes. But do *Black* folks act that way? Maybe not. What I mean is that white folks are good at disassociating our behavior from our identities, but what if that very ability was part of what is so dangerous as it concerns abuse? What if we learned this dissociation from our religious beliefs? Does not the mystery God become a "mystery" when YHWY refuses to name himself? Is not YHWY named YHWY because he fails to take ethnic and cultural responsibility for himself prior to the Exodus? In Exodus 3:6, YHWY does declare himself the God of Abraham, Isaac, and Jacob, who enabled release from the bondage of Egypt. Yet there is still the experience of wilderness, which represents geographic and therefore, ethnic dislocatedness. Where had YHWY been before and during the bondage in Egypt? Rather than naming himself with a specific totemic ethnic origin, YHWY leaves that identity ambiguous, preferring instead to name himself through genealogical affiliation. This basic covenantal arrangement, enabling transparent "movement" for YHWY and his believers, is then subsumed by the later Christian notion of the "new covenant," which further disconnects the monotheistic God from his genealogical relationship to the Israelites. While Assmann's notion of the "mosaic distinction" offers a location for marking when monotheism or the zeal surrounding it began promoting violence as a stop-gap against dysfunctional beliefs, it would be the Christian New Testament God presented in the Gospels that effectively whitewashed any remaining ethnic specificity away from YHWY. Hence, Long notes that "Paul Tillich in his *Systematic Theology* made explicit the meaning of transparency in his Christological formulation. In the crucifixion, Tillich affirms that Jesus became transparent so that through him the believer could see God."[16] Hence, the Christian ideal presented in Galatians 3:28: "There is neither Jew nor Greek, slave nor free, male nor female, for you are all one in Christ Jesus." While this shift in theological priority toward theological oneness may (or may not) have been well-intentioned, within many western Christian communities it plays out as the celebration of transparency, and the denial of social difference along with the harm done by that denial. Naming God "black" promotes opacity and forces "one to deal with the actuality of suffering itself, and with that human act whereby one human being or community forces another person or community to undergo an ordeal for the salvation of one or both."[17]

My experiences in the white church held in tension with my experiences with rap music saw to it that over time, I developed a perspective that saw a causal, intimate link between whiteness and monotheism. What I experienced in the church wasn't the generic ugliness of humans in community, but a specifically *white* mode of behavior characterized by the same lack of responsibility shown by YHWY in the face of the world's suffering. The other side of this lack of responsibility (for self) was expressed in the insidious effort on the part of believers to safeguard the mystery God above members of the community. Protecting the unity of the church was part of a process of identity formation, and my atheism was an effort to largely reject that *transparent* identity on the grounds that it was perverse. We might think we're just going to church to be saved for the hereafter, but we're making our white selves from those pulpits and pews as we preoccupy ourselves with the worship of the devil we know, YHWY. Unfortunately, we might even escape from that church space, but if everyone around us still looks like us, and if we have not thought deeply about the intersectional matrix of social identity where power is procured, concealed, and renegotiated, have we really escaped from anything?

Coming into an awareness of the idea that the black man was God forced an intersectional confrontation within myself. How would I appreciate, celebrate, or even believe in the divinity of blackness if my atheism had been the hatred of God all along? I had followed the teachings of Cone for a long time, whose work emphasizes the "ontological blackness" of God. My hatred of God dovetailed with the history and the legacy that I inherited as a white southern man in America. Now I was forced to reckon with the possibility that Cone's idea about the ontological blackness of God fit within my mind because of a more deep-seated learned anti-blackness at work alongside of my misotheism. Did Cone's work resonate with me because I sought to fight alongside black folks in the freedom struggle, or did it resonate with me because hating God felt so similar to the deeply codependent hatred of black folks taught to me in white churches and culture and reinforced by the abandonment and violence of YHWY? Over time, the inherent whiteness of misotheism or the inherent theological-ness of whiteness—found me rethinking my relationship toward hatred, in general. Could I escape the hell of hatred inculcated in white Judeo-Christian religion? I had hated God and called it disbelief, across the same years where I would turn to black Gods on the mic for wisdom and sustenance that the mystery God YHWY did not provide. Over time, I would come to draw a distinction between that mystery God and the true and living Gods of hip hop culture.

In coming into awareness of black divinity, not in Cone's ontological sense alone but in the embodied sense offered by both Five Percenters and the history of religions, I was confronted with an integral component of my Knowledge of Self. The intersectional synergy and overlap between race, gender, and religion became largely the subject of this book. In the chapters that follow, I work to unpack more of this codependent theological baggage.

4 I AM THAT I AM

The earliest English-language reference to devils being "white" seems to be John Webster's 1612/13 *The White Devil: Or, the Tragedy of Paulo Giordano Ursini, Duke of Brachiano*. From the play, the white devil came to refer to an aspect of one's character that might be improved but that did no acute, specific harm, something akin to what psychoanalyst Sigmund Freud would eventually call a "neurosis." For Webster, white devils are devils, but there are blacker ones, still (or so appears the idea from the seventeenth and eighteenth centuries). It appears even Martin Luther, the Christian reformer, used the term to refer to evil cloaked in good intentions or auspices. Like the idea of white lies in the popular imagination, "white" affixed to the idea of devil or Satan served as an adjective emphasizing the degree of severity or the danger of the lie or devil referenced.

One hundred or so years later, Daniel Defoe's 1726 *The Political History of the Devil* juxtaposes white and black devils, referring to the Devil as lord of the "black race" of all that is in hell. Like Webster a century earlier, in Defoe's text, "white" and "black" are used to convey severity, while black is also used as a general euphemism for evil. The book argued that the Devil has played a powerful role in human history, largely through the Devil's reliance on religion as a mechanism to divide and conquer. Defoe writes that the Devil is "a believer" having "more religion than some of our men of fame can at this time be charged with."[1] Important to Defoe is that the Devil "fears God," suggesting that sacred history and scripture attest to the Devil's fear of God. Defoe also addresses the theological substance of the Devil: is the Devil a singular being or are there many devils? Defoe answers by turning to the New Testament account in Matthew 24, noting that the Devil is a singular being that expresses itself as "Legion, for we are many."[2] Defoe also sketches the relationship between God and the Devil to believers, presenting something of a theological anthropology:

> The Truth is, *God and the Devil*, however opposite in their nature, and remote from one another in their place of abiding, seem to stand pretty much upon a level in our faith; For as to our believing the reality of their existence, he that denies one generally denies both; and he that believes one necessarily believes both.
>
> Very few, if any of those who believe there is a God, and acknowledge the debt of homage which mankind owes to the supreme Governor of the World, doubt the existence of the Devil, except here and there one, whom we call practical Atheists, and tis the character of an Atheist, if there is such a creature on Earth, that like my Lord Duke, he believes neither God or Devil.[3]

In all of Defoe's work, the devil is treated as a literal being, making its first appearance on Earth in the Garden of Eden as the serpent. Defoe is attempting to write an historical account, rather than a theological or otherwise analogical reflection. Race is surely coloring his basic worldview, to the extent race was operative in the eighteenth century, but does not seem to have been a motivating force in his presentation of the Devil.

One early reference to racialized devils is William Mason's 1765 *A Spiritual Treasury for the Children of God*, which refers to the "white devil of pride" and the "black devil of lust."[4] Early in the nineteenth century, explorer Hugh Clapperton's account of an expedition into Africa recounts a Yoruba tribe whose public theatre included a figure who the journal refers to as "the white devil, a meagre, shivering figure, so painted as to represent a European."[5] Yet this reference was seemingly not tinged with the moral weight we will come to associate with the white devil in the late nineteenth and twentieth centuries. It reads as a causal British euphemism akin to "chap" or "lad." Lastly, one of the earliest documented instances of the association of white men with devils comes from an obscure history of early American soldier and frontiersman Robert Rogers. The text sees fit to include the term "Wobi-Madaondo" in its index, explaining that this means "white devil" and was given to Rogers by "enemy French Indians."[6]

Also during the nineteenth century, David Walker's *Appeal to the Coloured Citizens of the World* (1829) mentions white people "'acting like devils.'"[7] The reference shows up again in 1866, in *Zion's Witness: Published Monthly, Exclusively for the Sect Which Is Everywhere Spoken Against—Acts. XXVIII. 22.*, edited by Arthur Wilcockson.[8] The author writes that

> Of all the devils in earth or hell the white devil is the most crafty. The black devil would follow me into the basest of sins, in filth and dirt with the swine of the world; but the white devil could follow me into the company of saints: and, from my experience, I boldly affirm, that there is more wickedness done under the garb of sanctity in unclean thoughts, lasciviousness, an evil eye, and hypocrisy in the house of God than in the most filthy of Satan's acknowledged dens on earth.[9]

Given the time periods and social contexts, it is reasonable to imagine these references carried racialized connotations. That same year, the term was used to refer to a white person by James Greenwood in his *Silas the Conjurer: His Travels and Perils* (1866).[10] Greenwood made a name for himself as a novelist, travel writer, and journalist of curios and oddities that often included accounts of prostitutes and "savages." Essentially, Greenwood peddled racist and misogynistic stories to an all-too-eager white Western audience. Another example is found in Volume 1 of 1870's *The Rural Carolinian*. In it, JNO. G. Williams reflects on the aftermath of the Civil War, namely Reconstruction:

> The South, like those unfortunate people mentioned in the Bible, has ever been 'possessed' by two fierce and unyielding demons, which, in respect to color, may be called the *black devil* and the *white devil*. The black devil, Abe Lincoln 'cast out,' or 'emancipated' us from his tyranny; and though the operation was very violent, and left us much bruised and sore, and though this terrible demon still returns to 'torment' us in the persons of his emissaries, yet we hope to be delivered from them finally, and our wounds all healed; but from the white devil there is no hope of deliverance for the poor South yet. What a heartless devil he is! He sports himself in the miseries of his unfortunate subject, makes her weak when she is naturally strong, starves her when she might be full of bread, and holds up to her a picture of boundless wealth, while at the same time he is making her bankrupt, takes away her reason and sense, and makes her one to be pitied, when she might be admired and envied. Could the South be exorcised of this white devil, as she has been of the black devil, she would soon be a greater country than she ever has been, greater in population, and greater in all the elements of a great country.[11]

Williams' reflection seems to be a reference to the end of slavery, if not the enslaved, as well as Reconstruction efforts along with northern "carpetbaggers." The association of white people or white men with devils seems to have intensified across the post-Reconstruction period in the United States. Journals from the turn of the twentieth century also offer similar references to white devils. A 1900 pamphlet written for white Christian missionaries reference Native Americans referring to white folks as "devils."[12] Another example appears in 1902 in Volume 85 of *The Churchman*, where white Americans are referred to as both "foreign devils" and "white devils," depending on the context and their locations.[13] A number of Christian mission periodicals actively and openly discuss the tendencies of non-whites to level the epithet of "devil" against white missionaries working domestically and abroad. Novels and other popular fiction played part in normalizing the idea, as well. Joseph Conrad's 1897 *The Nigger of the Narcissus* uses the term once, in direct racialized reference to a white man: "He talked about black devils—he is a devil—a white devil … ."[14] Edgar Rice Burroughs seems to have helped popularize the term in his Tarzan series. One of his books from 1916 wrote that the "black had recognized Tarzan as the white devil from the descriptions given by the whites and their black servants."[15] And, 1919's *Jungle Tales of Tarzan* refers to a "white devil-god" numerous times.[16]

Beyond the white/black binary, many references to "white devils" during the period are also associated with orientalism (in literature), emerging from the minds of authors as either a genuine perspective held by many Asians about white men in their dealings with Western white men or a racist caricature and projection of racial anxiety onto Asian populations by white authors. In fact, most references to white devils found in the early twentieth-century literary archives arise from white/Asian encounters.[17] Of many examples, the work of Lewis Stanton Palen stands out, including his *The White Devil of the Black Sea* (1924) and its sequel, *The White Devil's Mate* (1926). Globally, outside of black and brown American culture, one of the most prominent associations of white men with white devils is the Cantonese term *Gweilo*, which translates into either "white devil" or "foreign devil." Routine use of the term continues today in Hong Kong and across much of China. Depending on tone or context, the reference can be considered an insult or merely a description of a white foreign man. Etymologically, *Gwai* refers to either "ghost" or "devil," conveying the sense that white foreigners have earned a reputation for bringing harm to the indigenous populations of Asia. Most notable from this short genealogy of the presence of the white devil as a cultural trope for Westerners is recognizing that indigenous people in Asia, Africa, and the Americas were naming white men in ways that all translated into English as "devil" or "demon." In the eyes of all these others, we were being associated with evil. By the 1920s, our anxieties about that association had galvanized in popular culture. By then, many in the Anglophone world associated white men with devils and the association had become part of popular knowledge in the United States.

***

By the time of W.D. Fard Muhammad's arrival to Detroit, Michigan in 1930, the trope of the "white devil" was part of the popular American cultural imagination and available for his use. Along with the idea of the white devil, Fard also made use of various physical facts associated with the Earth, presenting them to followers as a series of lessons involving the true story of the human family. Fard's teachings would eventually be systematized and organized as the Lost-Found Lessons (120 Lessons) and elaborated upon in the books of the Honorable Elijah Muhammad. Studying these lessons promoted Knowledge of Self. This Knowledge of Self is both subjective knowledge for each individual self, and it can also be thought of as built around certain epistemological axioms packaged in the form of question and answer. Under Elijah Muhammad's leadership, the Nation of Islam would grow into a thriving religious community, organized in no small measure around the idea that black men were the original men of the earth and white men were devils. The Lost Found Lesson No. 1 is particularly instructive in its description of white devils as dangerous and (nearly) beyond salvation:

> Q: Who is the Original Man? A: The original man is the Asiatic Black man; the Maker; the Owner; the Cream of the planet Earth—Father of Civilization, God of the Universe.
>
> Q: Who is the Colored Man? A: The Colored man is the Caucasian (white man). Or, Yakub's grafted Devil—the Skunk of the planet Earth.[18]

These two questions begin the Lost Found Lessons and effectively define what Fard means by "Devil": "A grafted man which is made weak and wicked. Or, any grafted, life germ from the original is a devil."[19] Applying the basic biblical and mythical notion of the devil as a fallen angel who fell because it tried—and failed—to act like God, devils are inherently weak and dangerous largely because they do not accept their second-class status. They seek to act like God—or in this case, the Original Man—and in those actions inflict terror on themselves and others. Because awareness of this behavior could only possibly come from God, devils have not ears to hear of our devilish ways. This means that intervention is next to impossible, leading Fard to conclude that not a single devil can be reformed: "All the prophets have tried to reform him (devil), but were unable. So they have agreed that it cannot be done unless we graft him back to the original man which takes six hundred years. So instead of losing time grafting him back, they have decided to take him off the planet."[20] At times in the teachings, these rules of engagement with devils become even more severe. Fard suggested that Muhammad and Muslims were under the expectation to "murder the devil," stating that the duty of each Muslim is to "bring four devils." The 120 Lessons remark that "Muhammad learned that he could not reform the devils, so they had to be murdered. All Muslims will murder the devil they know he is a snake and, also, if he be allowed to live, he would sting someone else."[21] At best, devils can study theology and science between thirty-five and fifty years before "he can call himself a Muslim son" because he is so savage in his nature. Even then, the Original Man simply cannot trust white devils:

> A Muslim does not love the Devil regardless of how long he studies. After he has devoted thirty-five or fifty years trying to learn and do like the original man, he could come and do trading among us and we would not kill him as quick as we would the other Devils—that is, who have not gone under this Study.[22]

Fard's teachings mark a theological threshold whereupon black men are, at least, associated with divinity and, at most, establish themselves as Gods unto themselves. Black male Knowledge of Self, then, *is* divinity. Concomitantly, the Lost Found Lessons also offer Knowledge of Self to white men, only the story is much more severe. In clear terms, we are savage devils—"the Skunk of the planet Earth."[23] In the Lessons, "savage" refers to "a person that has lost the knowledge of himself and who is living a beast life." These savages, lacking Knowledge of Self, work to prevent the rest of the world's population from gaining their own Knowledge of Self. This basic social dynamic is distilled into percentages. Eighty-five percent of the world's population is ignorant of who they are, while 10 percent of the population are the devils who want to keep the 85 percent in ignorance. And, 5 percent are the Poor Righteous Teachers who seek to promote Knowledge of Self to the 85 percent. The Lessons present an image of the 10 percent as nearly beyond redemption.

Elijah Muhammad's 1965 text *Message to the Blackman in America* elaborates on much of what is found in the Lost-Found Lessons, at times expounding upon the raw information and at other times, explaining some of the answers and motivations for the severity of the perspectives offered by Fard. Parts of the book help to create a personality profile of white men. According to the text, Allah created white men to rule for 6000 years, a time that has come to an end. This 6000-year rule was characterized by murder, lying and other sorts of deception, all which "originated with the creators of evil and injustice—the white race."[24] Most instructive, Muhammad suggests that by our very nature, white people are "incapable of loving even themselves."[25] This psychological trait is exemplified in moments when white children make fun of black and brown children, analyzed in the text as the projection of self-hate onto others. Effectively, white devils were made through a grafting process organized around making social distinctions. Yakub taught us how to do this, and in a sense, it is all we seem to know how to do. "Yakub was the founder of unlike attracts and like repels."[26] Through the manipulation of magnetic attraction, Yakub created all the races, ultimately the white race being created last—therefore, holding within us the fewest natural healthy qualities. As a result, we must protect ourselves from the other races because if we do not, then the natural genetic dominance of the other races will win out and white people will be eradicated. Hence, the long-standing white demand for segregation and anti-miscegenation efforts. In this way, white devils created "Caucasian—which means, according to some of the Arab scholars, One whose evil effect is not confined to one's self alone, but affects others."[27]

Muhammad continues his psychological profile of the white man by turning to our history. According to the myth of Yakub, we were eventually exiled to Europe for a period of 2000 years. We lost all sense of civilization and became savages. We had no political leadership or artistic culture. "They lost all knowledge of civilization," according to Muhammad. "Being deprived of divine guidance for their disobedience, the making of mischief and causing bloodshed in the holy nation of the original black people by lies, they became so savage that they lost all their sense of shame … They became shameless."[28] Muhammad goes on to even explain the white man's enduring love of dogs, explaining that during our time in the caves of Europe, our "next and best weapons were the dogs." He writes that

> They tamed some of these dogs to live in the caves with their families, to help protect them from the wild beasts. After a time, the dog held a high place among the family because of his fearlessness to attack the enemies of his master. Today, the dog is still loved by the white race and is given more justice than the so-called Negroes, and, is called the white man's best friend. This comes from the cave days.[29]

Muhammad's psychological profile of white people ends with a basic comparison of white and black personality traits:

> Black people have a heart of gold, love and mercy. Such a heart, nature did not give to the white race. This is where the so-called Negroes are deceived in this devil race. They think they have the same kind of heart; but the white race knows better. They have kept it as a secret among themselves, that they may be able to deceive the black people.
> They have been, and still are, successful in deceiving the black man, under the disguise of being the ones who want peace, love and friendship with the world, and with God—at the same time making war with the world, to destroy peace, love and friendship of the black nation.[30]

Whether this comparison is literally true or not is not as significant as finding the truth within it. Muhammad's comparison hurts my white ears and eyes, but the basic distinction he poses resonates with the truth of my own experiences. Obviously, there are exceptions to any general rule, especially racial rules, but exceptions also prove rules. In my experiences, black folks have tended to express far more space in their hearts for others, including white folks. Conversely, far too many white folks struggle even to love ourselves. Many of us are too quick to write off others for moral failures, and rarely do we trust one another fully (even within white communities).

The image of white men presented here is hard to stomach for me as a white man. That difficulty presents me with a significant choice. I could deny the narrative, dismissing this entire religious system on the grounds that it convicts me in a negative light. At best, I might promote space for folks who do believe these stories while in my mind, I would maintain a distinction between those folks' freedom to believe what they want and my opinion that this story of us being devils is not true. At worst, the severity of the charge that I am a devil might be responded to by owning that description through new or renewed anti-black racism. "If they're telling me I'm a devil, then I'll show them they're right." Both of these possible responses are insufficient, however, because they undermine the veracity and legitimacy of the beliefs. I don't necessarily have to believe everything a Five Percenter believes, but I must create space in my mind for the beliefs to be valid for the believers. And to the extent those beliefs involve me as white devil, the beliefs invite me to turn inward and explore my Knowledge of Self. Or, my lack thereof. I want to find value in this material. But what would or could this value look like? How might a white response to the myth of Yakub and our status as white devils be developed? Would such a response require abandoning myself and my identity as a white man? How can I own up to who I am if owning up to it involves rejecting it?

***

Arguably the scholar who has written most extensively on the Nation of Gods and Earths is Michael Muhammad Knight. By far, Knight has written the most substantial material addressing the seeming paradox of a white man taking responsibility for the charge that we are a race of devils. Having authored several books that explore different dimensions of black American Islamic esoteric traditions, Knight's work is a powerful exploration of the deeply enmeshed nature of religious, ethnic, and at times, gendered identity, as well. In short, the white Knight comes to find that one potential response to whiteness is offered to white people in the form of conversion to Islam. Going so far as to profess (at times) that he is a member of the Nation of Gods and Earths, Knight's work is insightful, ground-breaking, and a vital aspect of any study of white devils.

Particularly instructive is Knight's notion of the "exceptional devil," a devil who does not want to be a devil anymore and tries to change their character and/or their reputation. For Knight, the prototype of the exceptional devil is William Lloyd Garrison, who was a strong abolitionist and for a time, friend, and mentor to Frederick Douglass. Knight conveys that Douglass once came to Garrison with the idea of starting a newspaper. Garrison responded by discouraging Douglass from the endeavor.

> Though deeply committed to the cause [of racial equality], Garrison became the Exceptional Devil by failing to consider that the struggle for black liberation might actually belong to black people—that it wasn't about *him*. Even as a freedom fighter, he still had to be a white guy about it and assume that his own voice was the most important in the room.[31]

While I struggle to see the connection between the example of discouraging Douglass and Knight's claim that Garrison was making it about himself, the concept of the exceptional devil is useful as a frame for exploring potential white responses to knowledge of ourselves as devils. In short, exceptional devils end up proving the rule, in that their efforts to not be or act like a devil inevitably create scenarios where their devilish behavior shows up. To this extent, by not accepting our nature, we risk showing our devilish nature to others more acutely than if we'd have just minded our business. Hence, even exceptional devils *still* act like white men, seeking to escape our ontology. Knight shares many stories of his own moments living into the archetype of the exceptional devil, before discussing other exceptional devils who have participated in the Nation of Gods and Earths.

The most famous "white God" is named Azrael, who Father Allah met while they were both in Matteawan State Hospital for the Criminally Insane. There, Father Allah befriended Azrael and recognized that "Azrael displayed no stake in white supremacy."[32] Azrael would come to be a mentor to Knight, as Knight explored the culture and his white relationship to the culture. Knight suggests Azrael "largely steered clear of the Exceptional Devil trap,"[33] although it is not clear how except that Azrael seems to have largely rejected many of the societal norms usually associated with white men. Knight also includes attention to "the first white person to join Warith Deen Mohammed's deracialized Nation of Islam," Dorothy Blake Fardan.[34] When asking her about the place of white people in black Islams, Fardan suggested Knight turn to Malcolm X's thoughts on the possibilities of white response. Malcolm X's words bear repeating here:

> I have these very deep feelings that white people who want to join black organizations are really just taking the escapist way to salve their consciences. By visibly hovering near us, they are "proving" they are "with us." But the hard truth is this isn't helping to solve America's racist problem. The Negroes aren't the racists. Where the really sincere white people have got to do their "proving" of themselves is not among the black victims, but out on the battle lines of where America's racism really is—and that's in their own home communities; America's racism is among their own fellow whites, that's where the sincere whites who really mean to accomplish something have got to work.[35]

Malcolm X calls white folks into renewed community with other white folks. Yet white folks who are escaping are not merely doing it for clearing our conscience—but often as a matter of safety. The tension between responsibility to safety of self and family over against the need to correct the actions and feelings of white people through activism is not easily resolved. This seems to have proven a constant challenge for Fardan, who sought theological escape in the story of white devils, going so far as to consider theological appeals to liberal inclusivity and equality as white lies. Knight recounts that Fardan initially joined a Sunni mosque but that it did not include the specific attention to American racist history that the Nation of Islam included as foundational. Essentially, the versions of Islam that were inclusive of her did not provide the theological emphasis on race and ethnicity that had initially led Fardan down her Damascus Road. Yet the versions of Islam attentive to that theological emphasis were largely exclusionary. Fardan ended up with mixed allegiances to Warith Deen's (then) more egalitarian community while also supporting what would become Louis Farrakhan's reorganization of the Nation of Islam. In short, Fardan's conversion left her socially dislocated, if spiritually nurtured.

Fardan's story as well as Knight's (and my own to an extent) exemplify an inescapable problem for white folks who want to respond responsibly to black esoteric wisdom and experience something of a conversion through that wisdom. In short, white people interested in these traditions cannot help but center ourselves (in certain spaces and moments). This is the problem of white particularity. Philosopher Robyn Wiegman characterizes this as a kind of paradox, "split in the white subject—between disaffiliation from white supremacist practices and disavowal of the ongoing reformation of white power and one's benefit from it."[36] In short, how can whites respond to our critics in a sympathetic way without centering ourselves in the discourse? Is it possible at all? More generally, how can whites today feel a stable identity when, in the wake of integration, we effectively lost our principal means of establishing our "white" identity, to begin with? In this way, I agree with Knight when he theologically concludes that "White people are devils not because of their origin or skin color but because of the meaning that they have given to whiteness and what this meaning has achieved in the world."[37] But this emphasis on behavior and belief as opposed to genetics and nature does not address the relationship between interracial/religious dialogue and Knowledge of Self. Knight, by my estimation, does what Fardan does as well—looks to black people for validation that there is salvation available to us. I have done this with hip hop culture and black culture, as well, turning to cultures not my own to provide a kind of rescue from the hell of the white world. In his case, Knight concludes that "this family can include the sons and daughters of devils,"[38] while leaving ambiguous just who he means by "this family." Comprehensively, these black esoteric traditions are built around the fundamental claim that the white man is the devil. While it is understandable that many of us would want to escape that charge, the escape effort can be read as the height of white devilish arrogance—hence, the "exceptional devil." In trying to escape the charge, we risk looking like worse versions of ourselves than if we would have just accepted, rather than rejected, our Knowledge of Self as devils. We white men cannot dictate how others perceive us, so in seeking validation in these communities, we reinforce a pathological psychosocial relationship to black knowledge and black opinions. In a word, we remain codependent. Knight knows this. Fardan knows this. Azrael may have known this, as well. Nevertheless, none of them seem to have responded fully to the charge leveled by Malcolm X about what sympathetic whites can do to begin responding to our devilish ways.

5 TROGLODYTES

An allegory is a true story. Usually, we think of the word "allegory" as conveying fictional information that teaches us a broader, real-world lesson, or as a story used to deliver a deeper, perhaps hidden message. George Orwell's *Animal Farm* is an allegory about political machinations in Russia. Hermann Melville's *Moby Dick* is an allegory of the United States wrestling with our legacy of slavery and racism. And Greek philosopher Plato's story of the cave is an allegory about our relationship to truth, our blindness to reality as it is, and our willingness to deny others and even kill them lest they reveal to us that we are living a lie. What needs to be "true" in an allegory for us to glean truth from it? Does the story need to be historically factual, or do the implications of the story on history matter? An allegory is a true story, but this recognition leaves open-ended the question of whose truth is conveyed and how our interpretations cause that truth to twist and turn across history.

Plato's "Allegory of the Cave" is foundational for the Western world, and it goes something like this: Plato, who is usually dated to about 350 BCE, writes that his teacher, Socrates, is talking with his companion Glaucon. Socrates tells Glaucon to imagine men chained in a cave, their faces pointing to the dark side of the cave (not the cave opening). They are chained in place; even their heads cannot turn fully from side to side. Socrates calls these men prisoners, but whose prisoners is never indicated. Chained to an embankment in the bottom of the cave, these men only know the reality that they see in front of them. Directly above and behind them, a stone wall is built that makes it difficult for natural light to make its way to the back wall of the cave. Further behind this wall, in the direction of the cave opening, is a lit fire. This fire supplies enough light to cast shadows onto the back wall of the cave. Other men—presumably free of chains—hoist objects above the stone wall and from the light provided by the fire, these objects cast their shadows onto the back of the cave wall. For the chained prisoners, "reality" would only be known from the shadows cast onto the wall, nothing more. Plato tells us that "such prisoners would deem reality to be nothing else than the shadows of the artificial objects."[1]

According to Plato, Socrates also encourages Glaucon to imagine a hypothetical intervention into this scene. What would happen if one of these prisoners were to escape or to be freed? Presumably, they would make their way slowly out of the cave and have difficulty understanding literally everything they discovered about reality. All of reality would be a problem for them, as they only had those past shadows to go by for orientation and understanding. We could imagine further that this escapee would make his way totally outside the cave and come to learn that what he had understood as reality was but a two-dimensional portrait (in black and white, no less) of reality. Accepting reality would take a long time and wouldn't come without hardship. Suppose further that after the former prisoner had acclimated to the *real* reality, he was discovered by guards and taken back into custody, to be put back with the other prisoners in the cave. Socrates concludes the story with some brief attention to the difficulties the briefly free prisoner would have acclimating back to the darkness of the cave, and equally, the difficulty the other prisoners would have at believing the one who had temporarily escaped, especially in those moments when he told the others the truth about each shadow cast upon the wall. Would they be able to understand the shadows as representations of realer objects? Could he even convey what he'd experienced outside the cave? The social dynamics would grow to be so severe inside of the cave, that the prisoners would meditate on killing the man responsible for trying to tell them the truth of their reality.

This "allegory" amounts to a distillation of one-half of the bedrock of how white Western men have understood *our own understanding* of the world around us. Plato's story tells us how our brains relate to the world and what we know about the world, and how both are connected to our personality and sense of self. It is a foundational theory for what we call "idealism" and "rationality" as much as it serves popular culture as the model of philosophical acumen undergirding *The Matrix* franchise. All of us struggle to escape the "caves" made by our own limitations, and many of us fear knowledge of the truth (even though we still aren't sure what that truth is). The allegory tells us something about our relationship to knowledge, in general, in the sense of recognizing that we only know a small amount of the information that makes up our reality. And just as importantly, as much as we assume much ado over the finding of information and facts, and emphasize the importance of education, most of us are happy with our limited knowledge, preferring relative ignorance and security of thought to *true* knowledge that would shake our existential foundations.

As an allegory, with its many parallelisms and comparisons, Plato asks us to think, and to think hard, by simply imagining the setting he describes, much less by making use of it for understanding *our* world. Harder still, but somewhat manageable, would be to apply the wisdom of the allegory to a more specific case than usual. Most often, people use the allegory to tell us something about the *human* condition. But could it say something about *particular* humans? One way we could evaluate the dexterity of the allegory is through the prism of race. Rather than a story about all of us, we could see a relationship between white ignorance and black realities. Suppose the allegory is applied to white folks. It could follow at least a couple different directions. One direction would be that black folks, today, are in bondage inside of a "cave," and as a result of the deep wounds of enslavement and racism, black folks are not yet attuned to reality. This would then account for what we call black pathology, the bad stuff some black folks do that we whites preoccupy ourselves with at an astounding rate. Following this perspective, we white men would be the "stone wall builders" from Plato's story, the makers of slavery and racism that have kept black folks in a cave of ignorance. It would be up to them to choose knowledge and freedom. White men would then be left in the tension between promoting black freedom from the cave, or awareness that ignorance is bliss, and consequentially, it is best to keep black folks ignorant.

Another way to use the allegory for understanding race and racism would point in a nearly opposite direction. White men, in our ignorance of black life and culture, and our indifference or hatred of blackness, choose bondage inside of our own cave of whiteness instead of accepting reality, as such. We lack Knowledge of Self. Slavery, then, amounts to the routinization of white immaturity, and the forcing of another more mature population (or populations) to work on our behalf because we did not yet have the skills to be fully human. White masculinity, in essence, could be considered this state of manufactured innocence based on ignorance, and blackness, the state of awareness of reality in its fullness and its complexity. We whites forced black people—first through slavery and then through segregation and racial oppression—to navigate all of reality as we remained in our "cave" of childlike ignorance.

We could come up with countless iterations of racialized reflection. But what if we took Plato's famous tale more literally than most would imagine useful. Would doing so tell us anything about who white people are or who we have been? What if the story is not only a parable about knowledge and what we do with it as humans—all of us—but tells us something of the actual history of white people?

Usually, we teach this allegory as a tale about *human* limits and motivations. All of us can see glimpses of ourselves chained to the cave, sometimes the free prisoner, and other times, the men hoisting the objects up above the wall. Some of the time, some of us even feel like that returned prisoner trying to convince his compatriots that the world is bigger and more beautiful and magnificent than they know. Plato's allegory is truthful in these and many other ways, and scholars have debated the implications of the allegory for centuries.

But what if the story was true in another sense?

***

There is no way to conclusively argue that Plato had white people in mind when relaying Socrates' "Allegory of the Cave." But it turns out that white people have a long history of our being associated with caves. The allegory offers the opportunity to tell a story about white folks that has been all but ignored over the last 100 years or so of Western scholarship. Today, many white men tend to respond to white racism and white supremacy (as a policy issue) as if to do right by our history of anti-black racism, we have to reject racialized thinking (rather than reject racism). The problem is rendered not so much as the hatred or oppression of another group, but the rendering of "us" and "them" into groups, at all. By this logic, we get to continue to hate and oppress people, only not under the auspices of race. At least not openly or without censure. On top of this moral effect of what we can loosely call liberalism's impact on racial understanding is that this logic makes it difficult to honestly track the history of racialized groups across time and space. In today's academic landscape, in fact, doing so is a bit of a fool's errand. If we want tenure or promotion in race studies, the history of white people only extends back about 500 years. There are understandable reasons why the politics of racial study has taken shape the way it has, but it doesn't tell the whole story of white people available in our religious archives. In fact, we do have a racial history widely available as our religious history. If we take seriously certain stories found in sacred texts associated with the West, we do have a story to tell. In fact, we can isolate evidence that demonstrates that as far back as antiquity, others tended to talk about white people in a particularly pernicious way. Indeed, that story often involves our penchant for cave-dwelling.

Few have told this story better or more often than Elijah Muhammad. In these tellings, the leader of the NOI is careful to note that the scientist Mr. Yakub was a "God." This moniker has implications for claiming a personal identity and for ascribing an identity onto someone based on utility (that is, on what they do to or for us). It is a reference to Yakub being himself an original man, a black man and it is also a statement about the black man being the creator God of the white man, an unruly race of devils. These devils were called "Caucasian," which Elijah Muhammad tells us refers to "one whose evil effect is not confined to oneself alone, but affects others."[2] Contrary to popular impressions, we whites are not named after the Caucasus mountains in eastern Europe.[3] Those mountains are named after us. Yakub created the race of white devils on the island of Patmos, and after some time, these devils headed to the mainland making their way, ultimately, to the Holy City of Mecca. Mecca had been where Yakub was from, and it was his plan to sow discord there among the citizenry. According to Elijah Muhammad, this discord would be sown through a strategy called "tricknology," which he describes here in a passage from 1965's *Message to the Blackman in America*:

> Mr. Yakub taught his made devils on Pelan: 'That—when you go back to the holy black nation, rent a room in their homes. Teach your wives to go out the

next morning around the neighbors of the people, and tell that you heard her talking about them last night.'

'When you have gotten them fighting and killing each other, then ask them to let you help settle their disputes, and restore peace among them. If they agree, then you will be able to rule them both.' This method the white race practices on the black nation, the world over.[4]

Once back in Mecca, it took about six months for the devils' terror to cause such discord that the original black people finally had to take the issue to their King. The King recognized that there would be no peace until Mecca was rid of the devils. And so, the King issued an edict:

'Gather every one of the devils up and strip them of our costume. Put an apron on them to hide their nakedness. Take all literature from them and take them by way of the desert. Send a caravan, armed with rifles, to keep the devils going westward. Don't allow one of them to turn back; and, if they are lucky enough to get across the Arabian Desert, let them go into the hills of West Asia, the place they now call Europe.'[5]

The King directed his military commander, named General Monk Monk, to collect the savage white race, bind them by chains, and set them in a straight line.[6] The general marched these whites across the hot burning sands of Arabia and what is today the Middle East—North and West into modern-day Turkey. Many of Yakub's white race died during the trip, and General Monk Monk would quickly execute any of the whites who sought to escape. After such a long journey, the white men and women who made it to Turkey were in a thoroughly decrepit, savage state. It was then that General Monk Monk freed them. Upon doing so, the whites fled across what is today Armenia, Azerbaijan, and Georgia into the caves of Europe. While the whites descended into total depravity, General Monk Monk's soldiers would stay in the area of Turkey for 2000 years, becoming the Turkish people, and preventing the white savages from escaping the wilds of Europe. Some speculate that the Gates of Alexander and the Sasanian defense lines were first ancient walls built by the Turks to keep these savages in Europe.

Unable to escape Europe, naked and forced to endure the dismal climate, whites found refuge in cave life. For 2000 years, the story goes that we whites lived as (and with) animals:

Being without a guide, they started walking on their hands and feet like all animals, and, learned to climb trees as well as any of the animals. At night, they would climb up into trees, carrying large stones and clubs, to fight the wild beasts that would come prowling around at night, to keep them from eating their families.

Their next and best weapons were the dogs. They tamed some of these dogs to live in the caves with their families, to help protect them from the wild beasts. After a time, the dog held a high place among the family because of his fearlessness to attack the enemies of his master. Today, the dog is still loved by the white race and is given more justice than the so-called Negroes, and is called the white man's best friend. This comes from the cave days.[7]

After 2000 years living in savage conditions, outside of civilization, Allah decided it was time the white man take over as punisher of the original man. It would be Moses, taught about civilization by the civilized Egyptians, who would then lead the white devils out of the wilderness. According to Elijah Muhammad, Moses taught these white people how to leave the caves, how to wear clothes and cook their food, and taught them many of the behaviors that we today refer to as religious rituals. Elijah Muhammad even refers to specific Jewish rituals like maintaining sabbath and certain dietary restrictions. This story offers an origin account for white people, whether Jew or Gentile, atheist or Christian. To paraphrase Muhammad, Moses taught all of us that if we would follow him and obey him, Allah would give them a place among the holy people. Most of us believed Moses, just to get out of the caves.[8]

If we look at the Quran, Sūrah Eighteen is called "The Cave" (Al-Kahf) and talks about a "People of the Cave," that tells an allegorical tale remarkably similar to Plato's allegory. The story goes that a group of young folks did not agree with the particular theology operative in their city at the time; and, as a response, they retreat to a cave, with their dogs in tow, who keep guard as the youth fall asleep for "300 and 9 years." Line twenty-two emphasizes how Muslims might be able to recognize white people (despite considerable variability in the size of the groups in which we travel): "They will say, 'Three, and their fourth being their dog.' And they will say, 'Five, and their sixth being their dog,' guessing at the unknown. And they will say, 'Seven, and their eighth being their dog.' Say, 'My Lord knows best their number.'"[9] Remarkably, it is literally written into the Quran that no matter how many white people are ever congregated in a single space, demographers will always have to count an additional dog. And of course, we do take our dogs everywhere. And we sleep with them, too.

Commentators on this Quranic story, also called the tale of the Seven Sleepers in both Christian and Muslim sources, tend to treat the story as if it were historical fact, debating over which moment and place in history it describes. Not everyone racializes the story but doing so produces interesting results. When read through the prism of race, the story of the Seven Sleepers is remarkably like Plato's allegory. Both are stories about the consequences of certain people maintaining a wrong-headed outlook on reality, and the difficulties of coming to terms with that reality and that wrong-headedness. In

Plato's story, Socrates refers to all of reality as such. In the Seven Sleepers story, the beef is over who is or is not God. Perhaps, a case might be made that the Seven Sleepers flee to the caves in response to their rejection of the divine status of the original man in the city. These uncountable white folks did not like that they lived in a world where the black man was God, or at least, where God held the visage of a black man.

Seven Sleepers shares certain elements with Elijah Muhammad's story and other features with Plato's story. All of them trade in assuming qualitative differences between groups of people. Until relatively recently in theological education, it was widely believed that the Genesis account of Adam and Eve referred to the creation of the white race. Others were here before us. The biblical story is not about *all* of us, but only *some* of us. Original Man was already on the planet, and as some have speculated, he was the creator of Adam and Eve, the first white people.

For instance, we know from various references in Genesis that caves were a common dwelling place for the descendants of Adam. Caves were used for living, defecating, congregating, fornicating, and burials. Genesis 23:11 refers to caves as a place to bury the dead. 1 Samuel: 24 recounts the story of Saul pooping in a cave. And Genesis 19 tells the story of Lot's drunken, incestuous sex with his daughters in their mountainous cave. Exodus 2:21 relays the story of Reuel/Raguel (best known as Jethro), who gave away his daughter Zipporah to Moses. According to Josephus' *The Antiquity of the Jews* (93 AD), Raguel was a troglodyte, corroborating Moses' work in the land of the cave dwellers and marking Moses as the husband of a troglodyte. The Hebrew Bible is replete with references to the groups of people we will eventually come to call "white people," and to those people originally living in caves.

To the extent "we" white people *are* being described in these stories, it wouldn't be difficult to conclude we were—as a feature of our identity, *our* Knowledge of Self—a people of the cave. We were troglodytes; and the Hebrew Bible can be interpreted as a chronicle of our coming out from the caves and slowly joining the ranks of the civilized whilst terrorizing the already civilized nations of the Earth.

***

Considering what we know from these sacred texts, could we imagine that Plato was making a comparative leap encouraging the people of his time and place to not act like the savage, blind white folks who lived in the caves north of Greece and Turkey? Was the "Allegory of the Cave" really a warning about white folks' savage limitations, and if so, is that why the story has resonated with us for so many centuries? It is fascinating to imagine Plato actively reflecting on white ignorance, in a Greek world that was much more diverse than we tend to imagine that it was, and in a time and space where white troglodytes were oppressed as either slaves or social problems of one sort or another.

Does an allegory need to be historically verifiable to tell us something useful about ourselves? In the nineteenth century, in the Anglophone world "Troglodyte" came to be a pedantic epithet for describing those who would exhibit savage or primitive behavior. Apparently, nobody wants to be a cave dweller. And so, we conveniently forgot who we were, inhibiting our efforts to know who we will be today. At what point do we realize that our autopoietic efforts to create ourselves sometimes meet limits imposed by who we were already? Elijah Muhammad reminds that "the devil is the 'devil' regardless of place and time."[10] In like manner, does a cave dweller ever stop hiding in caves? We no longer live in caves, this much is true. But have we escaped our primitive, cave-like thinking?

I tend to imagine that we have not escaped the cave, not least because of the perennial Western interest in cultural narratives that reiterate the "Allegory of the Cave." Over the last twenty-five-hundred years or so, this story came to be the gold standard of white wisdom-seeking and making, and for many of us, it remains so. The cave is our cultural inheritance. It is the key to deciphering our cognitive and social limitations as white folks. We also use it to garner coercion and understanding over others. It is a model of *us* that we apply to *them*. In this way, it is our principal cultural allegory.

> 'Quite inevitably,' he said. 'Consider, then, what would be the manner of the release and healing from these bonds and this folly if in the course of nature something of this sort should happen to them: When one was freed from his fetters and compelled to stand up suddenly and turn his head around and walk and to lift up his eyes to the light, and in doing all this felt pain ….'[11]

6 AUTHENTICITY

In a 1962 *New Yorker* article titled "Letter from a Region in My Mind," American writer James Baldwin recounts a time he had an audience with the Honorable Elijah Muhammad, the longtime leader of the black esoteric tradition known as the Nation of Islam. Whilst in Harlem to deliver a speech, the NOI leader and the young author shared a meal. During the meal, much of the talk was of the white man, and his devilish ways. "The white man sure is the devil. He proves that by his actions," Baldwin remembers overhearing.[1] This proposition—that the white man is the devil—was a difficult, but somewhat reasonable pill for Baldwin to swallow. The talk with Elijah Muhammad and some other members of the NOI was premised on a basic idea, that the white man is the devil, because his actions in history prove devilish. Elijah Muhammad's position, while "single-minded," was historically situated. No theological jumping-jacks were required. In fact, ever the astute ethnographer, Baldwin recognizes that "very little time was spent on theology, for one did not need to prove to a Harlem audience that all white men were devils."[2]

How do we lead an authentic life? Is the person living authentically the one who takes intentional cues from others and integrates them into their person? Or do we consider the person who rejects other people's opinions to be the authentic one? What do we mean by "authentic" to begin with? As it concerns white men, do we judge ourselves authentic when we express brash (and sometimes dangerous) honesty with respect to racial and gendered codes of belief and conduct? Or is authenticity at work for the white man who seeks to control their baser thoughts and behaviors to the point of repression of those racial and gendered norms and expectations? Which version of us, in the end, is morally justified? Does escape involve rejection of that moniker "devil" or acceptance of it? And upon acceptance, would it be that we are devils because of our innate character or because our actions are devilish?

Convincing run-of-the-mill America white men that we might be devils is an altogether different task than convincing a Harlemite from the 1960s. Not only does the idea of us being devils cause our defenses to perk up, understandably. Many others of us find the idea downright ridiculous. In this chapter, I want to consider the ontological and the moral limits of who we are as white men (considering the charge that we are devils). To put it simply, we can learn a lot if we bracket out our skepticism or defensiveness and instead treat the possibility as a thought experiment. And not for nothing, as Tupac Shakur once reminded, if we take the "D" out of devil it leaves us evil. Our talk of devils is ultimately a frame for exploring the concept of evil. Hermeneutician Paul Ricoeur suggests that evil has a particular symbolic value. In his study of evil, Ricoeur says that to begin "with a symbolism already there we give ourselves something to think about; but at the same time, we introduce a radical contingency into our discourse."[3] This introduction of a "radical contingency" is what I hope to accomplish in this chapter. The symbolic value of evil is part of our (white) cultural inheritance. In this way, the devil offers a useful interpretive frame for exploring who we are because we already know much of the semantic values associated with it. As an idea, "Devil" orients us in the world. In fact, Ricoeur emphasizes that here he means "cultural contingency." One can only ever find oneself where one is. Where we go upon orienting ourselves is contingent, that is, left up to chance and wide open with possibility; but it is radical in the sense that we can never change where our journey toward Knowledge of Self begins—in deep, intersubjective reliance on the interpretations of others.

Ricoeur also offers us a definition of evil as "defilement or sin,"[4] along with guilt. By defilement, he means to experience a "blemish that infects from without."[5] By sin, we can take the most basic popular definition of "separation from God," or as Ricoeur puts it, the idea of sin "indicates the *real* situation of man before God, whether man knows it or not."[6] In short, white men exist at and as a radical distance from God—considered here as the black man, but the same holds true if considered in light of a mystery God. The mystery God, in total, is an expression of this radical distance from the rest of our human family. The violent history of monotheism bears this out. Ricoeur also elaborates what he means by guilt. Guilt is, as he characterizes, "to become oneself the tribunal of oneself," emphasizing that such a state is alienating.[7] "Guilt is not synonymous with fault," for Ricoeur.[8] In fact, confusing the two often leads to a misrecognition of not only the human responsibility for action, but also the responsibility for accepting what one's separation from God demands of white men. Guilt is an emotional response to our distance from God, it is the "anticipated chastisement"[9] that is promised because of fall/fault. To experience guilt is "to make oneself the subject of the chastisement."[10]

All this talk of evil and sin is deeply symbolic, religious language, in fact the proper name we give to such material is myth. But following Ricoeur, myth doesn't mean it isn't true. While a myth might be historically false, similar to an allegory a myth is something that tells a different sort of truth. For Ricoeur, this religious language helps teach us *how* to respond to those aspects of ourselves that others may know better than we do. The language of myth, here considered in light of human evil, works for Ricoeur as a kind of confession. To see ourselves as devils is not to hide behind mythical thought. Rather, it allows us to tap into a deep cultural trope in order to claim responsibility for ourselves through a confession impacting our reputation, and to transmute that confession into possibility. Defilement, sin, and guilt are the primary symbols of any such "confession."[11] Taking seriously the possibility of our being devils might be one of these "confessions." Such a confession would include attention to how we have undermined our intrinsic existential situation, how we have misrecognized what it means to be separate from God, and how being at such fault might contribute to an abundance of counterproductive guilt. The French existentialist philosopher Jean-Paul Sartre asks a similar set of questions in his 1951 play *The Devil and the Good Lord*.

***

How might any of us respond to a situation where our longstanding assumptions about ourselves and others have been forever destabilized? What if a person has always thought our own perspective correct, and our lives and communities morally right and justified? Perhaps just as significantly, if we had the option, could we come to terms with who we are to ourselves, and who we appear to be to others? Could I still consider myself "good" while someone else deemed me "evil?"

These ideas are at the center of Jean-Paul Sartre's 1951 play *The Devil and the Good Lord*. Originally presented at the Theatre Antoine in Paris in June 1951, Sartre tells the story of three principal characters: Goetz, Heinrich, and Nasti.[12] The setting for the play is Worms, Germany during the middle of the Renaissance. During this moment of the Renaissance, the various German states are embroiled in two distinct, but related, social crises: The Peasants' Revolt and the beginning of the Martin Luther Protestant Reformation. In many respects, religion connects these two distinct crises. Popularly, many of us tend to remember the "Church" as a morally good institution. Many of us, even if we don't ourselves believe or practice Christianity, think about the church as a well-intentioned institution with a spotty or even bad track record—but that "it's heart is in the right place." Sartre wants us to reconsider this basic assumption based on the evils in Europe during the Reformation. Phenomenology—Sartre's most basic philosophical method—tells us something very different about the church and many within it. Phenomenology begins from the premise that we must assess phenomena as they happen, focusing on experiences in the concrete and not assumptions about innate goodness or good intentions. We ought not accept as self-evident the values we associate with objects or people out in the world. Shifting our attention away from our preconceived notions about what the church is, or whether it is good or bad, enables us to ask critical questions about the church and other institutions and individuals. Such a phenomenological critique of the church and Western Christianity is at the heart of *The Devil and the Good Lord*.

What would it mean for our understanding of ourselves to reconsider something so seemingly obvious as the notion that Christianity does good in the world? Just because Christians say they are working for good in the world does not mean that they are. Just because Christians might believe they are working for good in the world does not mean that they are, either. Such a simple logical point is hard to maintain in real-world settings where so many of us simply assume the best intentions of Christians. Sartre's play suggests that the Protestant Reformation was the result of a series of abuses of power, including but extending beyond the issue of indulgences—that is, buying one's way into heaven. Sartre throws us into the moment of the Reformation for us to consider questions of identity and morality, and social normativity. Particularly, the play presents a social paradox that plays out in terms of individual psychology. Are we determined by an essence, or by our actions? Do my actions determine my essence, or does my essence dictate my actions? This ambiguity on display in the play is ironic because every character believes in some version of right and wrong. But when thrown together, they produce tensions that deconstruct everyone's assumptions about right and wrong and who has access to right and wrong thinking and behavior. Does our nature or do our actions determine our moral value to self and others? Is our moral value based on working for the good of all or is it determined by birthright? The question is similar to the basic theological dichotomy remembered today as a debate during the European Christian Reformation—are we totally depraved or do our actions carry merit in determining whether we are saved? Essentially, Sartre offers an existentialist theological anthropology. Is the decision about whether we are morally righteous or bankrupt a decision to live into one's preordained fate, or is it a decision at all? Ultimately, do our actions determine whether we are good or bad, or do our actions in the world follow from whether we are good or bad deep down in our heart of hearts based on the way God made us?

In the play, the city of Worms is in crisis. The action of the play occurs across a year and some months, whilst Worms is closed-off expecting war. The peasants have revolted, partly against the bishops and nuns of the city. The peasants have thrown some 200 members of the clergy into jail—all but one of the working clergy of Worms. The peasants have also forbidden anyone from leaving the city, as they prepare for an assault from an encroaching army. Heinrich is the name of the lone priest who is spared jail-time because he is considered the "priest of the poor."[13] It will turn out he is a hypocrite. Heinrich maintains a critical voice against the religious establishment, but still believes there is a "right" way to be in relationship to others. He represents moral ambiguity as he embodies the tensions between the poor and the church, fulfilling the needs of the physically and spiritually hungry. Early on, we're told Heinrich's perspective on suffering: "Nothing on earth occurs without the will of God. And God is goodness itself, therefore everything happens for the best."[14] His character forces the audience to consider whose faith is the "right" faith? The bishop called Heinrich a traitor for supporting the poor, and this weighs on Heinrich's psychological well-being. As the play unfolds, Heinrich ends up pessimistic, concluding that justice is altogether impossible.

Nasti is the name of the peasant leader, a baker by trade, who goes against the priest Heinrich directly, suggesting that evil does not come from God, and "for that [very] reason, God needs our help."[15] He is a self-righteous and a religious man who believes in the utility of piety. Faith without works is dead. Good and evil are not preordained but result from the actions we take here and now. He is an advocate of the poor and thinks it is God's will that all people are equal. From Nasti's perspective, Heinrich does not really care about the poor, but is trying to get the priests out of harm's way, out of the way of the Peasants' Revolt. The two find themselves in various theological debates. At one point, Heinrich retorts to Nasti: "If God is on your side, why do the peasants always lose?"

Arguably, evil in the play is personified best by Goetz, the military commander set on conquering the city of Worms. Goetz is merciless and considered to be the "devil" by many around him. His reputation is pure evil, and figuratively, he also represents the loss of stability. He is very contrarian, someone who will say the opposite of what is expected of him in any given moment. He is spiteful and makes decisions based on who or how many they will hurt. Goetz is self-loathing and most motivated to spite God—working to do what he thinks God does not want. Definitionally, that makes him the devil, to the extent that his object of preoccupation is God, and his defining behavior is creating distance from God by pretending to be God. Essentially, Goetz represents the classic formula for the devil, or Satan. Nasti, on the other hand, who prioritizes the needs of the poor, wants to make strategic use of Goetz' evil, suggesting that Goetz should go and kill the rich.

In his freedom, Heinrich betrays the poor by offering to provide the invading Goetz entry into the city, in exchange for the rescue of the 200 priests in jail. Through this barter, Heinrich protects the rich priests and the church at the expense of the peasant masses who would be slaughtered if Goetz attacks. Heinrich, wanting to absolve himself of guilt, urges Goetz to spare the peasants upon the siege, but Goetz never agrees. Nevertheless, self-interest overwhelms good intentions and Heinrich provides Goetz with a key that will aid in his entry into the city. In the back and forth, Heinrich suggests that it is action that determines fault, while Goetz—understanding himself as evil—suggests we are all evil or good, and that our state of being (who we are fated by the Gods to be) determines our actions. Presumably, Heinrich is rationalizing his self-interest and hoping to convince Goetz that the power to do good is a choice available to the military commander. Goetz, on the other hand, rationalizes himself as naturally evil and therefore, considers it his duty to do evil things. Goetz concludes that he is obligated to aid Heinrich in becoming a Judas-figure and equally obligated to destroy the peasants.

Learning of Heinrich's betrayal, the actual peasant-leader Nasti pays a visit to Goetz. Goetz quickly claims to be the devil, incarnate. Nasti, hoping to spare the peasants, appeals to the possibility that it is not Goetz' fate to inflict such harm on the peasants. Here, Nasti introduces the audience to yet a different rationalization for evil. Evil and goodness are still bound by fate, but through free will we have direct or a semblance of agency to determine our relationship to evil and goodness. Certain people exist in the world and those people have behaviors attached to them intrinsically. They cannot help but act in a specific way corresponding to their identity. But what if we were unsure of who's who? In this way, Nasti opens the possibility that even Goetz can choose good and therefore do good deeds. Goetz can still choose a different path.

A moral and practical military standoff ensues between Goetz, Nasti, and Heinrich. Goetz emphasizes that Heinrich's betrayal is precisely why the attack must occur, because receiving the key is a sign that he is doing his duty unto God. Receiving the key is proof that Goetz is doing God's work. Goetz is God's evil man, and he does not want to question that fate—"because I cannot be other than myself."[16] Then, to meliorate his own guilty feelings, Heinrich begins distinguishing his brand of evil from that of Goetz. All the world is evil. All humans are evil—totally depraved. Choice only determines what sort of evil to do. All of us are devils, in the end. Goetz isn't special, after all. This ontological possibility troubles Goetz, so much so that he decides to question both fate and his long-assumed God-given purpose on earth. Goetz bets Heinrich that he can be good for a year. If he wins the bet, then Goetz will besiege the city. If he loses, Heinrich will have spared both the priests and the peasants—he will have atoned for his betrayal of the poor and of the priests.

Across the year, Goetz gains the reputation of a miracle worker, even receiving the stigmata as a sign of his powers. He comes to be known for doing good. Tension mounts between those who knew Goetz before his "transformation" and many of the peasants who have become his religious followers and devotees. People continue to follow Goetz, but out of adoration rather than fear. Whilst working for good, Goetz tries to give away his lands to the peasants. Nasti refuses, on behalf of the poor. The tensions around Worms are indicative of the broader states, as more peasant revolts and responses spring up relentlessly. Soon, the peasants of Worms need a military commander because other would-be invaders are on the march. Responding to the threat of new invaders, Nasti tries to convince Goetz to resume his military duties. Ahh, but there is a catch: to do well in battle one must be a bastard. Goetz refuses to lead his new followers as it would require him to surrender good to evil. But, according to Nasti, doing limited evil as a military general would be for the greater good, saving more people into the future.

Refusing to lead the peasants, 25,000 are killed in battle, and the survivors come to blame Goetz, for his failure to act, his failure to do evil so that good would prevail in the end. The full year passes, and Heinrich and Goetz return to reflect, where Goetz poses an ontological question: "If Thou dost refuse us the means of doing good, why hast Thou made us desire it so keenly? If Thou didst not permit that I should become good, why shouldst Thou have taken from me the desire to be wicked? Strange that there should be no way out of this."[17] Listening to Goetz's diatribe against God, Heinrich is filled with rage, and attacks the military commander. "Heinrich, I am going to tell you a colossal joke: God doesn't exist," Goetz tells the priest before stabbing him to death.[18] Goetz then finds himself back in the company of Nasti, whose political leadership has transformed into military leadership as well. Resigning himself to humble service under the leadership of Nasti, it took Goetz losing belief in God to gain insights on goodness. Nasti asks him to lead the soldiers, to which Goetz begrudgingly agrees. Immediately, Goetz stabs Nasti's captain to death.

In many respects, Goetz and Heinrich together represent white men, particularly those of us who filter our moral identity through some version of monotheistic belief. Qualitatively, for Sartre, there is no distinction to be made between the person doing "good" because they've been told to do so by God and the person who may be evil "in their heart," but who does good out of spite. Appealing to good intention does not matter. In fact, such appeals at best muddy the moral waters or at worst, constitute the most basic preoccupation of devils who have always used religion to control others and to deny responsibility for that control. To what extent do our intentions matter when we consider whether we've been devils? How do we take stock of our moral failures, if there is no static point of orientation? A person can have good intentions and bad outcomes, or bad intentions and good outcomes. This paradox amounts to the central philosophical challenge levelled to the play's audience. Before he is killed by Goetz, Heinrich tells him that "What matters whether the harm was done? It is my intention that matters."[19] How are we justified in life? Heinrich, the church bishop, represents the perspective that intentions are all that matter—outcomes do not. Goetz, on the other hand, questions this logic, imagining that if no harm is done, what then is a bad heart or intent? In many respects, Heinrich and Goetz represent two warring ideals within the white man's imagination historically. Are we good, and therefore, removed from responsibility for our actions? Or ought we reject the idealistic claim to goodness, and instead, concern ourselves with good outcomes? Historically, at least over the last 400 years, neither option has produced helpful results for others. Together, Heinrich and Goetz outline the "look" of white men's ethical deliberation, historically. Heinrich represents the harm done by a Christian idealism all too often the impetus and *post facto* justification for atrocities, including the historic peasant revolts of Europe—as discussed in the play—but also many other historic events occurring during the age of conquest, colonialism, and American Manifest

Destiny and Occidental enslavement. On the other hand, Goetz represents the white man's instrumentalization of goodness and righteousness, as if it could be so simple as making the right decisions of action: 'I'll do good because none of us think I can do good.' Knowing full well that good deeds from the devil are never treated as such, Goetz addresses the paradox with an assault on the very notion of good intentions:

> GOETZ: The gold pieces of the Devil change into dead leaves when you try to spend them; my good deeds are like them: when you touch them, they turn into corpses. But what about the intention? Eh? If I really meant to do good, neither God nor the Devil can take that away. Attack the intention. Tear the intention to pieces.[20]

Goetz is the victim of our efforts to define ourselves through morality, and morality through intention. But, neither can he fully escape the notion of intention at the level of his own identity. He knows that despite his intentions, he will be treated as the devil. And so, he attacks the logic of relying on good intentions to determine a person's moral identity. Yet he still maintains an ontological belief in good and evil, because it makes him who he is—or, because he cannot imagine something after moral identification. On the whole point, he arrives at a kind of resignation of identity that will feel familiar to many white men:

> GOETZ: I am no longer sure of anything. [Pause.] If I gratify my desires, I sin, but I free myself of desire; if I refuse to satisfy them, they will infect the whole soul ... Night is falling; at twilight a man needs good eyesight to distinguish the good Lord from the Devil.[21]

To what extent do our good intentions matter? As Sartre accomplishes with *The Devil and the Good Lord*, this ontological question can be framed in terms of the history of Christianity and the religious wars that ravaged Europe for centuries. Perhaps, the Christian church has had the best of intentions, but it has done some dastardly things in history. Conversely, devils among us are surely guilty of doing good deeds alongside their history of evil. Therefore, how do we make moral judgments about who we are when intentions are added to the equation?

Sartre ends the play with Goetz representing the human boundaries clarified when we begin to accept ourselves, regardless. Resigned to no longer ask the question of whether Goetz is good or evil, the audience sees in Goetz a hermeneutical shift akin to what Ricoeur is calling for, awareness that evil is part of our cultural inheritance. What does taking responsibility through guilt really look like? What would it sound like? In one final powerful soliloquy, Goetz uses Heinrich's criticism of him to cultivate Knowledge of Self. To the extent we have been devils in the eyes of others, the identity-based about-face made by Goetz might be instructive:

GOETZ: Listen, Priest: I had betrayed everyone, including my own brother, but my appetite for betrayal was not yet assuaged; so, one night, before the ramparts of Worms, I thought up a way to betray Evil, that's the whole story. Only Evil doesn't let itself be betrayed quite so easily; it wasn't Good that jumped out of the dicebox; it was a worse Evil. What does it matter anyway? Monster or saint, I didn't give a damn, I wanted to be inhuman. Say it, Heinrich, say I was mad with shame, and wanted to amaze Heaven to escape men's scorn. Come along! What are you waiting for? Speak! Ah, it's true, you cannot speak any more; I have your voice in my mouth. [Imitating HEINRICH] You didn't change your skin, Goetz, you altered your language. You called your hatred of men love, your rage for destruction you called generosity. But you remained unchanged; nothing but a bastard. [Resuming his natural voice] My God, I bear witness that he speaks the truth; I, the accused, acknowledge myself guilty.[22]

7 NEUROSES

There seems to exist two types of white men in the United States: those who do not believe black men when they refer to themselves as Gods. And those who do not believe black men when they refer to themselves as Gods *and* who also feel the need to punish, pathologize, or protect against these claims. No white men seem to fully believe it. But some of us get all worked up about it, while others of us keep it moving. During the 1960s, a few white men tried to understand or see past the seemingly bizarre claims, but most who interacted with Father Allah and the Five Percenters seem to have been terrified or out for blood.

Father Allah, aka Clarence Edward Smith, aka Clarence Smith Jowars,[1] was arrested on June 1, 1965, along with five other Five Percenters, for a disturbance the day before. One memorandum written to FBI director J. Edgar Hoover with the subject "Puddin" (Allah's old nickname) describes Allah as "a self-proclaimed leader of the 'Five Percenters', who are the 5% of the Muslims who smoke and drink."[2] The same memorandum goes on to describe Allah as one "among six male negroes who were blocking the sidewalks and were interfering with street traffic in front of the Hotel Theresa, 2090 7th Avenue, NYC. When told to move on by two police officers, they turned on the officers, called on bystanders to attack the officers, and shouted anti-white and anti-police invectives."[3] Later, Allah would relay to friends that the arrest had been because he overturned a garbage can.[4] The actual charges for Allah included "felonious assault, conspiracy to commit same, resisting arrest, assault with deadly weapon, disorderly conduct, as leader of Negro youth gang called 'Five Percenters'" along with "possession of a marijuana cigarette and malicious mischief."[5] Being the leader of the "gang," Allah's bail was set at $9500.00. During his hearing, Allah "claimed that he was God and stated that the court could not charge him with anything since 'you can't charge Allah.'" Allah was then "confined to Bellevue Hospital" where he was diagnosed as psychotic. His original diagnosis was described as schizophrenic reaction, paranoid type, expressing delusions of grandeur of a religious nature and of persecution. His claim that he was God was not believed, but Hoover and others still perceived him as a threat. Through a tragic irony seemingly lost on the white folks involved in his case, Allah was the one diagnosed as schizophrenic.

Another memorandum from the following week of October 22, 1965, also sent to Hoover, describes Jowars as a decorated Korean war veteran, honorably discharged after service in Japan and Korea, having been "awarded Korean Service Medal with one Bronze Service Star, Combat Infantryman's Badge, Presidential Unit Citation (Republic of Korea), United Nations Service Medal, and the National Defense Service Medal."[6] Several weeks later, another memorandum issued to Director Hoover writes that "it is expected that when subject appears in above court on 11/16/65, subject will be adjudged criminally insane and will be committed to a mental institution."[7] The memo continues in reminding of the original crime, where it notes that Jowars "was arrested on 5/31/65, by the NYCPD as being the ringleader of a group called the 'Five Percenters,' a Negro youth gang in the Harlem section of NYC."[8] Another FBI file remarks that "Clarence Edward Smith aka, a former NOI member who called himself 'Allah.' Under his influence these youths became indoctrinated in the perverted NOI form of Muslim ideology with anti-white racial overtones."[9] The same document states that the "NYCPD is continuing to conduct a full-time, extensive investigation of the 'Five Percenters' which includes daily interrogation of gang members and nightly surveillances of them."[10] At times, the documents note that the FBI considered the Five Percenters to be a concern for local police, and no formal FBI investigation into the group was necessary. Yet it is obvious there was FBI interest in Allah, reaching a seeming crescendo in the days leading up to Allah's November trial. A document with FBI letterhead sent to the director of the United States Secret Service and signed by Hoover lists Allah as having been "under active investigation as member of other group or organization inimical to U.S." and characterizes him as "Subversives, untrarightists, racists and fascists who meet one or more of the following criteria," including "Evidence of emotional instability (including unstable residence and employment record) or irrational or suicidal behavior" and "Prior acts (including arrests or convictions) or conduct or statements indicating a propensity for violence and antipathy toward good order and government."[11]

As has been suggested by Michael Muhammad Knight, "Allah's classification as insane was better for the authorities than a guilty verdict; without a fixed sentence, he could be held at Matteawan 'for his own good until the end of time.'"[12] Many of the available FBI files go in depth into Allah's association with the Nation of Islam and with Malcolm X, before pivoting to simply elaborate on the teachings of Elijah Muhammad or the incendiary statements of Malcolm X. The files present an image of Allah being guilty by association. The files also make it clear that the NYPD and FBI officers had been following the activities of Allah for years.

Allah was held across the summer and fall, with various trial dates pushed back over and over under the auspices that he was unfit to stand trial as psychiatrists had not concluded their full diagnosis. Just as predicted in the FBI memo, on November 16, 1965, the New York court found him "unable to understand the charges against him," and he was "remanded to the custody of the New York State Department of Mental Health for an indefinite confinement."[13] FBI records indicate that he was admitted to Matteawan State Hospital for the Criminally Insane on November 26, 1965. He was held at Matteawan until March 6, 1967, at which time he was moved out of the system, and by April of that year, he eventually pleaded guilty to several of the remaining charges from the initial incident, where he ultimately received a suspended sentence and was released.

Within weeks of Allah's release, a white aide to then-New York mayor John Lindsay befriended Allah as part of the mayor's effort to reach out to the dispossessed black population of New York City. Barry Gottehrer had the task of mitigating the potential unrest of racial tensions in the city as they boiled across the United States in the 1960s. Part of his strategy was to build genuine relationships with unlikely folks, including the Five Percenters. Gottehrer recounts that "In these pre-Panther days, no group struck fear into whites more than the Five Percenters. Allah and his group had a reputation for being unreachable, anti-white criminals and these qualities were exactly the ones that interested me."[14] Having been warned about Allah by the police and many others, Gottehrer was undeterred and managed to meet Allah at a Harlem bar called the Glamour Inn. The two would meet there often over the next two years.

Gottehrer was fascinated by the claims to divinity, spending many conversations discussing the theological implications of black men being God with Allah, himself. During one discussion, Allah celebrated the people at Matteawan as having helped to "validate his status" as Allah. Gottehrer was so curious about the claim that he called hospital officials and received confirmation from them that they considered Allah "crazy."[15] The labels people placed onto Allah did not scare Gottehrer off from wanting to collaborate with him and the Five Percenters. They became friends. In fact, after spending time with Allah, Gottehrer came to consider people's fear of Allah to be misguided, noting that "Someone like Allah didn't kill people, in no dealings with me was he ever anti-white … The people I knew were all trying to survive in their different ways."[16] Presumably, theological pronouncements to divinity counted among these strategies. Gottehrer recounts one Christmas party where Allah was in attendance with a variety of other types of people in the city. Allah got into a discussion with Bronx super-district attorney Burt Roberts. Roberts, in jest but also seemingly earnest, told Allah: "You can be Allah all you want—in Manhattan, in Queens, in Kings County. But you come up to Bronx County and tell people you're Allah and I'll have your black ass in jail."[17]

An argument can be made that Allah referring to himself *as Allah*—or believing it to be true—was an easy excuse for Hoover and other powerful white men to keep Allah locked up as a political prisoner. In short, this forced bondage was not *because* of the claims to divinity, but Allah's claims to divinity made an easy target for suggestions of mental illness. The comment from Roberts suggests that there is something dangerous and fear-inducing about the theological pronouncement, itself. What? Perhaps, something of religious rhetoric enables social and cultural movement—something Five Percenters recognize and make use of in claiming that they are Gods. The rhetoric of religion tends to matter to white folks, and so, it offers a means of intersubjective communication across race (and gender). Essentially, Allah's claims to divinity force a (more) even field for intersubjective communication. Perhaps, this is what was so terrifying to Hoover and the FBI about black religions, in general.[18] Gottehrer recounts a fond conversation in which Allah offered the mayoral aide a job:

> "Why don't you quit working for the mayor and come work with me?"
> 'As much as I'd like to say yes,' I answered, 'I don't know what kind of work I could do for you.'
> Allah said, "That's easy. If you come up to Harlem, you can be Moses."
> I wasn't always sure if Allah was serious or joking or totally crazy. He looked absolutely serious now. "It's all very well for you to be Allah," I said, "but I *know* I'm not Moses."[19]
> Allah thought that over and then said, "But Barry, if you're not Moses—*who is?*"

The repartee between the two men makes use of religious rhetoric and honorifics in response to existential and social concerns. As has come to be common of Five Percenter rhetoric, religious language signifies social conditions and realities. As this language, it provided the two men a foundation for forging community and relationship. It was not necessary for Gottehrer to believe that Allah was God incarnate. It was enough to believe that Allah believed it. What was there to second guess? Allah was Allah.

What is at stake for us as white men when we police the beliefs and behaviors of black and brown men? What is the threat to us? How and why do some of us end up on the side of Hoover and his FBI who sought to control and know all that was knowable or controllable among black esoteric religious traditions like the Nation of Islam and the Nation of Gods and Earths? What's the big deal? And, what determines who of us will simply keep it moving and who of us will spend time and energy working to ensure that black men think twice before making such an audacious statement as "I am a God?"

***

I want to flatten the qualitative distinctions usually maintained between whiteness, patriarchy, and alcoholism by locating the roots of these issues in a codependency crisis among white Western men fostered through monotheistic religion. By growing up in homes and communities that practiced monotheism, and by often responding to situations of absentee fathers through a renewed interest in monotheistic religions, many white men have essentially been wired to maintain codependent relationships with others. In short, monotheism has underdeveloped our Egos. As a result, many white men overdetermine our own sense of self in terms of other people. In this section, I turn to the work of Sigmund Freud and Anna Freud to situate patriarchy and whiteness—what I have elsewhere labeled as god-idols[20]—as particular psychological neuroses that reinforce and perhaps arise from a destructive codependency among white men. Rather than promoting an intersubjectively oriented sense of self, monotheism, masculinity, and whiteness all collide in the person of the white man and produce in us a series of psychical deficits. The impact from these god-idols isn't uniform, and not every white man will be impacted by all three or even by each. I'm not making an exhaustive statement but speaking to tendencies among white men.

Whiteness. Masculinity. Monotheism. These can be considered ideological dispositions or states of being, based on behavior, essence, or a combination of what we do and who we consider ourselves to be. I want to treat them here as salient identities. As salient identities, they are artificial constructions that do not correspond to anything intrinsic and tangible in the real world. Being artificial constructions doesn't stop them from exerting a considerable influence on the way that we understand ourselves, our relationship to our environment and to one another in that environment. In this chapter, I explore these salient identities in terms laid out by famous psychologist Sigmund Freud. Freud is a complicated and even dangerous figure, but in his quest for Knowledge of Self through the lens of psychoanalysis, he exemplifies certain features of who we have been as white men. Essentially, his theories may not work for all of us, or correspond to empirical findings, even, but they offer an example of a white man reflecting critically on himself. I also turn to the work of Freud's daughter, Anna Freud, who helped to methodologically organize Freudian psychoanalysis. For Anna Freud, "the task of analysis" is "to acquire the fullest possible knowledge of all the three institutions of which we believe the psychic personality to be constituted and to learn what are their relations to one another and to the outside world."[21] Freud and Freud help in moving beyond the phenomenological appraisal of white men offered by the Five Percenters, and toward an assessment of how white men might begin to cultivate a response to the claim that we are devils.

Sigmund Freud was an atheist. Religion, for him, was an illusion. But this illusion had a particular psychological purpose. He argued that society has as its goal to protect us from nature. Essentially, we are helpless against nature. It is wild and expansive and big. And if we let it, nature will kill us. One of the ways that we protect ourselves psychologically is by attributing human qualities to nature. Religion allowed people to deal with the manifested hostilities of nature by humanizing them via a father figure, in the form of God. Religion, for Freud, is a response to a sense of helplessness first faced in childhood, and then cultivated in one's adult life and expressed as various neuroses.

In Freud's system, the white man's psyche, or mind, is divided into three parts: the Id, the Ego, and the Superego. If you crack open your head, you won't find these three pieces. They are a model for understanding how our selves work, but they are not actual physical parts of our brains. The Id is our instinctual self, the version of us that is focused on preserving our life. This aspect of our self is often called the "lizard" or "reptilian" brain inside of us. It's our instinct toward life and away from death. Our Id is that part of us that seeks sex and avoids death. Often, it does both at the same time, using death (in the form of the murder of a competitor) to achieve sex with a potential mating partner. The Ego is our conscious reflection of our self. The Ego is the thing that talks to you, when you talk to yourself inside of your own head, the thing interested in balancing internal feelings with external expectations. Then, the Superego is the moral compass of our minds. If the Id is based on base instincts like survival and desire, the Superego marks out the limits imposed on us by society as we try to fulfill our desires. For a crude example, if we see an attractive woman walking toward us with a man, our Id might instinctively desire to attack the man and start sexually assaulting her. Our Superego, on the other hand, is comprised of all we know of societal expectations, and it tries to ensure we stay part of the society (because society is what protects us from nature). Our Superego is what keeps our Id from attacking the couple. With our Id shaped by nature, and our Superego shaped by society, a tension emerges in our Ego. Our Ego is left to balance itself in the middle. Our Ego is where we feel guilt or desire, while our Id and our Superego are *why* and how we feel those things. As adults, the Ego is in a constant battle to not be overrun by the Id. The Superego is how the Ego keeps the Id at bay. But there is also a tension between the Ego and the Superego because the distance between them is insurmountable. The Ego can never arrive to where the Superego points us. We can never actually escape our reptilian instincts to the degree demanded by our Superego. The psychologically healthy person, for Freud, has an Ego that balances these demands from the Id and Superego through what are called "defense mechanisms." Anna Freud lists ten, including "regression, repression, reaction formation, isolation, undoing, projection, introjection, turning against the self, reversal," and "sublimation, or displacement of instinctual aims."[22] These defenses respond to various feelings of anxiety. As infants, and as we grow, we experience objective anxiety. As we develop, our anxiety differentiates into instinctual anxiety and Superego anxiety. A healthy Ego is anxious of its Id, for fear of being overrun by reptilian instincts. A healthy Ego is also anxious of its Superego, for fear of not living up to its impossible demands.

"Neurosis," for Freud, is the name for situations when behaviors or thoughts arising from instinctual, or Superego, anxiety outweigh the consequences of the initial threat from the Id or demand from the Superego. Essentially, a neurosis is an overcorrection. Neuroses are patterns that emerge in people where a fear of some aspect of our Id causes "unvarying use of a special method of defense, when confronted with a particular instinctual demand, and the repetition of exactly the same procedure every time that demand recurs."[23] Verbal stuttering and obsessive, intrusive thoughts are two examples. Anna Freud suggests that neuroses amount to a compromise[24] between the Id and Superego. At root of both neuroses and the basic defenses is anxiety, in that "whether it be dread of the outside world or dread of the superego, it is the anxiety which sets the defensive process going."[25] Principally, denial is the defense mechanism most often associated with anxiety arising from acute, actual, or potential dangers existing out in the world. Divorce, rape, the loss of a child—these disparate situations are all possible, but usually not probable. As they are not probable, we defend ourselves against them through denial. "When we find denial, we know that it is a reaction to external danger; when repression takes place, the ego is struggling with instinctual stimuli."[26] On the other hand, when we are faced with instinctual dangers, such as wanting to run away from a boring spouse, the desire to have sex with someone against their will, or even infanticide, we repress those ideas or feelings in order to stave off the actions or the negative feelings associated with confronting those instinctual desires. Anna Freud even suggests that a rule of thumb for the severity of any given defense mechanism can be found "by the strength of the resistance which we encounter when we seek to lift them."[27] Anna Freud continues:

> The existence of neurotic symptoms in itself indicates that the Ego has been overpowered, and every return of repressed impulses, with its sequel in compromise formation, shows that some plan for defense has miscarried and the Ego has suffered a defeat. But the Ego is victorious when its defensive measures effect their purpose, i.e., when they enable it to restrict the development of anxiety and unpleasure and so to transform the instincts that, even in difficult circumstances, some measure of gratification is secured, thereby establishing the most harmonious relations possible between the Id, the Superego, and the forces of the outside world.[28]

Freud's theory of personality is geared primarily toward understanding individual selves. However, he also applied the idea of a neurosis to the subject of religion, in general. Freud famously defined religion as a "universal neurosis."[29] What he meant by this is that it was a social system arising as an outgrowth of psychological defense mechanisms run amok. To the extent these defenses developed into a full-scale social institution of belief and practice, it took on a *universally* neurotic character. Initially an effort to mitigate anxiety, religion came to add to the sum total of anxiety experienced by adherents. If religion was practiced by one person alone, psychoanalysts would easily consider it a neurosis or a full-blown psychosis as was the case when state psychologists diagnosed Father Allah with schizophrenia. Yet, because millions and billions practice and believe the same basic things, some expressions of religion are treated as psychologically "normal" and are not regarded in the same way as other neuroses such as depression or obsessive-compulsive disorder. If only one person was walking around talking about a man 2000 years ago who turned water to wine, was crucified and resurrected after three days to save us from the suffering in the world, the person would be deemed neurotic or psychotic for holding a belief in something magical and imaginary. But because we all do some version of this—or, at least billions of us do—we turn a blind eye to the neuroses arising of and as religion. What if these other aspects of human social life such as masculinity, and whiteness work in this same neurotic fashion?

Before moving any further, let me be clear in noting that Freud's theories are not based on science. They are, like most theories, based on myths of one sort or another, which are then mapped onto the world or scientific data and either confirmed or denied based on how we interpret that data. And, as we are increasingly learning about somatics between the mind and body and the trauma and memories stored in our bodies, Freud's theories are only part of a larger puzzle useful for addressing white men's mental health. His theories remain useful because they created a shared grammar and vocabulary for a therapist and patient, an analyst and an analysand, to achieve certain psychologically beneficial results through talk-based therapy. Like religion providing a foundation for Gottehrer and Father Allah to communicate, Freud's theories enable intersubjective communication between patient and therapist. While much of Freud's work has been rejected by contemporary psychology, many scholars of religion still hold that he offers a useful theory for understanding where religion comes from. For my part, I also think that these theories remain helpful if we qualify that they only apply (and even then, perhaps, loosely) to western white men. I'm using him here for precisely this reason. Essentially, Freud came up with stories that helped us understand the way that white men's minds operated. Currently, we have no way to "prove" the veracity of the theories he offered. In this way, his theory of religion and the neuroses functions kind of like religion—we must believe it for it to work. Because some of us believe in the same set of stories (propagated by Freud), we can come into the space of a clinic and engage in talk therapy and have our shared assumptions about those stories lead to rehabilitation.

Freud turns to Greek playwright Sophocles' *Oedipus Rex* (c. 430 BCE) to suggest that the origins of religion emerge in the interpersonal dynamics between a father, mother, and child. The play tells the story of Oedipus, prince of Thebes, who was the son of king Laius and queen Jocasta. Upon becoming a man, Oedipus visits the oracle at Delphi who tells him that he is fated to murder his father and seduce his mother. The young Oedipus scoffs at the idea and fashions his life steps in such a way as to ensure he does not do either of these things. Despite his best defenses and avoidances, Oedipus fails at this effort, and does in fact kill his father and sleep with his mother. For Oedipus, tragedy arises because of the effort to fight the tides of fate.

Oedipus Rex articulated complicated dynamics within our natal families. Neuroses begin in childhood, as we move through different developmental phases. As babies and toddlers, we first bond with our mothers. This is a psychological and physiological bond. As we now know it is a chemical bond, as well. The mother, through this bond, addresses the immediate needs of the baby, and the baby develops a desire for the mother. Yet the baby is the result of a preexisting relationship between the mother and the father. This means that the baby first experiences the father as a romantic rival and as an all-powerful figure who can surely cause harm to the baby. Moreover, the mother is not equipped to protect the baby from potential invaders, and so must rely on the father. A second social bond is forged, then, between baby and father, as fathers meet the needs babies have to feel a sense of safety and security while they also represent that danger. The baby and father, therefore, cultivate a relationship leading to unfulfilled desires. The baby transforms the fear of the father into a promise of safety. The baby, needing protection, must have their desires for the mother mitigated. To make matters worse, as we further develop and experience pain in life, it is further proved to us that our fathers fail in keeping us safe and secure. Inevitably, they fail us, and in their failing contribute to our neuroses. We then do the same thing with our children. The process continues across generations. For Freud, there were psycho-social explanations for why the God depicted in the Judeo-Christian tradition acted so much like an actual father.[30] The God of patriarchal religions was a stand-in for the patriarch of each family.

Freud presents us with a story about the generational transmission of neuroses. This primal family sets in motion the actions and ideas of subsequent families to the point that civilization emerges as much as a response to these inherited collective neuroses, as it is shaped by these neuroses. Ultimately, for Freud, religion amounts to those things, which "are given out as teachings, are not precipitates of experience or end-results of thinking: they are illusions, fulfilments of the oldest, strongest and most urgent wishes of mankind. The secret of their strength lies in the strength of those wishes."[31] In the service of these wishes—safety, sustenance, overcoming death, sexual satisfaction—religion emerges as a neurotic response to the failure of our fathers to fulfill these wishes. Because they fail us, we imagine a bigger, better, more capable father (up in the sky, or somewhere), and many of us bring this with us into adulthood. For Freud, the Oedipus Saga, or the Oedipal Complex (as he comes to call it), provides not only a way of allegorically framing our social relationships between our families, but also for explaining where religion comes from, when it describes what he calls the "primordial" or the primeval family. For instance, imagine the literal beginning of the human story, a hypothetical "first" family at the beginning of human history. At some point, it was the case that a man and a woman came together in a sexual union. In that union, they ended up with a son. But at this point in human history, there were no other people around and no semblance of society to shape our Superegos. The child bonds with its mother, only to recognize that its needs for safety are not met. Further, he comes to compete with the father for the mother's attention. Childhood for the boy consists of receiving safety in exchange for repressing his desires. At some point during or after puberty, the boy realizes he is the physical equal of his father. Then one day, tensions escalate, and the son picks up a rock and hits the father over the head. The son has conquered his rival, but now is left to keep himself safe in a hostile natural world. Needing comfort for the overwhelming psychological weight of recognizing oneself as existentially alone, the son creates God in the image of the missing father. The beliefs and practices of religion, according to Freud, emerge from this first "primal" murder. God comes to be an idea, representative of our actual natal Fathers. Like our actual fathers, God can provide safety, but God is going to get in the way of our desires. Our desire for our mother is emblematic of desires, in general, what Freud situates in terms of wishes. God comes to "work" or function as we come to realize the best strategy for dealing with rivals is not always to murder them, but to compromise with them. God ends up a means of having one's desires organized according to the circumstances on the ground that may inhibit or make possible realization of these desires. God, therefore, is born in the image of our fathers, meaning that our relationship with our actual fathers will deeply impact our relationship with God. For many of us, a deadbeat father will turn into a deadbeat God. And for others of us still, mothers will turn to religion to provide guidance to young boys whose fathers are not around. It bears scrutiny, then, what sort of stories we are told about God.

***

Deuteronomy 28 offers an incomplete psychological profile of the monotheistic God, and if we're honest about the profile, it makes me wonder if monotheism has not been a wholesale failure in terms of developing within many believers the capacity to make healthy decisions centered in terms of our ego development. In short, it looks like an insecure God might promote insecurity of self. Hence, we'd be threatened when a lone black man in Harlem starts telling us that he is God.

Essentially, Deuteronomy 28 tells us that if we do everything "the Lord your God" tells us to do, then we will be treated as special. If we obey everything God tells us, then "Blessed shall be the fruit of your body, and the fruit of your ground, and the fruit of your beasts ... Blessed shall you be when you come in, and blessed shall you be when you go out."[32] The chapter also promises all of our enemies to be defeated, going so far as to say that "all the peoples of the earth shall see that you are called by the name of the Lord; and they shall be afraid of you."[33] All of this will be ours *if* we follow "all his commandments." God's favor with us is deeply conditional. God's interactions with us or with the Israelites—depending on how much historicizing we do with our interpretation—will be determined based on whether we follow God's rules.

Would it be considered healthy or appropriate if our actual fathers—whether biological or through marriage—determined our worth based on whether we followed all their rules? Many would-be fathers have surely tried, and failed, at enforcing similar demands. At the very least, such a dynamic would place an undue burden upon the Egos of we—the children—in that we would understand our essential value through the lens of our fathers' pleasure with our actions. This would create a condition of codependency among us as the children. Quite literally, such an arrangement unfolding at the family-level would amount to an abusive threat of abandonment. Yet, at the level of religious information or identification, many of us do not think twice about this arrangement made between God and God's believers.

Further in Deuteronomy 28, the emotional abuse grows more severe, in that the bulk of the chapter is dedicated to outlining what will happen *to believers* if they do not follow God's rules. The biblical chapter describes all that will happen to family members who disobey the father God. In short, they will be treated as outsiders, as enemies to the family, as was promised would happen to the family's enemies upon the family adequately obeying God's rules. "The Lord will send upon you curses, confusion, and frustration, in all that you undertake to do, until you are destroyed and perish quickly, on account of the evil of your doings, because you have forsaken me."[34] The passage is startling, in no small part, because the writers clearly have a sense of the all-too-human anxieties that shape the religious motivation:

> The Lord will cause you to be defeated before your enemies; you shall go out one way against them, and flee seven ways before them; and you shall be a horror to all the kingdoms of the earth. And your dead body shall be food for all birds of the air, and for the beasts of the earth; and there shall be no one to frighten them away.[35]

This passage speaks to both acute anxieties surrounding safety, and the feelings of guilt and shame that arise when white men feel inadequate to the task of ensuring their own or their families' safety.

> The Lord will smite you with the boils of Egypt, and with the ulcers and the scurvy and the itch, of which you cannot be healed. The Lord will smite you with madness and blindness and confusion of mind; and you shall grope at noonday, as the blind grope in darkness, and you shall not prosper in your ways; and you shall be only oppressed and robbed continually, and there shall be no one to help you.[36]

This passage continues with threats from the father and catalogs some of the physical and psychological harm that might befall someone who has been banished or treated with shame as a result of their disbelief or disobedience toward the father. This works at multiple levels, both pedagogical and punitive. Suppose an actual father knows best how to keep their son or daughter safe. Some of the harm described here could be a practical consequence of not following the father's rules. Some rules are healthy and designed to promote safety. Others are meant to teach a lesson. It is impossible to separate the pedagogical from the punitive, here in the biblical account. Whether or not the rules are reasonable is a different issue than whether the father has a healthy relationship to these rules. Here, God has a deeply pathological relationship to his own rules, such that his identity *as God* seems connected to whether the rule is followed. The rule is no longer about actually keeping children safe, but ensuring the children fear the father.

> You shall betroth a wife, and another man shall lie with her; you shall build a house, and you shall not dwell in it; you shall plant a vineyard, and you shall not use the fruit of it. Your ox shall be slain before your eyes, and you shall not eat of it; your ass shall be violently taken away before your face, and shall not be restored to you; your sheep shall be given to your enemies, and there shall be no one to help you.[37]

This passage promises emotional pain in the form of taking away or damaging property, beginning with treating women as property. Simultaneously, it teaches men to objectify women—beginning with our mothers—and to connect our psychological well-being to possession of those objects. This is another expression of codependency, in that God is using our relationships to other people (as objects) to threaten us. Patriarchal religion is patriarchal, in part, because women are objects, and men are valuable to the extent we procure and control such objects.

> Your sons and your daughters shall be given to another people, while your eyes look on and fail with longing for them all the day; and it shall not be in the power of your hand to prevent it.[38]

It is worth reminding that these threats are coming from God, in the form of a father speaking to his children. What does it suggest about this God that threats toward children would be permissible? At the least, this father is consistent, and seems to be the same father who was willing to turn Isaac into a sacrifice on Mount Moriah to prove a point to Abraham. This father loves to use children as means toward assuaging his own anxieties of identity, even and especially his own children. Few would blame the children of such a father if they ended up succumbing to madness and other mental and physical maladies. Both the rules of engagement demanded by God, and the severity of breaches to these rules, are too severe to be maintained without serious neuroses developing. Indeed, such a father would be responsible for the arrested emotional development of his children's egos and the subsequent codependent dysfunction resulting from those underdeveloped egos.

It is my basic hypothesis that this "religious" failure, epitomized by (but in no way exclusively demonstrated in) Deuteronomy 28, created one or more communities within the world's population that would be predisposed to codependency of thought and action. Our engagement with non-monotheistic and other monotheistic traditions would be organized around codependent threats of violence, on the one hand, and objective instrumentalization, on the other. If we cannot use the other to our benefit, then we will destroy the other. All the world's others would be ours for use, in practical terms related to material resources and in terms of assuaging our underdeveloped Egos. Indeed, such communities of belief would be responsible for producing the "Other" as an idea to be exploited in the social world and in our minds. Antiblackness and patriarchy would be two additional, albethey distinct, expressions of this basic theological failure on the part of monotheism to enable healthy interpersonal and cultural development among us. Indeed, the remainder of Deuteronomy 28 largely involves extended justification for enslavement as punishment for our disobedience of God. Across the last centuries, racism and misogyny and other forms of severe "othering" have been the model we white men have followed in our religious dysfunction.

8 **CODEPENDENT**

Biblical scholar Elaine Pagels wrote the definitive history of Satan in the 1995 text *The Origin of Satan*. In that book, Pagels demonstrates how "Satan" is a Hebrew term, and that early in the biblical sources, Satan "describes an adversarial role" rather than any "particular character."[1] The Christian West would eventually render Satan into a single figure, often used in service to antisemitism. Pagels recounts that initially "Hebrew storytellers" would use the term to refer to "any one of the angels sent by God for the specific purpose of blocking or obstructing human activity."[2] In fact, the root word from which Satan emerges "means 'one who opposes, obstructs, or acts as adversary.'"[3] "The Greek term diabolos," Pagels continues, "later translated 'devil,' literally means 'one who throws something across one's path.'"[4] From this, we can arrive at a couple basic points. First, devils are creatures of God. They exist as expressions of God's will. Second, they are obstacles standing in the way of the paths of others.

Across the historical timeline as expressed in the Hebrew Bible, by the time one reaches the book of 1 Maccabees (which was written about 100 BCE), the idea of Satan had come to represent "Jewish opponents,"[5] both internal and external. For centuries, Israel had defined itself in terms of its opposition to "the nations," a reference to the broader imperial forces impacting Jewish life and custom. Initially, the Israelites were organized in opposition to their bondage in Egypt. Their relationship to God, and to one another, was organized in terms of their shared negative relationship to Egypt, and then in terms of the selfish demands of YHWY. In Exodus, YHWY defines Godself in terms of having come down "to rescue" the Israelites "from the hand of the Egyptians and to bring them up out of that land into a good and spacious land, a land flowing with milk and honey."[6] God's initial identification with the Israelites is born in the crisis of Egyptian enslavement. The relationship is organized in terms of both functional rescue (or, codependency) and identification as the savior. The price of this relationship with YHWY is that no longer can any of the people maintain relationships with other gods. After the

Exodus, for centuries the colonizing forces "had been the Babylonians, then the Persians, and, after 323 BCE, the Hellenistic dynasty established by Alexander."[7] At the time of Maccabees, Israel was largely under Greek rule and a practical need emerged among the Israelites to find ways to govern themselves while placating the Greek colonizers. This need, effectively, created an internal faction within the Israelites, those who were remaining true to the traditional teachings and customs, and those who had become "Hellenized." That is, those who cared too much for Greek customs. As this and other dissenting voices emerged, the idea of Satan was increasingly deployed as a means of characterizing opponents.[8] At first, Satan had been more allegorical; then, it offered a way of describing peoples of the non-Israelite nations; "in the process they turned this rather unpleasant angel into a far grander—and far more malevolent—figure."[9]

With this usage came various origin accounts of Satan available in the sacred books of monotheism, all with similar moral tales to exemplify. First, as occurs in Isaiah 14, Satan sought the heights of God, only to be brought down so far into darkness, into the underworld, Sheol, or hell (depending on one's tradition of affinity).[10] Genesis 6 offers another account, as it came to be read as a tale of god-like beings mating with human women, creating a hybrid race that "took over the earth and polluted it."[11] Lastly, a third story develops as what Pagels frames as a sibling rivalry (of sorts), in that upon humans being created by God, God asks the angels to submit to the humans. "Satan refused," one apocryphal book concedes. There, Satan tells God that he "will not worship one who is younger than I am, and inferior. I am older than he is; he ought to worship me!"[12] While different, each of these stories convey a similar theme, according to Pagels. No longer does "Satan" refer to "an outsider, an alien, or a stranger. Satan is not the distant enemy but the intimate enemy—one's trusted colleague, close associate, brother."[13] Born as a means of distinguishing outsider group or dissident belief from insider belief, Satan had become a means of marking or shaming factions *within* a community. This shift is the effective precondition for the subsequent weaponization of the idea of Satan as a means of distinguishing (as the New Testament writers often did) between those who followed the Old Law and those who followed the New Law of Christ. In the very use of the term Satan, it carries the connotation of family resemblance. The concept did not refer to a truly foreign alien, but a person from one's own community who was not acting in an orthodox or morally appropriate way. By the time the New Testament writers are drafting their Gospels, even the Jewish Jesus uses the term Satan to distinguish himself and his followers from "his Jewish opponents."[14]

Across medieval and Modern Europe, Satanic imagery was used as a powerful antisemitic trope. Given this history, it is reasonable that many commentators have considered some of the teachings within black esoteric traditions, particularly the Nation of Islam, as antisemitic. The Southern Poverty Law Center, one contemporary organization that seeks to police and account for hate groups in the

United States, characterizes the Nation of Islam as "organized hate."[15] There is no doubt that the notion of the white devil, particularly its theological and mythical origin located in the biblical figure Yakub/Jacob, is inherently incendiary in a broader society that understands itself as Judeo-Christian. Equally, many of the comments of prominent members of the Nation of Islam, including Malcolm X, Muhammad Ali, and the eventual leader Louis Farrakhan, can easily be understood as anti-Jewish and anti-white. Largely, this language seems meant to draw out the intrinsic connection between contemporary Israel (as a nation), its negative impact on many parts of the black and brown world, and western whiteness (in general). To the extent white supremacy has an obvious history of antisemitism, Farrakhan and others within the organization seem to want to emphasize the *theological* roots of white hatred, which have *also* played out historically as white-on-white violence (in the form of European and American antisemitism and even genocide). The incendiary comments put white people—Jew, Christian, and Secular, alike—in the position to make an ethical choice: Would we have ears to hear that the theological roots of hatred rest in our own culture? Would we be more willing to be honest about those roots than we would feel it necessary to defend ourselves against the accusations? If we've been acting like Satan, would we have ears to hear the cries of our victims? And in the case of European Jews, would they be willing to see past their pain to recognize the pain that they may or may not be involved in producing among black and brown people? Would-be commentators and critics are forced into a hermeneutical and ethical choice, and in that moment, we either live into our role as Satan by denying our status as Satan in the eyes of others; or we begin to own up to our role as Satan, historically, and account for the deep religious racial whiteness that binds so many Western Christians and Jews, alike to codependent reliance on and resentment toward black and brown people. To this extent, whether the NOI and its members are considered a hate organization seems besides the concern of Farrakhan and other officials. These traditions like the NOI and NGE offer white Christians and Jews alike an opportunity to reflect on how certain theological concepts like chosenness, grace, and passover play out historically for the rest of the world's population.

Exploring our status as Satan tells us as much about our opponents as it does our need or reliance on those opponents. Ultimately, for Pagels, thinking of ourselves as Satan offers "a reflection of how we perceive ourselves and those we call 'others.'"[16] Pagels writes that "originally he was one of God's angels, but a fallen one. Now He stands in open rebellion against God, and in his frustrated rage he mirrors aspects of our own confrontations with otherness."[17] If our racial, ethnic, or religious opponents consider us Satan, rather than refuting the charge in a fit of denial, we might benefit from accepting the criticism and learning from it. If Satan represents the "intimate enemy," then the charge that we have been or are Satan is also a call to renewed or repaired relationship. If we are in the moment of such an invitation, it bears examination what our past and current relationships with others have felt like for us and them.

***

Psychological codependency offers a way to make sense of the long patterns of behavior that have earned white men the reputation of devils. The devil, ever anxious of his own status among his and other groups, preoccupies himself with the thoughts, feelings, and behaviors of others, seeking to control them and in doing so, mitigate his own feelings of inadequacy. This is codependency, and I think it offers a lot for understanding white masculinity historically, and today. Codependency is characterized by "constantly looking outside of ourselves for love, affirmation, and attention from people who cannot provide it."[18] As those people, for whatever reason, cannot provide this love, codependents seek to control others. What if the basic pattern of relating to others described in the biblical and mythical record of Satan was scalable and applicable to broader social issues and to the behaviors of some of us in response to those issues? I want to entertain the possibility that similar patterns might be scalable to help analyze white masculinity, historically. Could it be that we are Satan because devilish dysfunctional patterns of relationship have been passed down from one generation of white men to the next, to the next, and to the next? Could it be that whiteness's reliance on blackness, and masculinity's reliance on the production of an othered woman, leaves white men today with dysfunctional behaviors and emotions and thoughts as it concerns women and all people of color? In our constant theft and exploitation of the labor of others, could it be that we white men have been addicted to others in a manner similar to psychological codependency?

In the last few years, sociologist Robin DiAngelo has propagated the idea of "white fragility" as a means of capturing the psychological and social mechanisms of denial that make it hard(er) for white people to want to address our inherited racism, privilege, and the like. For DiAngelo,

> White Fragility is a state in which even a minimum amount of racial stress becomes intolerable, triggering a range of defensive moves. These moves include the outward display of emotions such as anger, fear, and guilt, and behaviors such as argumentation, silence, and leaving the stress-inducing situation. These behaviors, in turn, function to reinstate white racial equilibrium.[19]

The white racial equilibrium here reinstated is akin to a dysfunctional worldview, reinforced through denial. When issues of knowledge or morality criticize that dysfunctional worldview, the white person feels threatened in ways akin to how a child will feel when an outsider criticizes their father for being an alcoholic. The defensive moves discussed by DiAngelo are like the psychological mechanisms working within or alongside of codependency denial—ultimately involving efforts to control others in a misguided effort to minimize our own feelings of "uncertainty."[20] For decades now, a select few in the study of religion and race have rendered whiteness as a "denial structure." James Perkinson, following the work of Charles Long, has argued that such a structure imposes a boundary between the being of human and those in denial of the responsibilities required of humanness.[21] White fragility shows something of denial of one's responsibility to others. A kind of accidental, yet learned and willful narcissism unfolds, in that the perpetrator is too psychologically fragile to maintain a healthy sense of their own ego alongside recognition of this shared moral responsibility. Whether this dysfunction plays out as a confrontation with internalized antipathy toward black people or women of any color, or as a confrontation with someone telling us honestly about how dangerous and dysfunctional a parent is because of that parent's dependency on substances, it plays out through similar psychological patterns. Family dysfunction, typified in (but not exclusive to) the alcoholic family, is generational, meaning it is passed down across multiple generations within a family. While there is both a genetic and a situational component to this transmission, here I simply want to emphasize that dysfunctional parents often make dysfunctional children who make dysfunctional children, etc. For instance, as it expresses itself with alcoholism, "the prohibition against speaking honestly about the alcoholism or about one's feelings becomes an expectation on those who wish to be accepted as members of the family."[22] Not all family members of alcoholics look or think exactly alike, but certain shared patterns of behavior or personality traits are discernable that seem to emerge in the dysfunctional natal environment. The same sorts of patterns are discernable with other forms of addiction, and ultimately, codependent behavior. This codependence (at a family level) is toxic; one of the members of the family might have the "problem," but all the family members are shaped in the same way at behavioral and emotional levels. A family might only have one heroin addict, but usually, every member of that family would essentially act like they were the addict due to the emotional dysfunction learned from the addict parent and the codependent parent. Across the years and generations, family members absorb "generational shame, abandonment, and rage only to grow up and recreate similar families or relationships."[23]

"Codependency," writes psychologist Timmen L. Cermak, as a concept "is intended to communicate that a *recognizable pattern* of traits does exist within most members of an alcoholic family."[24] Not all members of a family with alcoholism will turn into alcoholics, but many children of alcoholics will marry alcoholics or other people who are emotionally unavailable to them. This fulfills what is ultimately a self-fulfilling psychological need to relive our childhood abandonment. What is true of alcoholism might also be true of racism and patriarchy by way of monotheism. The alcoholic or addict—as we might conceptualize—is the slave master of long ago and the patriarch who initially engaged women as subordinate and in need of constant rescue and protection. These patriarchs and these slaveowners would represent the source of the dysfunction, the actual addict or drunk. Even if we may feel or hope to feel differently than our forefathers about black and brown people and all women, it could be that we still have not stopped engaging black and brown people, and all women, from the same codependent position of victim. Importantly, in this framing, we white men take the victim position even if reality suggests otherwise. It is enough that we *feel* victimized.

Codependency offers a psychological explanation for the white fragility that DiAngelo situates at the level of social engagement. Codependent denial answers the question of why so many of us are so fragile when it comes to talking about white masculinity. In codependent family structures, there is usually a person dependent on alcohol or drugs, who has preexisting emotional dysregulation issues. They choose to self-medicate through drugs and/or alcohol. The same family usually has one or more (often, the other parent) who is codependently attached to the alcoholic or addict. They are also emotionally dysregulated. But rather than becoming an alcoholic or addict, their identity comes to be fundamentally bound up in taking care of the alcoholic or addict. The codependent suppresses their own feelings and needs and teaches their children to do the same—such that Abraham would willingly sacrifice Isaac. The only person whose feelings or actions matter to the family is the alcoholic or addict. The result is that the entire family grows and lives not knowing how to express themselves in a healthy, balanced way—God dictates the terms of emotional engagement for the whole family, forcing everyone around them to walk on eggshells. Abraham and the other family members are left to defend God above themselves. Like God is depicted in Deuteronomy 28, the only person who matters to the family is the alcoholic, who doesn't want to share their full self with the family to begin with. The alcoholic is also, often, guilty of various moral failures. Codependents come to model these same failures as everyone in the family is taught to emotionally regulate as if they were all alcoholics or addicts. The entire family comes to depend on the alcoholic as the frame for understanding normalcy. What is true of many contemporary alcoholic families may be true of monotheistic cultures, too.

Cermak offers five diagnostic criteria of the codependent person. Try to consider how these features might be expressed in terms of Judeo-Christian monotheism and white masculinity, alike:

> (1) continual investment of self-esteem in the ability to influence/control feelings and behavior in self and others in the face of obvious adverse consequences; (2) assumption of responsibility for meeting other's needs to the exclusion of acknowledging one's own needs; (3) anxiety and boundary distortions in situations of intimacy and separation; (4) enmeshment in relationships with personality disordered, drug dependent and impulse disoriented individuals; and (5) exhibits (in any combination of three or more) constriction of emotions

with or without dramatic outbursts, depression, hypervigilance, compulsions, anxiety, excessive reliance on denial, substance abuse, recurrent physical or sexual abuse, stress-related medical illnesses, and/or a primary relationship with an active substance abuser for at least two years without seeking outside support.[25]

A word might be said that personality traits do not equate to personality disorders. As Cermak reminds, any of us might express narcissism from time to time but that doesn't diagnose us with narcissistic personality disorder.[26] The *Diagnostic and Statistical Manual of Mental Disorders* (*DSM—5*) labels "dependent personality disorder" as a "Cluster C Personality Disorder."[27] Conversely, what is popularly referred to as a "codependent personality" or "codependency" is not treated in the *DSM—5* at all. In fact, the very idea of codependency has caused debates in literature since it began to be used in the 1980s as an umbrella-term for "coalcoholic," which described the "recognizable pattern of behavior and attitudes characteristically found in family members of an alcoholic."[28] But Cermak's criteria offer an opportunity for self-assessment.

For instance, the first criterion includes "continual investment of self-esteem in the ability to influence/control feelings and behavior in self and others in the face of obvious adverse consequences."[29] Historically, white men's primary mode of engagement with women and the rest of the world has been through efforts at control. W.E.B. DuBois talks about this in "The Souls of White Folk," in that a kind of intercultural albeit familial dysfunction among white men would go on to produce world war. "The hatred and despising of human beings from whom Europe wishes to extort her luxuries" created such jealousy and animosity among the European nations that "they have fallen afoul of each other and have fought like crazed beasts."[30] Is not one way to understand DuBois, here, offered in terms of the idea of family dysfunction? Because of Europe's codependent reliance on Africa and the psychological demand to justify and mitigate the effects of that codependency, Europe descended into world war. This first criterion plays out interpersonally, as well. Many white men and women continue to rely on racialized others. Lower-level health care workers, food service industry workers, and custodial/domestic workers continue to be disproportionately black and brown, and while many white Westerners may not necessarily rely on these workers *because of* race, racial codependency is reinforced, nevertheless. Their task is to take care of us; our task is to act with charity in moments when we perceive them in a situation of hardship. So goes our usual rationale. The next criterion of "assumption of responsibility for meeting other's needs to the exclusion of acknowledging one's own needs" is possibly expressed in all the development and NGO work and culture found throughout the developing world. Nineteenth- and twentieth-century church mission work comes to mind, as well. It makes sense that many references to white devils show up in missionary accounts of the nineteenth and early twentieth centuries. In their criticism, indigenous peoples were offering a diagnosis of this white codependency in terms of how it impacted their communities.

Cermak also notes "anxiety and boundary distortions in situations of intimacy and separation"[31] as a marker of codependency. Many white people feel anxiety when we are apart from the object of our codependent identification. When we do not have their black body or woman's body nearby, we white men don't know how to orient ourselves toward the world or others in it without help (from them). The book and film *The Help* illustrate this tendency well. The little white girl in that story is raised to be codependent on the black woman. Her entire sense of self and wellbeing is literally wrapped up in that black woman telling her that she is a somebody. Meanwhile, the black body that provides this psychological salve does not even have the same legibility or rights or existential circumstances that the little white girl experiences. This is the same basic pattern of codependency: Black folks take care of us, while we think and act like we are taking care of them.

Completely inefficient and dysfunctional in both psychological and sociological senses, this codependent dynamic has come at the expense of addressing our own existential needs. Simply put, we've relied on others to provide for us a sense of who we are, and for so long, that we don't know who we are without "Others." We have lived into our moniker "Devil." We simply do not have an identity outside of our codependent bond to others. We do not have Knowledge of Self. Through all our controlling behavior, to prop up and define our social identities and our egos, we have preoccupied ourselves with others, just as our God taught us to do. In turn, our actual Judeo-Christian identity remains an empty signifier. It is an identification via negation, an apophatic identity, remaining to be filled with content that is not derived from others. The fourth and fifth criteria discussed by Cermak may also be applicable. Many white men have maintained severely enmeshed "relationships with personality disordered, drug dependent and impulse disoriented individuals."[32] We could apply this to countless white families that deal with substance abuse, while we could also think creatively about all the excuses and justifications we have collectively offered for nearly sociopathic public policy decisions made by so many of our white leaders, historically, that so often seek to neutralize a black or brown threat and/or ignore black and brown concerns altogether.

Lastly, Cermak suggests any combination of three of the following patterns of experience help to mark the codependent person. These include "dramatic outbursts, depression, hypervigilance, compulsions, anxiety, excessive reliance on denial, substance abuse, recurrent physical or sexual abuse, stress-related medical illnesses, and/or a primary relationship with an active substance abuser for at least two years without seeking outside support."[33] These sorts of interpersonal and social outcomes may not be isolated to white men, but anecdotally, I know more white men for whom this fifth criteria would apply than I know white men for whom it would not apply.

What if the codependent dysfunction seen here correlates to both the racism and patriarchy in the Western world? What if racism or patriarchy could literally be addressed—in part, at least—with talk therapy or an antidepressant? Could talk therapy make us less racist or sexist? In contemporary clinical psychology, more attention is given to rehabilitation and healing from experiencing racial and gendered trauma than ever before (e.g., a black woman healing from the PTSD caused by an experience of racism and sexism). Racism and sexism produce both depression and dysfunction in their victims. Couldn't the opposite also be true, that depression and dysfunction produce racism and sexism, too? Perhaps, if more white men were to confront our root codependency issues, we might become more able and willing to be in fuller, mutually healthy relationships with other people. But are we talking about these issues in our therapy sessions? And are our therapists bringing them up?

***

Suppose we consider Sigmund Freud's perspective on religion in tandem with German philosopher Karl Marx's theory of religion? Freud considered religion a "universal neurosis," that is, if only one or a few of us across any given society believed in a mystery God in the sky, we would be treated like we were crazy. But, because so many of us believe in this mystery God, we give ourselves a collective pass on our neurotic behavior. What would be deemed pathological comes to be considered normal. What if white masculinity works somewhat similarly? Elsewhere I have compared whiteness with theism, suggesting that they are of the same sort of ideological markers.[34] They function similarly, and in tandem. What is true, categorically, of one of them is also true of the other. Perhaps, we white men *do* exhibit the signs of a codependency disorder, only we've yet to be so-labeled as having this disorder because the numbers still work in our favor? Marx, decades earlier than Freud, had suggested that "religion is the self-consciousness and self-feeling of man who has either not yet found himself or has already lost himself again ... *religious* distress is at the same time the *expression* of real distress and the *protest* against real distress."[35] In this way, Marx suggests that people preoccupy themselves with religion as a response to psychological distress brought about by social inequality. In doing so, religion makes it harder to address that same social inequality. God, in these terms, is a codependent object. Marx also emphasizes that because religion is modelled on this real world, then it can impact that world as well. Hence, if we are learning about how to act and think codependently from God or religion, such a dynamic will impact the real world and our dealings with other people. Marx continues with one of the most famous passages in western philosophy that "Religion is the sigh of the oppressed creature, the heart of a heartless world, just as it is the spirit of a spiritless situation. It is the *opium* of the people."[36] That Marx would turn to drug dependency as a model for religion suggests a quality of codependency at work in the religious person's life. Like opium, religion prevents adequate and healthy relationships between people from forming. It prevents awareness of the need for revolution because it tricks people into not realizing they are sick. Religion is the ultimate denial mechanism. At the very least, then, religion might also be guilty of undermining individual emotional regulation, conditioning many of us toward codependency. If addiction dependency is at the root of codependency, wouldn't that suggest that religious codependency exists, bringing with it all manner of dysfunction?

Growing up, I was taught that God would solve all problems. I was to rely on God. I was to pray during times of hardship and give thanks in those same moments (as well as in all the other moments). God was good, all the time, and all the time, God was good. We would be at church so often, and each visit was like a hit of oxytocin or dopamine or outright opium. It would literally leave us feeling good, like we'd accomplished something to stand apart from others. Over time, I came to be suspicious of religion. But not before I had been raised as a full-blown religious codependent. My entire identity was built around a perceived relationship between my belief in God and my self-esteem. If God loved me, I could love myself. But the truth was that I rarely actually felt God's love for me. If anything, I blamed God for the harm that befell me. God wasn't looking out for me. God was in bed with the alcoholics and the sexual abusers. Over time, I came to fashion myself as an atheist, but this was a hard fit. How could I be so angry at something I didn't believe in? Eventually, I came across a little-known theological discourse called, Misotheism—that is, the hatred of God. I wasn't a disbeliever, after all. I just had not had the language to articulate my theological outlook.

Something about coming to terms with my hatred of God enabled me to see my relationship to God as essentially codependent. Granted, I wasn't responsible for my hardships, but it wasn't God's place to save me from my circumstances (even if I didn't deserve those circumstances). I spent years assuming this very thing, that God or Jesus was my savior. I was no different than millions of white American Christians. Don't white Christians underscore that Jesus is their savior? And as a precondition to accepting that savior, don't white Christians also assume responsibility for addressing the (assumed) needs of others instead of our own? My basic point was made by the German philosopher Ludwig Feuerbach in the mid-1800s.[37] The problem with Christianity was that it projected human problems onto a cosmic screen, disconnecting us from our ability to take responsibility for ourselves. Feuerbach wasn't thinking in terms of codependency, of course, and his own antisemitism is an indication that ideology doesn't only play out in terms of the things we call "religion," but Feuerbach's work really exemplifies how a certain brand of Christianity distorts boundaries. White Christians end up overidentifying with the suffering of others (suffering they often have not faced at all), and underidentifying with their own social and psychological circumstances. Marx, informed by Feuerbach, helps in understanding why and how white

Christian religious codependency develops. Essentially, white Christianity equips those of us in its cultural web to live life like victims in denial, and as sinners with a constant get-out-of-jail-free card. Growing up, this codependency played out concretely when we (as a family) told ourselves and everyone around us that our father had a drinking problem, but we're good religious people. And it played out as we told ourselves and others that God loves non-Christians and gay people, and has a plan for them, too. Our God was too righteous to leave them behind, even as other iterations of the white Christian God sought to exclude these groups. But in talking about ourselves, theologically or otherwise, we always talked about others. Christian theology is a codependent discourse arising from the dysfunctional effort to find and understand a cohesive, salient identity that does not exist. Thinking theologically, our family functioned by playing the victim with my dad or God serving as principal scapegoats, and my sister, mother, and me all escaping into religion. We would blame others or work to rescue others. There was very little room for nuance. How many white Christians can resonate with this? How many former Christians can resonate with this? Is there any escape for us from this codependent dynamic?

9 SHADOW WORK

When one tries desperately to be good and wonderful and perfect, then all the more the shadow develops a definite will to be black and evil and destructive. People cannot see that; they are always striving to be marvellous, and then they discover that terrible destructive things happen which they cannot understand, and they either deny that such facts have anything to do with them, or if they admit them, they take them for natural afflictions, or they try to minimize them and to shift the responsibility elsewhere. The fact is that if one tries beyond one's capacity to be perfect, the shadow descends into hell and becomes the devil.[1]

CARL JUNG

Cultivating an intersubjective sense of self begins by taking responsibility for our behavior. But what, exactly, is a "Self"? How do we take responsibility for repairing our self-image, self-confidence, and capacity to respect those features in others? It is relatively easy for any group of scientifically minded people to admit to statistical and historical data suggesting that white folks, collectively, exhibit anti-black prejudice, even *if* white people are no longer as explicitly racist (as we once were).[2] According to philosopher Paul Taylor, one way we continue to show anti-black prejudice is not through explicit hatred of black folks, anymore, but through indifference to the hardships they face.[3] These days, our racism is often organized in terms of our dismissiveness of black and brown folks, not outright hatred. Suppose, further, that many of us might also be willing to accept sociological data suggesting that white men have a collective problem with anger, rage, and emotional regulation. Sociologist Michael Kimmel notes that this anger is largely the result of "aggrieved entitlement that can no longer be assumed and that is unlikely to be fulfilled."[4] According to Kimmel, scores of white men are angry because the Mad Men days of not having to compete with black and brown folks, and of simultaneously screwing our wives and our co-workers with impunity, have ended. White men understand that those days weren't fair for everyone, but what's most unfair (to many of us) is that those days ended before many of us enjoyed their perks. Some of us are nostalgic for the good ole days that we never got to participate in while others of us self-righteously act like we do not harbor these feelings of resentment. Many of us do not actually participate in those ways of relating to women and black folks, at least we don't think we do. When we consider our own involvement in racism or sexism, our individual egos tend to regard ourselves as exceptions to the norm. Some of us wish we could have been devils. Others of us act like we would have never been devils. Very few of us take responsibility for our "shadow that descends into hell and becomes the devil."

German psychoanalyst Carl Jung's notion of the shadow and Nation of Gods and Earths teachings are both predicated on cultivating proper Knowledge of Self. Proper Knowledge of Self involves awareness of who one is (from one's own standpoint) but also who one is through the eyes and interpretations of others. Dangerously, we ignore our unconscious out of a latent awareness that deep down we don't like who we are—which, in a mythical register, is precisely the story of how devils are made. In denying our shadows, we turn self-hatred into externalized aggression.

Jung wrote that "most people confuse 'self-knowledge' with knowledge of their conscious ego-personalities," making most "self-knowledge" "a very limited knowledge, most of it dependent on social factors, of what goes on in the human psyche. Hence, one is always coming up against the prejudice that such and such a thing does not happen 'with us' or 'in our family' or among our friends and acquaintances."[5] Jung indicates that people have a difficulty with self-knowledge because we have a difficulty with comparison. Yet, self-knowledge is possible only through comparison of ourselves with others.[6]

Many of us ground our Knowledge of Self on our conscious awareness, but from a psychoanalytic standpoint, we are also a product of our unconscious. According to Jung, we deny our unconscious reality out of fear and consider ourselves exceptions to collective rules. Effectively, every devil perceives themselves as an "exceptional devil."[7] Racism and misogyny are two of myriad social issues where white men could benefit by doing what is popularly called "shadow work." Many of us make use of clinical psychology. That is, we go see shrinks. And we talk about our problems. But how many of us use that space to talk about our involvement in white supremacy or patriarchy? In like manner, how many of us go to marriage counseling and discuss dismantling patriarchy and toxic masculinity? I want to consider the possible therapeutic value of shadow work for cultivating Knowledge of Self among white men. How is it that many of us can more easily handle discussions of our most agonizing individual moral failures than we can recognize some of our unconscious feelings or behaviors toward black and brown folks? Would a confrontation with our shadow better equip white men to take responsibility for our devilish *behavior*?

In 1957's *The Undiscovered Self*, Jung considered coming into greater self-knowledge to be of utmost importance so that the heightened moral and epistemological possibilities of the individual would hold various collectivities in check. This was, however, only possible if the shadows of our unconscious were brought into conscious relief. For his part, Jung thought that this denial of our unconscious—more precisely, the denial of our capacity to know (and then, synthesize) our unconscious—was socially dangerous, leading to both despotic fascist regimes as well as depersonalized socialist governments. The scenario is made more complicated, however, because we *can* see our shadow in other people (or regimes); but we cannot see it in ourselves.[8] Jung writes that

> Separation from his instinctual nature inevitably plunges civilized man into the conflict between conscious and unconscious, spirit and nature, knowledge and faith, a split that becomes pathological the moment his consciousness is no longer able to neglect or suppress his instinctual side.[9]

Having not sought to incorporate these traits volitionally, they erupt outwardly in the form of what Jung euphemistically refers to as revolutionary behavior, in that the aggrieved person who is coming to know their shadow *unwillingly* can only blame outside forces, for example, the government, or women, or black folks, etc. Bear in mind, the very notion of the shadow is informed by Jung's racism. Jung is talking about black folks as he's developing the notion of a shadow. Quite literally, he associates the shadow with black men, and our antipathy toward black men as rooted in our projecting onto them all the qualities that we fear in ourselves, suggesting at times that "savages" amounted to "an embodiment of the primitive shadow."[10] I want to more forcefully disrupt his racism and chauvinism and apply his theory squarely to white men. It is easier to project onto external forces than to—quoting Jung—"solve the much deeper problem of split personality."[11] Even if hurtful and racist, Jung is more honest than many of us today about who we really are as white men. Jung continues,

> What then happens is a simple reversal: the underside comes to the top and the shadow takes the place of the light, and since the former is always anarchic and turbulent, the freedom of the 'liberated' underdog must suffer Draconian curtailment. The devil is cast out with Beelzebub.[12]

The pot calls the kettle black. In demonizing and blaming others, we are protected from confronting the devil within. Unsurprisingly, part of this dual nature can even be seen in Jung's own perspective, in his exaggerated ethnocentric concern for the West. Early in *The Undiscovered Self*, Jung warns that "Everywhere in the West there are subversive minorities who, sheltered by our humanitarianism and our sense of justice, hold the incendiary torches ready, with nothing to stop the spread of their ideas except the critical reason of a single, fairly intelligent, mentally stable stratus of the population"[13] (meaning, himself). In some respects, his perspective sounds like white nationalist and alt-right groups seeking to preserve Western or European values. But if we're honest, many of us probably feel something truthful in his words. They convey our denied baser concern to protect (ourselves) through affiliation. In another respect, many white men turn in the other direction, overidentifying ourselves as race-traitors, allies, or simply progressive white men who have transcended racism and sexism. "Others may need to do work on themselves, but not us," we feel. We know ourselves well enough to deny ourselves. For many of us on both sides of response, we seek to separate ourselves from the other white men. Wanting to cultivate honesty, if not adequate responsibility, Jung's ethnocentrism is *somewhat* balanced by his critical awareness of the problem. He notes that "quite apart from the barbarities and blood baths perpetrated by the Christian nations among themselves throughout European history, the European has also to answer for all the crimes he has committed against the coloured races during the process of colonization. In this respect the white man carries a very heavy burden indeed."[14] Failure to confront our shadows means we will remain in denial, unable to account for the toll of our codependency on others, historically. Later in the text, Jung elaborates,

> Did not a well-known statesman recently confess that he had 'no imagination for evil'? In the name of the multitude he was expressing the fact that Western man is in danger of losing his shadow altogether, of identifying himself with his fictive personality and the world with the abstract picture painted by scientific rationalism. ... where religious orientation has grown ineffective, not even a god can check the sovereign sway of unleashed psychic functions.[15]

At what point does our sense of civic responsibility as white western men collide with our critical awareness of our feelings of individual innocence and resentment? Much could be said here of liberalism's failure from assuming that all social problems can be solved. Psychologist (and public lightening rod) Jordan Peterson has come to represent in the popular imagination a staunch critic of the collective failures of the liberal establishment to advocate for the whole psychological person of white men. Peterson often discusses Jung's concept of the shadow, emphasizing that the synthesis of our baser selves into our Knowledge of Self is integral lest we are overcome by those baser impulses represented by the shadow. While I think much of the public debate about and by Peterson is sensationalized, liberalism deserves scrutiny. Within the western liberal paradigm, religion has been particularly pernicious. Liberal religion has proven an escape route for white western men who turn to religion to justify all our moral and social failures and to megalomaniacally convince ourselves that we can solve all social problems. It also, in dysfunctional fashion, has failed to adequately provide for the existential needs of white men even though it promises that very thing, historically.

For Jung, however, religion also offers creative strategies. Jung understands religion to be a space where confrontations with (and therefore, synthesis of) one's shadow are made possible. In religious experience, we are left feeling a sense of awe and fear in the face of mystery, enabling greater self-knowledge. And for its part, religious experience then protects against unmitigated collectivism and uncritical group thinking (of various sorts). Assuming Jung is onto something, what then for white men who might reject the possibility of religious experience and (likely) the premise that religious experience is required for protecting society from itself? For Jung, actual belief in the biblical God is beside the point, insofar as all religious symbol and myth is an outgrowth of the unconscious. What we "do" when we are "being" religious is learn about and reinforce who we are. This can happen in troubling ways or life-affirming ways. Monotheism, as I have argued, constitutes a harmful expression of belief in that it inhibits intersubjective exchange through a chronic codependent instrumentalization of others. Moving beyond or before these dangers of monotheism, instead, offers an opportunity for spiritual development. For Jung, it is through wrestling with the *human* meanings associated with religion, where we enable a synthesis of our unconscious shadows with our conscious selves. While certain expressions of religion conceal our shadow, others reveal it.

Enter back, the Nation of Gods and Earths, the black esoteric community of men who fashion themselves as Gods, black women as earths, and white men as devils. The Five Percenter talk of white men as devils is in keeping with Jung's emphasis on understanding evil as "lodged in human nature itself."[16] To the extent we deny this religious register of meaning, "our lack of insight deprives us of the *capacity to deal with evil*" (emphasis in original).[17] What could be regarded as an absurd proposition, that the white man is the devil, is, according to Jungian logic, a potentially healthy idea, as Jung notes that "the great advantage of this view is that it exonerates man's conscious [mind] of too heavy a responsibility and foists it off on the devil, in correct psychological appreciation of the fact that man is much more the victim of his psychic constitution than its inventor."[18] Jung, at once, offers the ability for white men to critically engage with Five Percenters, while also contextualizing the claims made by the Five Percenters. Jung's notion of the shadow aids in our capacity to have ears to hear the critiques of white men as we experience them in our intersubjective exchanges with black and brown folks as well as all women. As if describing how many black and brown folks and women have experienced white men, Jung writes that

> Since it is universally believed that man *is* merely what his consciousness knows of itself, he regards himself as harmless and so adds stupidity to iniquity. He does not deny that terrible things have happened and still go on happening, but it is

> always 'the others' who do them. And when such deeds belong to the recent or remote past, they quickly and conveniently sink into the sea of forgetfulness, and that state of chronic wooly-mindedness returns which we describe as 'normality.' In shocking contrast to this is the fact that nothing has finally disappeared and nothing has been made good. The evil, the guilt, the profound unease of conscience, the dark foreboding, are there before our eyes, if only we would see. Man has done these things; I am a man, who has his share of human nature; therefore I am guilty with the rest and bear unaltered and indelibly within me the capacity and the inclination to do them again at any time.[19]

This is the confrontation with his shadow. Such a confrontation is not possible from the bad faith claims of innocence, but through honest reflection of our propensity for violence, indifference, and all manner of evil. In admitting all of this to ourselves, we open ourselves to not being overrun by these forces. To the extent Five Percenter cosmology enables such a confrontation for white men, we owe the Gods all our praise. Jung continues,

> Even if, juristically speaking, we were not accessories to the crime, we are always, thanks to our human nature, potential criminals. In reality we merely lacked a suitable opportunity to be drawn into the infernal melee. None of us stands outside humanity's black collective shadow. Whether the crime occurred many generations back or happens today, it remains the symptom of a disposition that is always and everywhere present—and one would therefore do well to possess some 'imagination for evil,' for only the fool can permanently disregard the conditions of his own nature. In fact, this negligence is the best means of making him an instrument of evil. Harmlessness and naivete are as little helpful as it would be for a cholera patient and those in his vicinity to remain unconscious of the contagiousness of the disease. On the contrary, they lead to projection of the unrecognized evil into the 'other.' This strengthens the opponent's position in the most effective way, because the projection carries the *fear* which we involuntarily and secretly feel for our own evil over to the other side and considerably increases the formidableness of his threat.[20]

Considered in Jungian terms of the shadow, the ontological notion of the white devil promotes psychological well-being on both sides of any racial divide. If only more white men would be willing to see the ugliness within ourselves.

***

The problem with talking about whiteness with white people or masculinity with men is that we get so upset over the charges that we have offended or otherwise hurt women and people of color that we react abusively toward others and conversations shut down. For example, in 2019 US Congressional Hearings, Donald Trump's proclaimed "personal fixer" Michael Cohen testified that Trump was a racist. He made this point repeatedly in over seven hours of testimony. At one point during the proceedings, Republican from North Carolina Mark Meadows brought Lynne Patton, an African American woman who worked within the Trump administration, to serve as an emblem—or as some later called it, a "prop"—in arguing that Trump is not racist. If he was racist, why would Patton have worked in the administration? Such was Meadows's logic. He was hiding behind his shadow rather than confronting it. Later in the proceedings, Democrat freshman congresswoman from Michigan Rashida Tlaib spoke out against Meadows' use of Patton as a "prop," saying that "the fact that someone would actually use a prop—a black woman—in this chamber, in this committee is alone, racist in itself."[21] Meadows nearly had a fit at Tlaib's suggestion, effectively colonizing the next few minutes of the proceedings to ensure that the "record" vindicated his character. He went so far as to argue that he wasn't racist, but that Tlaib's accusation was actually a racist offense. Meadows sounded like the white folks analyzed so well in Robin DiAngelo's 2011 article "White Fragility." There, she writes that

> White people in North America live in a social environment that protects and insulates them from race-based stress. This insulated environment of racial protection builds white expectations for racial comfort while at the same time lowering the ability to tolerate racial stress, leading to what I refer to as White Fragility. White Fragility is a state in which even a minimum amount of racial stress becomes intolerable, triggering a range of defensive moves. These moves include the outward display of emotions such as anger, fear, and guilt, and behaviors such as argumentation, silence, and leaving the stress-inducing situation.[22]

I don't want to belabor an analysis of white fragility—DiAngelo has done yeoman's work for us already. I can only add now what the white DiAngelo (and countless black folk) knows well—her focused attention on "fragility" is as much an academic exercise in nuance as it is a euphemism and signification for all the brutality and pain that our defensive denial has inflicted on others for centuries. We're not devils for the harm we do to self and other—everybody knows something of moral failure—but for the defensive lies we tell about our innocence. These lies, effectively, are what mark us as "white." Largely, this defensiveness has to do with the strange relationship between discrimination and objectification of others and the construction of our own, white, identity. Although "white" has been treated as a racial and ethnic classification for a few centuries, in some respects, there is no such thing as "white" people. "White" emerges in the context of the New World as a means of marking social acceptance and normativity. It emerges as a "racial" category based on the demographic and phenotypical information representing those who have passed into social acceptance and normativity, and ultimately, power.

In another respect, the term "white" does signal a set of confederated tribes who have lived in and around Europe for about 6000 years and who have forged identity by understanding ourselves in a constant tension with others. Across most of human history, tribal identity has been forged through a geographic totem. A rock formation or mountain, a river or other natural feature, or even an artificial construction like a pyramid, came to be the means of a tribe coming to understand itself, and the means of an individual inside that community understanding their place in the larger tribe. But for landless, homeless, white people—lost in a perpetual wilderness experience—identity was forged through antagonism. In the Hebrew Bible, God promised not only the protection of his chosen people, but also the destruction of their enemies. I am because they are not; we are because them over there are not. For many white folks, this plays out in terms of intense individualism. We're a group by way of negation; we don't belong together intrinsically, but because we all agree that we are individuals first and share a history based on that individualism. Our only connection is by default. I call this an "apophatic impulse," based on the theological idea of identifying attributes of God through assertions about what God is not. Whiteness expresses itself in history as a kind of cultural affiliation and social identification by way of negation. It is not a *functionally* positive embrace of one's tribal, totemic, identity once theorized by Emile Durkheim. Rather, it is a way of identifying a tribe or confederation through a denial of one's "tribe" and a perpetual deferral of responsibility for that denied tribal affiliation. Often, what is denied is cultural continuity and heritage (as in, "they are not me") as well as a denial of ownership of the consequences of that cultural continuity and heritage, historically (as in, "slavery was a long time ago"). But this denial is more extensive than these examples, amounting ultimately to the *denial of difference*—not the fear of difference or the hatred of difference, but the denial of it. Most tribes, or "Ethnoi" to use the Greek, know something of competing with other tribes—the beaver tribe fights with the snake tribe over finite resources. But ostensibly, our white wilderness confederation of European tribes has situated fighting with other tribes as a feature of who we are, as a group, because we have relied on antagonism with outsiders (or outsiders within our ranks) to define ourselves apophatically. We claim universality with all other people, and in doing so, jettison any culturally specific identity. Antagonism becomes our identity as we deny difference (all the while fighting others over it). The effect of this apophatic impulse toward naming by othering has meant that the history of white people involves European tribes fighting with one another until we meet black, brown, and yellow people, who we then turn our aggressive tendencies toward (all the while still fighting amongst ourselves until the end of the Second World War). In moments today when we are charged with acting like a racial group, we then deny that group affiliation and appeal to the most individual aspect of who we are, our interior—our good intentions, our heart of hearts, our character.

Little over three years ago, I sat at the foot of God in the flesh, at Allah School in Mecca, the *axis mundi* for the Nation of Gods and Earths. As I engaged in dialogue with one of these Gods, he reiterated to me that what I needed to understand about the experience I was having with him was that it was a theophany. He said, over and over, "Now, what you need to understand is that you are in the presence of a God." This "you" was pregnant with markers of his awareness of my social situativity. I was with a black woman. I was there, embracing black culture as a white person, which meant I was either lost and needed Knowledge of Self or I knew very well exactly where I was and meant to do harm. I was either in complete lack of what the NGE refers to as "knowledge of self," or I was a narc, working for a governmental agency surveilling the group. This latter possibility is not conjecture or conspiracy-theory, but documentable thanks to the invaluable historical investigations of scholar of Africana religions Sylvester Johnson and others.[23] We know that government and law enforcement have long been interested in any group claiming a relationship between blackness and divinity. This includes the NGE, as FBI files discussed earlier attest. As I spoke with this God, his major refrain to me was simply: "What you need to understand is that you are in the presence of a God." Our conversation tacked in various directions across about forty-five minutes, but about every five minutes, he would come back to the same refrain: "What you need to understand is that you are in the presence of a God." At times, he would include the indirect article "a" before "God" and at other times, he would leave it out. The implications of the slippage to my metaphysically preoccupied mind were immense.

According to psychologist of religion Anthony Storr, God, for Jung, "is neither an idea in need of proof nor an object to be blindly believed in but" rather "an experience, the most immediate and certain of all experiences."[24] In my experience with God at Allah School in Mecca, indeed I was coming into awareness of the reality of God in the form of intersubjective exchange. Jung finds that "when no longer projected as a God distinct from the psyche and inhabiting external space, the self is described as a supreme union of opposites."[25] That day in Mecca, Black men and white men were united in a religious experience of intersubjective communication. I decided at that moment, at the height of my confusion as to the implications of *this* theophany on my understanding of God, that I would take this God at his word. I would force myself to believe him until I did so without hesitation. I came to an understanding of perhaps the logic behind his refrain that I was in the presence of God. His situating of my experience with him as one of a theophany, an experience with black divinity, was his way of giving me the thing that he knew—better than I knew myself—I needed at a psychical level. Jung offers insights about the impact of this theophany, writing that

> Through the negation of God one becomes deified, i.e., god-almighty-like, and then one knows what is good for mankind. That is how destruction begins.

The intellectual schoolmasters in the Kremlin are a classic example. The danger of following the same path is very great indeed. It begins with the lie, i.e., the projection of the shadow.

There is need of people knowing about their shadow, because there must be somebody who does not project. They ought to be in a visible position where they would be expected to project and unexpectedly they do not project! They can thus set a visible example which would not be seen if they were invisible.[26]

Both Tlaib and the God in Harlem represent the "somebody who does not project." They told a truth not only considering their experiences but with attention to the interconnectedness of their and our (white men's) experiences. Jung's racist caricature of black people representing a primal shadow is tragic, but truthful for white men. In our encounters with powerful difference, many white men are confronted with or consumed by our shadows. The God's act of naming himself as the locus of divinity was not an act of hubris or arrogance. It was not self-aggrandizing in the way it might initially hit our ears or impressions when we hear someone claim themselves as God. In hindsight, I can see now and partially articulate what I only felt then with fear and trembling. His naming himself as God was one of the most compassionate moments of my life. In that brief span of time, he and I both were able to share an interior experience of mutual understanding of where we come from and where we belong. I had been operating according to the Biblical notion of God, the God of my father who was a psychological stand-in for my father. In my actual father's failures, I had blamed God. In our collective white male failures, we have blamed women and black men. Miraculously, in my theophany with the God at Allah School in Mecca, I came into an experience of a different kind of God, one that Jung understood, that would become the foundation for reimagining my *self*. Essentially, my willingness to accept this black man as God along with the knowledge of myself as a devil enabled the opportunity for intersubjective communication across various lines of social difference. Our individual autonomous selves did not merge into one conglomerate mass, but something of his impact on myself came into awareness within me.

As Gods do, the Five Percenter God made "understanding understood." In claiming *his* divinity, this black man became my teacher. I had been a scholar of religion focusing on race and religion, and with an axe to grind, a soapbox to stand upon while channeling my devilish fury in an industrious and ironic direction, toward anti-racist agendas. If whiteness had taught me to hate blackness, I would keep the hatred but point it in the opposite direction. This had been my perspective—I was going to keep on hating YHWY, my actual father Charles, women, and black men all for having abandoned me. My experience that day in Harlem, however, pointed me in a new direction of healing and an eventual understanding of myself as an expression of my many intersubjective experiences with other selves.

10 SHAME

My father may as well have been the Pied Piper, the German folk figure who worked as a ratcatcher. The Pied Piper would play a magical flute and rats would follow the sounds. In some versions of the story, the Piper works as a paid bounty-hunter for the town of Hamelin, Germany. Upon commission by the mayor to address the town's rat infestation, the Piper trotted through town playing his flute, with all the rats following in line. Summarily, he marched the rats into a nearby river drowning them. In longer versions of the tale, the mayor and citizens of the town turn out to be unscrupulous and refuse to pay the Piper for his services. Wanting revenge for his unpaid labor, the Piper devised a plan. On the following Sunday, the Piper showed up in the city street playing his fife. Instead of rats, the town's children surrounded him. While all the town's adults are in church, the Pied Piper marched the children out of town and into a cave on the side of a nearby mountain. Neither the Piper nor the children were seen again by the townspeople.[1]

Rats would follow my dad everywhere. Some of my earliest memories involve rats. One evening, my sister, mother, father, and I were returning home from a restaurant. My father was holding me as he walked up to our back door, me having fallen asleep on the ride home. Inserting his key into the door, a shadowy figure scurried across the floor of the sunroom. My dad dropped me and both parents started yelling. Groggy-eyed and terrified by the melee, my sister and I watched as my dad grabbed a broom and chased the rat all around the house. This scene happened more than once in my early childhood. Another early memory I have is waking up in my bed and turning my head to the side, where I was face to face with a rat. It was staring at me perched on my pillow. I must have been five years old. My sister has a similar story of lying in bed and seeing a rat trot across the foot of her bed. Our mom tried to convince her it had all been a dream.

Rats were an unwanted family member for most of my upbringing. Moving into adolescence and my teenage years, my dad or I would take to using poison to solve the rat problem, only for the rats to die in the walls of the house. The poison only made the situation worse. My sister and I would be embarrassed to have friends over, because certain parts of our houses smelled of decaying rats. At one point, when I was twelve or thirteen, I tracked down the smell of death to the bottom of our oven. Pulling back the bottom panel of the gas oven to expose the burner, underneath it was a charred rat carcass. It still creeps me out to think about how many frozen pizzas were cooked and eaten with that dead rat in the oven.

When I was nineteen, I once found my dad drunk in his underwear, sitting in a recliner in the living room, holding his .38 Special Ruger revolver. "What the hell are you doing?" I asked him. "Hunting rats," he replied. In that moment, he may as well have been perched high on a deer stand out in the woods. "What are you shooting," I pressed him further. "Snake shot," he replied. A few months later, I walked up to the back door of our house—the same one he'd dropped me at years earlier. No rodents scurried as I jiggled my keys. I opened the door and walked through the sunroom—the same one that had been a makeshift bedroom for me where I had come face to face with a rat—into the kitchen. The house was silent. Not a rat in sight or sound. Calling out my dad's name, repeatedly, I quickly realized I had just walked into a recurring nightmare I had been having of finding my dad's dead body. I walked slowly back into the sunroom, which also attached to my dad's bedroom from an adjacent door. Grabbing the doorknob, I took a breath and called out "Daddy!" I must have said it half-a-dozen times, louder with each utterance. I was practically yelling. I opened the door and found him in the same recliner that had months earlier served as a makeshift hunting stand. He had moved it from the living room to his bedroom. I called his name. There was only silence. Laying on the bed next to him was his .38 Special. I walked up to him and tried to check for a pulse. His neck was stiff and cold. He had been dead for a while. The coroner would eventually place his death twenty-four to thirty-six hours prior to me finding him. I walked out into the back yard and called 911. Then, I called my mom and sister. They were together at church.

***

Nothing exemplifies family trauma and dysfunction quite like rats. Using rat poison to address the rat problem only to have it backfire in the form of noxious odors is a great metaphor for understanding the emotional reactivity I learned growing up. I still feel shame for not having known how to get rid of rats without them getting stuck in walls and ovens. To this day, rats remind me of the intense shame and grief that followed me from childhood into adulthood. Shame is a powerful, difficult-to-recognize emotion. Basically, it is the feeling of being unworthy of a social group. Shame often causes people to do things that create the unworthy feelings, like self-fulfilling prophecies. Therapist and author Darlene Lander writes that

The need to belong and feel accepted is one of the most basic and primal of all human needs, and it dates back to the beginning of time, when security was a tribal effort. Belonging provides a sense of internal security. When that is interrupted, the magnitude of feeling different, inadequate, or inferior can be unbearable. When shame becomes chronic, it can take over our identity and our ability to enjoy life, chipping away at the trust we have in ourselves and the world. It is the feeling of being a bad or unworthy person. And it underlies all addiction.[2]

My father never finished catching rats, and he was never really paid for his services, either. As a result, he kind of did to my sister and me what the Pied Piper did to the town of Hamelin. He took away our childhood by forcing us to take care of ourselves. This created in us certain patterns of emotional and social dysfunction. It arrested our emotional development. Children in these and similar circumstances experience a constant emotional rollercoaster and become preoccupied with our parents' emotional needs. We grow up too fast in some ways, and not fast enough in other ways. The alcoholic parent will abandon their children in any number of ways, and supposing the other parent is not an alcoholic (or addict), that "healthy" parent will often codependently preoccupy themselves with the emotional stability of the alcoholic—often, in an effort to not "rock the boat." With the alcoholic obsessed with themselves and the codependent parent obsessed with the alcoholic, the children are left to experience physical and emotional neglect and abandonment. We learn that we aren't lovable intrinsically, that we don't matter as much as other people (who we often are told are broken). We come to understand our value as related to whether the addict and the codependent parent are experiencing emotional equilibrium. As children, "we want to heal our drunken or dysfunctional parents by acting good, silent, or by taking care of them."[3] We stuff our feelings until they explode in neurotic ways down the road. In our love for our parents, we learn to love ourselves only to the extent we can address these perceived needs in others. Many of us end up living our adult lives seeking relationships that allow us to recreate this destructive, dysfunctional natal dynamic.

Throughout my adult life, I have struggled to maintain healthy relationships with lovers and with friends. I never knew why until I came across the Twelve-Step Program of Adult Children of Alcoholics (ACA). Essentially, my father's alcoholism and the codependency it inculcated in my family had produced what ACA refers to as an "Adult Child," an adult with the emotional regulation capacities and social boundaries of a child. As Adult Children, our parents' "disease of dysfunction" comes to be our own.[4] As I imagine happened to the children kidnapped to the cave by the Pied Piper, my psychosocial development had been arrested. As a result, throughout adulthood, I literally have never known what a normal family situation involved. Some readers might balk at this claim, and be thinking "but what is normal?" True, every family is different, but health and wellness are concrete situations that families each have more or less of. Mine had lots of love but not enough health. As a result, I lived many years of my adult life not even realizing that I did not know how to regulate myself emotionally. What I thought had been healthy, normal behavior turned out to be denial of the spiritual disease of codependency.

My introduction to ACA began with reading the "Laundry List" (14 Traits of an Adult Child), a set of criteria helpful for determining if a person could benefit from the Program. The Laundry List brought me out of denial of self. These traits, worth quoting in total here, include:

1. We became isolated and afraid of people and authority figures.
2. We became approval seekers and lost our identity in the process.
3. We are frightened by angry people and any personal criticism.
4. We either become alcoholics, marry them or both, or find another compulsive personality such as a workaholic to fulfill our sick abandonment needs.
5. We live life from the viewpoint of victims and are attracted by that weakness in our love and friendship relationships.
6. We have an overdeveloped sense of responsibility, and it is easier for us to be concerned with others rather than ourselves; this enables us not to look too closely at our own faults, etc.
7. We get guilt feelings when we stand up for ourselves instead of giving in to others.
8. We became addicted to excitement.
9. We confuse love and pity and tend to "love" people we can "pity" and "rescue."
10. We have "stuffed" our feelings from our traumatic childhoods and have lost the ability to feel or express our feelings because it hurts so much (Denial).
11. We judge ourselves harshly and have a very low sense of self-esteem.
12. We are dependent personalities who are terrified of abandonment and will do anything to hold on to a relationship in order not to experience painful abandonment feelings, which we received from living with sick people who were never there emotionally for us.
13. Alcoholism is a family disease; we became para-alcoholics and took on the characteristics of that disease even though we did not pick up the drink.
14. Para-alcoholics are reactors rather than actors.[5]

Ten of these fourteen behavioral traits resonated with me deeply and still do. Identifying with as few as three of these traits may mean a person could benefit from the Program. As a result of the various traumas experienced in my early childhood, my adult relationships were dysfunctional and marked by this laundry list of defective character traits. Essentially, these traits were dispositions within me (within my*self*) that have inevitably led to emotional and practical life turmoil and pain. I was not responsible for these character defects, but I now was responsible for recognizing how they impacted me and those around me. In a "mistaken belief that I could have changed my parents' circumstances," I developed codependency, referred to as "para-alcoholism" in ACA (as seen in trait 13 and 14). In ACA, codependency means that

> we constantly look outside of ourselves for love, affirmation, and attention from people who cannot provide it. At the same time, we believe that we are not truly worthy of love or attention. In our view, codependence is driven by childhood fear and distorted thinking known as para-alcoholism. We choose dependent people who abandon us and lack clarity in their own lives because it matches our childhood experiences.[6]

It is not that our parents did not love us; mine and many parents of Adult Children love their children deeply. But given the generational transmission of codependency, many of these parents simply do not know how to love in a healthy fashion. Confusing love with codependent preoccupation with others, the parents teach this to the children across generations.

ACA also offers a "Solution" to all this codependent dysfunction. Through a modified version of the twelve steps of Alcoholics Anonymous, Adult Children "become [our] own loving parent."[7] By working the steps and attending meetings, Adult Children begin to release stored trauma, shame, and grief, and in doing so, it becomes more possible for us to learn how to love ourselves fully. The Solution makes it clear that

> Healing begins when we risk moving out of isolation. Feelings and buried memories will return. By gradually releasing the burden of unexpressed grief, we slowly move out of the past. We learn to reparent ourselves with gentleness, humor, love, and respect. This process allows us to see our biological parents as the instruments of our existence. Our actual parent is a Higher Power whom some of us choose to call God.[8]

A lot is happening in this passage. It confronts us with the wisdom that became the foundation for this book—healing requires "leaning in" to intersubjective experiences with other people. I spent the first two decades of my adult life hiding from the rest of the world, usually hiding behind my work. One reason I adore the thinking of existentialist philosopher Jean-Paul Sartre is because he understood that "hell is other people."[9] Sharing my feelings with other people was an impossible possibility because of the fear I held at the pain and shame that would emerge from within me. Like many Adult Children, I rationalized my upbringing as being not as bad as many peoples', so who was I to feel grief or rage or shame. Friends, family, and lovers became either people with problems that I would seek to fix, or they were to be avoided. ACA forced me out of isolation, and slowly, I have learned to appreciate intersubjective communication with others. Indeed, intersubjective communication came to be a workaround for me, in the face of the other drastic challenge posed in this Solution and in any twelve-step recovery: submission to a higher power.

In the passage above from the "Solution," a subtle but important distinction is made between God and our parents. Thinking back to Freud's theory of the origin of God in the father figure, the Solution here allowed for both parents and God to get off the moral hook, so to speak. They were not the same thing. Freud may or may not be right about how the idea of a monotheistic God develops, but what good God offers in our lives depends on our relationships with our parents. In the ACA Program, participants come to realize that our actual parents provide nothing more than the opportunity for our existence. They do the best they can. All of them. Empathy toward our parents becomes possible as we focus on the generational transmission of shame. This has the effect of helping to heal our relationships with our actual parents because we begin to see that they—like us—were doing the best they could do. Their best may have undermined our capacities at emotional regulation. But they did not do it on purpose. Where God is concerned, for me, the Solution made possible a new relationship with God. For years, I had fashioned myself an atheist. It had been a caustic fit, in that an actual atheist does not believe in God at all. To the extent I spent years hating God, I never stopped believing in God. The ACA Solution was available to me if I would be honest about my theological outlook and cultivate a notion of God suitable to my past trauma as well as my philosophical and theological expectations. I would be damned if God was an old white man in the sky or a mystery God. As I got to know more and more members of ACA, I was not alone in my past hatred of God.

Many within ACA have experienced family dysfunction precisely because of the religious beliefs of parents and other family members. My trouble with God was theodical, in nature, as in "Why did God allow my suffering?" To the extent God was able to stop it but didn't, God was a bastard. Many ACA members held similar feelings. But many members were also there because at the heart of our monotheistic formation were notions of shame that played out in terms like the dysfunction experienced by alcoholic or addict families. In my family, pathological codependent reliance on God and religion had set in motion sexual abuse I experienced at the hands of my pastor's son. That religious zeal was itself an escape from alcoholism and other dysfunction in family generations' past. Yet, for many, the actual substance of religion plays out as shame-based codependency. ACA is in a precarious situation as it concerns isolating and naming religious dysfunction. As a scholar of religion, much of my work, including *White Devils, Black Gods*, seeks to name and describe religious dysfunction. I try to judge which beliefs and practices are productive and which are harmful. However, "ACA respects all the religions and spiritual belief systems of the world" as well as it prioritizes not providing critical feedback to members—feedback comes through the Steps (and, to a lesser degree, a person's Sponsor). Practically, I know several members of ACA who understand their family dysfunction to be rooted in the religious beliefs and practices taught to them as children. I count myself as one of these ACA members. To reiterate a common theme in this book, there *are* bad ways to be religious just like there are practical psychological and medical norms that constitute healthy family dynamics. ACA helped to clarify my thinking on the culpability of God and religion on my Knowledge of Self. Through the program, I found a God I could rely on.

As I explored my theological options, I came to understand God in the sense of abstract intersubjective communication with others. For me, today the idea of God means the sharing of energy with other people. This means that God is not responsible for pain and suffering, neither does God receive the benefits when good things happen. Rather, I have come to understand God as a fundamental principle of how the universe works. Submitting to a higher power simply means aligning myself with the order of the universe. Experiencing God involves the transmission of energy between myself and other people. To the extent we are all energy, energy likes to move. To the extent we remain still and in isolation from other energy, our energy will find destructive ways to express itself. By coming to terms with this basic ontological axiom—that we are energy and energy likes to interact with other energy—I have slowly taken ownership of my well-being and my life. Ironically, in submitting to the idea of God (in the form of intersubjective communication), I became empowered to make choices that were life-affirming for me and those I love. My long-standing hatred of God had been the result of feeling like a victim and hoping against hope that God would intervene and simply solve my problems. Coming out of denial about who I was as an Adult Child opened the possibility of "truly letting go and letting God work in"[10] my life through and as intersubjective communication.

Denial is the psycho-social mechanism that passes dysfunction across one generation to the next. Across time in the program, and in my research, I have come into greater awareness of the patterns that all-but-ensured that my parents would pass their dysfunction down to my sister and me. Today, I am both encouraged by the empathy and compassion I feel toward my parents, grandparents, great-grandparents, and the parents before them, while I am apprehensive about what my Knowledge of Self as an Adult Child might mean about the likelihood that I will pass down dysfunction to my own children. Between these two realities, I work on finding balance.

***

I have "good" memories of my dad. Our time spent together was not all rats and rigor mortis. My sister and I always knew that he loved us even if we didn't always feel like he did. He really did do the best he could. One powerful set of memories I have of him showing us love and of me feeling that love involves Blockbuster video. Like countless American families in the 1980s and 1990s, we spent many Friday nights renting movies and ordering pizza. My mom still lights up whenever we bring up Pizza King pizza, no doubt because they did have the best pizza in the city but also because it brings to mind some of the good times we experienced as a family. We would watch *Willow*, *Darby O'Gill and the Little People*, the *Herby* movies, *Field of Dreams*, and so many more, renting our favorites over and over.

One movie, *Song of the South*, offered more pathos than the rest of them, because it starred my dad's second cousin, Bobby Driscoll. Bobby had been one of Hollywood's first child stars. In the early 1940s, my dad's great uncle Cletus Driscoll took his family from Cedar Rapids, Iowa out to Southern California. Bobby was discovered by Walt Disney and starred in a host of incredibly popular early Disney movies including 1950's *Treasure Island*, 1953's *Peter Pan*, and before them all, 1946's *Song of the South*.

Song of the South was the movie that made Bobby famous. It was controversial since its first release. Some folks consider it so racist that Disney no longer makes it available to the public. The film is based on a collection of African American folk tales centering on Br'er Fox and Br'er Rabbit, stories that presented morality and other proverbial life lessons to black children. The stories were passed down from one generation to the next in black families. These stories had been collected by a white man named Joel Chandler Harris who created the character Uncle Remus as a vehicle for the telling of these stories. Harris's book provided the foundation for the film. Between people frustrated that white folks would benefit financially from black cultural products and offended at the idyllic depiction of Reconstruction-era plantation life, the film was (and remains) deeply controversial. None of the controversy mattered when we were picking out a movie to rent.

We would sing the hit song from the film, "Zip-a-Dee-Doo-Dah," together as a family. My dad would use the film to introduce Bobby to us and use the family connection to teach us one thing or another about our extended family. It was, for him, a window into who the Driscolls of Cedar Rapids, Iowa were. And it made us feel good. It brought us together as a family. Literally, that movie represents some of the happiest times of my childhood. At no point during all those family Friday nights did my dad tell me whatever eventually happened to Bobby or explain why we had never met him. I had even asked because Bobby was famous. In like manner, at no point do I remember my mom or dad pausing the movie to explain the complicated social circumstances of Reconstruction or white supremacy or even racism. Celebrated writer Alice Walker wrote that "Uncle Remus in the movie saw fit to ignore, basically, his own children and grandchildren in order to pass on our heritage—indeed, our birthright—to patronizing white children who seemed to regard him as a kind of talking teddy bear."[11] Something in my parents' failure to tell the whole story about Bobby or Reconstruction rings of parental neglect just as Walker suggests was forced on the children of the character Uncle Remus. Both black and white kids were neglected by our parents because of white supremacy. Walker remembers the film as an experience of "vast alienation" at the hands of an "oppressive culture."[12] The worst part of it all, for Walker, was that the film produced in her feelings of shame.[13] Walker's description of vast alienation is also somewhat applicable to the relationship white children maintained toward our identity, but in an inverse way. Black children's identities were stolen, and white identity came to be clouded by the shame of the theft. For my sister and me, the film taught us to deny the shame buried deep down in the hearts of white children. Whiteness, white supremacy, however we want to frame the white relationship to *Song of the South*, like the overall ideology of the "lost cause" in the American South that inspires so much white nostalgia, the film reinforced white denial of intergenerationally-transmitted shame. Lancer suggests that "denial is the biggest obstacle to healing, and the denial of shame is immense."[14] Like what had been taught to our parents, we were taught to repress and ignore feelings of shame during these family moments. I still regard these movie nights as some of the warmest moments of my white life while I recognize the dysfunction these moments were programming into me. "Shame typically begins at an early age," Lancer continues, noting that "Some parents teach their children to keep secrets to maintain appearances and to hide family shame about addiction, mental illness, criminality, infidelity, poverty, and more."[15] My parents did not do all of this on purpose, but because they had been taught it by my grandparents, who had been taught it by my great-grandparents. Who knows how long white families have been in denial of self? What Lancer does not include in her thoughtful analysis of shame, but that seems obvious from Walker's wisdom and my life circumstances, is that shame for white kids is also about whiteness, masculinity, heteronormativity, and all the other "isms" that white people participate in. It was not all about alcoholism. Alcoholism is as much about all those other isms, too.

Shame is deeply intersectional. For instance, Michael Muhammad Knight, scholar of religion and one of the few white members of the Five Percenters, turned to Islam as a way of responding to the white supremacy espoused by his father. Islam provided Knight an avenue for critical response to the strictures of race. Upon participation in the Nation of Gods and Earths, however, Knight was confronted with the status of women as "Earths," "secondary but most necessary," according to prominent hip hop artist and God Lord Jamar.[16] Realizing the intersectional nature of both dysfunctional racism and sexism, Knight was confronted with an ethical challenge: Did his being somewhat of an outsider to the NGE (because he is white) mean he had to stay silent on the gender issue? He concluded that "to say that whiteness prevents me from speaking on maleness means that I owe something to my whiteness that I do not owe to my maleness."[17]

Knight continues, writing that he is "also pulled in the other direction, with the knowledge that challenging maleness does not entitle me to ignore my whiteness."[18] Despite, or maybe because of Knight's awareness, he came to recognize that at times, his "Islamic antiracism gave shelter to [his] sexism."[19] Knight is honest and compelling in his concluding thoughts on the sexism that was his antiracism, and its implications: "Taking the devil off the planet" means "recognizing the ways in which sexism and racism feed each other, causing black men to be hurt by sexism, white women to be hurt by racism, and everyone's lives to be shaped by both,"[20] and I would add, black and brown women hurt and ignored altogether. Knight's intersectional analysis provides a strong foundation for anyone interested in accounting for interlocking systems of oppression. In the style of confession, Knight recognizes the deep impact of racism and sexism on white men's identity, even and especially including those white men who want to do and be better:

> As the beneficiary of both racism and sexism, I have seen my reality written by them. Apart from the countless ways in which whiteness and maleness define me every day, I can trace histories through which racism and sexism lured me into each other. Taking my views on gender as a teenager from Malcolm X, my treatment of women was therefore influenced by the psychological impact of slavery, poverty, and disenfranchisement upon black men: the legacy of racism made me a sexist. Similarly, if commitment to antisexism causes me to forget my whiteness and all that comes with it when in dialogue with Muslim communities or the Five Percent, then the legacy of sexism has made me a white supremacist. I have to respect what Malcolm X and Mary Daly could say to me, but also what they would say to each other.[21]

In many respects, my story is like Knight's, but in my telling, I want to imagine what it would mean to include alcoholism and addiction as co-morbidities alongside of racism and sexism (and homophobia) in an overall shame matrix shaping white families. If we take away the limiting notion of individual vs. corporate-level issues, then all of these "isms" appear to be rooted in feelings of shame and the codependency and abuses that unfold in response to deeply denied trauma and shame. Well-intentioned codependent behavior might lead a child to grow up and become an alcoholic. An alcoholic parent might lead a child to find solace in the priesthood and eventually molest parishioners. A cocaine-addicted parent might lead their child to grow psychologically-dependent on misogyny. An explicit white supremacist parent might lead their child into alcoholism or shame-based adherence to God and religion. Denial is at work in these transmissions. The notion of para-alcoholism is helpful for keeping attention on alcohol as a point of origin for so much family dysfunction, but it doesn't really account for the roots of so many white people's alcoholism and addiction, nor does it give adequate attention to the many other spaces in social life where dysfunction expresses itself. Shame is at work in these transmissions of dysfunction.

For practical example, most of the explicitly racist behaviors that I have witnessed or participated in throughout my life have been the result of white men being triggered by an altogether different situation or circumstance, where they then projected their feelings onto black and brown people. Many white men use racism as a valve to release unprocessed emotions in dysfunctional, toxic fashion. For another example, many men across race who have perpetrated abuses against intimate partners are often dealing with life pressures and circumstances outside of the home that turns them into ticking time bombs, so to speak. Then, upon interaction with their intimate partners, the partners do or say something that triggers an explosion. The partners are not responsible for the building pressure much less the explosions. The misogynistic and patriarchal treatment comes to be a pathological valve releasing stored energy unaddressed and unregulated by emotionally dysfunctional, shame-filled men.

Shame is a pandemic we do not discuss adequately as families or as a society. So many scholars, journalists, and other interested parties tend to treat these issues as if distinct from one another. Racism. Sexism. Monotheism. Homophobia. These are all expressions of emotional dysregulation that play out in terms of various salient identities. Accounting for such abuses—and thinking about racist and sexist and homophobic behaviors as abuse—aids in recognizing the scope of the overall pandemic. Whether we think about these issues as interpersonal violence against individuals or groups, or whether we think about these abuses as structural and systemic, their point of origin is emotional dysregulation at work among many white men. Ostensibly, white men are Adult Children in many ways. It is not necessary to argue that all white men are codependent, emotionally dysregulated, shame-based individuals. That only some of us would come from dysfunctional families, where dysfunction is transmitted across generations, is enough to suggest that emotional dysregulation is a pandemic. Providing adequate attention to the deeply intersectional quality of shame, moreover, might then suggest that a kind of toxic dysfunction is at work among white men, having shaped aspects of what it has meant to be a white man, historically and today. In what follows of this book, I offer practical frames for beginning the process of rehabilitation—recovering the child within white men and learning to love them.

It is impossible to exist in today's world as a white man without confronting stories from others about us that would—and will—bring up feelings of shame within ourselves. Yet, so many white men continue to act as if we are impervious to shame. This is denial. My parents were likely in too deep of denial to speak openly and honestly about the circumstances surrounding Bobby or *Song of the South*. In fairness, it is hard to talk about tragedy with children. It is hard to discuss it at all. It is even more so difficult when we attach so much shame to ourselves. My father was in denial of his own shame connected to his own drinking, his family's drinking, and the abandonment his family left him to feel. As a result, my father was not in the position to face, much less share with his children, the story of what happened to Bobby or what may have happened to my father and his brothers at the hands of a Catholic priest when they were children in Iowa. Relatedly, neither of my white parents were in the psychological position to adequately and openly confront the shame that whiteness brings. To admit to whiteness and white supremacy is to admit defeat, failure, and victimhood that very few white people are in an overall healthy-enough state to address. If more of us expect more white people to take seriously racism and patriarchy, we must address "the whole person." We must address all the spaces in our lives where shame is at work. In getting to the root cause, we will then be better equipped to do anti-racist or anti-sexist work within ourselves and communities. Quite literally, unless white people begin to love ourselves without codependent reliance on the use or feelings of others, we will be emotionally unavailable for participation in justice work, today. It won't be out of lack of concern, per se, but a lack of emotional capacity.

So, what *did* happen to Bobby? As an adult, I have cobbled together the scaffolding of his story. By 1949, the year both of my parents were born, Bobby was quickly entering into puberty. With puberty came changes to his body type and size, and acne appeared on his face. Soon, he was not nearly as bookable as he once was. It seems that Bobby was not psychologically developed fully enough to weather the storm that his dimming star created inside of himself. I can only wonder what intergenerational Driscoll family dynamics were also at work for him during these years. Across the 1950s, Bobby became a drug addict and lost contact with much of his family. Eventually, he moved to New York City, becoming destitute and estranged from the lives he had known in Southern California and Iowa. In 1968, he died in a drug den somewhere in Manhattan's East Village. The City of New York buried him in an unmarked pauper's grave at Hart's Island.

11 ABUSE

Philosopher Peter Sloterdijk has, in recent years, drawn a series of causal linkages between western culture and the rage exemplified so often by many white westerners, today. Astutely, he notes that rage is present as an idea in the very first sentence of the very first book classically regarded as the foundation of western culture. Homer's *Iliad* begins with a statement of Achilles' rage.[1] The "first" westerner, Achilles, Homer associates with rage and wrath, to such an extent that the poet is left asking, "What God drove them to fight with such a fury?"[2] While Zeus and all the rest of the ancient pantheon will play a part in answering Homer's question, it is notable that Homer associates rage with both Achilles and the Gods. Perhaps, Homer is telling us something about the qualities of character of those of us who will end up counted as white western men. To know us is to know our rage.

Many white men feel like we are being persecuted by societal forces. The feelings are sincere. I feel them, too. And at times, I find myself thinking and believing in these feelings. But we shouldn't *believe* everything we think or feel. Feelings are to be felt and processed, not "believed." Contrary to these feelings that so many of us hold, it is more historically accurate to argue that we white men have a long history of rage-filled, abusive outbursts and our feelings of persecution have been with us for a very long time. They are not new. History shows us that many white men have had a strange chip on our shoulder for, literally, thousands of years. And this feeling that the world is out to get us is what has, so often, caused some of our most devilish behavior.

One thing that *has* changed in recent decades in the west is that there is now a critical mass of folks—scholars, journalists, teachers, activists, and even some politicians—who are honest about who white men have been in history. One of these is historian Carol Anderson, who has argued quite convincingly that white people—white men, especially—today continue to embody the same rage that Sloterdijk tracks back to Achilles. And similarly to how some have sought, to varying levels of success, to paint the *Iliad* as a racial or ethnic conflict, we as Achilles-figures are enraged by the seeming advances of dusky-hued Ionians:

> The trigger for white rage, inevitably, is black advancement. It is not the mere presence of black people that is the problem; rather, it is blackness with ambition, with drive, with purpose, with aspirations, and with demands for full and equal citizenship. It is blackness that refuses to accept subjugation, to give up. A formidable array of policy assaults and legal contortions has consistently punished black resilience, black resolve.[3]

As Anderson finds it, competition with historically marginalized racial and ethnic others triggers white men to rage. Anderson offers a wealth of examples to bolster her claims, most compellingly centered around the seismic event of Barack Obama's presidency. Another scholar, sociologist Michael Kimmel, has studied the possible social conditions resting underneath what explodes from white men as racial resentment and anti-black violence. In exploring figures within the men's rights movement, Kimmell finds that participants often blame the women's rights movement and feminist movements of the 1960s and beyond for men's emotional duress. Essentially, men's rights activists act codependently, blaming other people for their own problems. Moreover, Kimmell recognizes that within the men's rights movement, rarely are the rights of black and brown, or queer men discussed, nor are men of color common participants within the movement. Those men marginalized in terms of race or sexuality outside of this movement that choose to participate are often tokenized within the movement. Overall, these men angry enough to mobilize against women's political activity are decidedly white, and feel a similar persecution felt by Achilles. Moving beyond the historical analysis offered by Anderson, Kimmell suggests that

> It is important to acknowledge the authenticity of the pain and anguish that propel their misguided empirical analysis. That's real and important. Many men do not feel very good about their lives. They're casting about for someone to blame, some explanation for their anguish, confusion, malaise. In a sense, I think some of the original men's liberation rhetoric hit closer to the mark. Traditional masculinity can be a fool's errand, an effort to live up to standards set by others that leave you feeling empty, friendless, a Willy Loman surrounded by Mitt Romneys—shallow, happy cartoon characters. They feel themselves to be the "hollow men" in the T.S. Eliot poem. They're scared their lives are going to amount to little. That malaise is real and important—and able to be politically manipulated and mobilized. Failure to hear that pain means that rational assessments of these men's plights will never be heard.[4]

Summarizing his findings, Kimmell notes that

> The "enemies" of white American men are not really women and men of color. Our enemy is an ideology of masculinity that we inherited from our

fathers, and their fathers before them, an ideology that promises unparalleled acquisition coupled with a tragically impoverished emotional intelligence. We have accepted an ideology of masculinity that leaves us feeling empty and alone when we do it right, and even worse when we feel we're doing it wrong. Worst of all, though, is when we feel we've done it right and still do not get the rewards to which we believe we are entitled. Then we have to blame somebody. Somebody else.[5]

Essentially, many of these critical voices like Anderson and Kimmell are trying to bring white men out of denial about our abusive codependent reliance on others. Anderson does the tragic work of holding history up to us as a mirror. Kimmell does the thankless work of maintaining a compassionate posture toward folks who are often insufferably unworthy of receiving it. In turn, no matter how such critics present the information to us, many white men react as if we were drug addicts experiencing an intervention. The current effort to ban critical race theory from state-funded schools is one of many attempts to deny our abusive history. Literally, all critical race theory does is correct the historical record and reveal how our legal system has failed all of us (in its having only been designed to protect white men). The latter is not an opinion, but an historical fact. The denial of abuse runs so deep because our history has been so violent. It simply has. We might fashion ourselves as problem-solvers, but in the eyes of the rest of the world, white men have been problem-makers and problem-blamers.

Once we have let go and begun the process of accepting who we have been, it opens us up to explore *why* we have been this way. What causes us to be so devilish, so often? As Kimmell suggests is true of masculinity, I want to add to this in suggesting that a comprehensive problem with emotional regulation is at the heart of so much of our devilish behavior. We have severely atrophied emotional intelligence capacities. Many white men simply do not know how we feel, and so, we are unable to regulate ourselves in a healthy fashion. The result of this dysregulation is rage and the abusive behaviors that result from the many moments when we explode.

If rage is a feature of white men dating all the way back to the mythical figure Achilles, what could possibly be the cause of it? One of the insights offered by the myth of Yakub, which posits white men to be devils created by a mad black scientist, is that it provides an open-ended analogy to explain white men's abusive behavior. Devils abuse, in no small part, because they feel resentment toward God. To this extent, the story works as an analogy for understanding our behavior toward others. Yet, the Yakub story goes one step further than analogy in opening us to the possibility that there are biological or genetic factors contributing to our devilish ways. As is commonly reminded in the teachings of Elijah Muhammad, the grafting process that created white men sought to isolate the recessive genetic traits in such a way that would have a consequence on personality and psychology.

In short, while I have not seen solid or enough scientific evidence to make the claim that higher rates of melanin lead to higher capacities of compassion, emotional intelligence, and toleration of social frustrations, anecdotally, many of us have seen such evidence in the form of black compassion and white rage, generally. White marauders still trod our streets in the form of nosy "Karens" eager to police black behavior, and in the form of killer white men committing massacres with assault rifles. Taking the topic into the space of genetics brings up complicated concerns about drawing causal connections between our biology and our proclivity for violence, which is problematic for several reasons. Causal arguments can be problematic because white men have used very similar arguments, historically, to marginalize and oppress black and brown folks, and women. Today, we call this scientific racism. Phrenology was one such effort, the attempt to draw behavioral conclusions about people based on measurements of the cranium. Drawing such causal genetic conclusions is also problematic, for some, because it could potentially get the perpetrators off the moral hook. If, it happens that, white men are genetically predisposed to abusive rage-filled outbursts, then it could excuse that behavior in history. For my part, I feel that the potential benefits of having greater *genetic* Knowledge of Self outweigh the potential abuses or excuses that may come from it. With respect to the problem of white men abusing others, is our priority to cast adequate blame (the issue of blame seems rather obvious, historically speaking) or is it to promote the cessation of abusive behavior?

One author who has offered a genetic explanation for the abusive behavior of white men is Michael Bradley. Bradley takes causal biological arguments in an altogether different direction than their nineteenth century scientific racism counterparts. In *The Iceman Inheritance*, Bradley proposes that a genetic link between contemporary white people and Neanderthals has created what some have referred to as an "aggressive" or "warrior gene."[6] As with genetics in general, there will be exceptions to the rule of who has this aggressive gene or who is missing a compassion gene, but Bradley suggests that history along with paleontology, and the growing science of epigenetics, offers enough evidence together to make the case that white men, generally, are more aggressive than the rest of the world's population.[7] While I leave it to readers to judge for themselves the merit of Bradley's argument, it is notable that his book was first published in 1991, at a time when Neanderthals were popularly regarded as culturally backwards and biologically disconnected from the human genome. I can only speculate that the contemporary social whitewashing of the notorious reputation of the Neanderthal in our collective western imagination is due to the growing scientific recognition that they are part of us; Part of some of us, at least. Bradley concludes that "our"—yes, he is a white man—"psychology is treacherous and self-protective."[8]

While I am imminently fascinated by the possibility of locating a genetic origin for our treacherous psychology, I am much more motivated to create an immediate behavioral wedge between white male aggressors and our victims. Breakthroughs in epigenetics could lead to future recognition that some of us are predisposed toward apathy or sociopathology, while others of us have more proclivity toward compassion and empathy. It could end up the case that many, many white men need antidepressants to stabilize what has for centuries and generations been a chemical imbalance within our brains. While I do not draw conclusions based on Bradley's work, ironically, his willingness to continue to use race (even if socially constructed) as a means of asking behavioral questions is an example of the kind of courageous, counterintuitive thinking that will only aid in collective efforts to address white abuse.

Bradley, Kimmell, Anderson, and many other scholars, as well as Elijah Muhammad and other religious and community leaders across the last decades, are part of a cacophony of voices who are seeking to end the abuses of white men. In what follows of this chapter, I hope to join their efforts by discussing practical tools white men like me can use to better ensure we contribute to these efforts.

***

The first behavioral intervention into white abuse is recognition of the black-and-white, all-or-none thinking common among so many white men. One way of defining abuse is as the imposition of a reality onto a person. Most fundamentally, white men often impose totalizing, zero-sum, binary logics of value and meaning onto everyone around us. Responding to our abuse begins with expanding what we understand as possible within our relationships.

Part of codependency includes a lack of self-love and self-esteem that are the result of neglect and abandonment experienced as children. Internally, codependent people struggle to feel important because as children, we responded to neglect by imagining our parents having more important things to do and people to spend their time with. Trained at an early age to compete with our parents' priorities, codependent people tend to approach others as if we are in a competition with them. As a result, one coping strategy we develop is seeking the approval of others while also resenting others as our competition. There is nothing intrinsically wrong with wanting to feel special, but for many white men, we feel as if our ability to be validated in the eyes of a mother or lover or an entire professional field or an entire race will come at someone else's expense. This sense of competition—that the value shared between people is a zero-sum quantity—is based on childhood logics at work in our minds as children (or later in life when we are arrested to childhood emotional skills). This isn't to say we—as codependent white men—desire it to be this way. We *perceive* the world to be this way, and we often violently impose our perception of the world onto others, in what becomes an abusive self-fulfilling prophecy. Perceiving ourselves in a competition, we create it in our social relationships, coming to have a love/hate relationship with those around us.

Responding to our history of abuse begins with expanding what we understand as possible within relationships. For instance, many codependents will feel intense neglect and anxiety when their love-interest or their professional contact (of one sort or another) is not in constant contact with them. Let's call this other person their "qualifier"—the person for whom the codependent person draws their self-esteem. Suppose a codependent person is "talking" to a potential partner. They may be messaging off and on back and forth. For the non-codependent person, the spaces in between texts might usually produce feelings of happy anticipation, a light curiosity about what is around the next corner, and an overall sense of excitement. For a codependent person, waiting for the next text message or phone call can be a fraught experience. Fear of neglect and abandonment short-circuit our capacity to appreciate or be fully present for the intersubjective exchange taking place. Instead, fear and dread flood our minds. "What if I said the wrong thing and now they are not interested?" "What if something happened to them?" "What if they are just busy and don't get to respond now, but then later forget to respond, do I then text message them again?" Surely, many of us think about these hypotheticals. They are the fodder for the plots of romantic comedies and the like. Yet, these scenarios can torment codependent people, who struggle with feelings of impending abandonment. The biggest fear becomes losing the people we "catch" or avoiding everyone to dodge the emotional ambiguity of social interactions. As a result, most of our emotional and practical energies end up directed toward not losing the person rather than sharing in experiences with them (and others). In this way, we struggle to be present in the relationships we work so hard to preserve. While the person on the other end is (presumably) doing their thing, the codependent person is operating from a fight-or-flight mode.

Personality psychologist Robert Kegan writes of a "zone of mediation where meaning is made," "that most human of 'regions' *between* an event and a reaction to it—the place where the event is privately composed, made sense of, the place where it actually *becomes* an event for that person."[9] For codependent people, this space of meaning-making is terrifying, and black and white, good vs. evil logics offer a way to psychologically avoid the terror of uncertainty and emotional ambiguity. The aesthetic style or the "value" (as I am using the term here) is limited to two kinds, that which will harm us and that which will sustain us. Fight-or-flight is the name given to the times when our nervous system dictates our thinking and our behavior. In Freudian language, it is part of our Id, our reptilian, reactive mind, and body that responds to perceived threats. Historically, fight-or-flight functioning has helped us to stay alive. But it doesn't do well at enabling our psychological health or peace of mind, in the long term or in society, today. "Alive" and "Healthy" aren't the same thing. Our fight-or-flight response trades in black-and-white thinking. Reacting to social interactions with anxiety, any intersubjective encounter becomes an all-good or all-bad experience. Those we deem "all-good" end up without any negative feedback informing our shared experiences. At the same time, those deemed "all-bad" are completely avoided. For codependents, whether we are running from a dinosaur or text messaging our girlfriend, much of what we experience as sensory stimuli is responded to with this binary logic—good or bad, safe or harmful. Little nuance or ambiguity is allowed, within the codependent mind.

Technically, this "zone" as Kegan describes is not the space where a "self" is located *a priori*. Rather, all expressions of myself are constituted in this zone, in real time, based on a variety of factors. What Kegan helps to emphasize is that the "self" doing the codependent behavior is not really an autonomous entity as such. "Persons," for Kegan, are "understood to refer as much to an activity as to a thing—an ever-progressive motion engaged in giving itself a new form ... human being as an activity."[10] Selves are not so much entities that do things but are constellations of doings that we treat as distinct entities. This way of understanding the self, or personality, lends itself to flexibility and malleability. There are no "codependent people" but amalgamations of intersubjective exchanges that organize as "people" in our everyday experiences. Fight-or-flight experiences take for granted the static expression of a self precisely as an effort to keep that self safe. The autonomic nervous system—responsible for the flight-or-fight response—is not overly concerned with the thinking and feeling being that understands itself as either static or an evolving intersubjective being. Rather, it seeks to keep those thinking and feeling beings out of danger. What results during activation of the nervous system is the limiting of options down to two—good or bad. Selves become static, singular things, and each one is then measured based on their proximity to perceived safety or danger. A multiplicity of expected outcomes for our identities, as well as a multiplicity of values we associate with our identities, is truncated for the codependent person, ever feeling persecuted and victimized by the sheer variety of potential selves. Insofar as human selves are expressed through our intersubjective experiences with other potential selves, codependent white men ultimately inhibit our capacity to express our full selves because we live in near-constant fear of other selves.

The emotional state of fight-or-flight is not necessarily problematic because there are real moments when we must protect ourselves from those who would do us harm. But for many people, the nervous system stays activated when threats are no longer occurring. Emotions have no understanding of history or the passing of time, and so at an emotional level, many who have experienced acute instances of abuse and neglect can live in a state of feeling perpetual fear and anxiety. Many experiencers of trauma, neglect, or abandonment end up living within the boundaries imposed by their trauma. This is one way of describing the condition of post-traumatic stress disorder, a condition that follows many codependent people. Others, still, can be triggered easily and set into a fight-or-flight response because of the mere *perception* of trauma. For the codependent person, who has a love–hate relationship with other people, basic social interactions can be deeply triggering. What might otherwise be a healthy emotional response in terms of responding to acute dangers and threats comes to be expressed as emotional dysregulation or dysfunction for the codependent person, insofar as they treat most or all zones of intersubjective exchange as threatening even when there is no actual danger or likelihood for danger. Beginning to think in terms of a multiplicity of values possible within any given intersubjective experience offers an aspirational frame for moving into a new ontology, an inclusive ontology not predicated on divisiveness or zero-sum logics. As codependent people, we do matter, and we are special—but we prevent our (and others) recognition of why and how we matter when we operate from the faulty premise that our ability to feel important requires others to feel unimportant.

***

White men are not the only men who abuse. Men across race and ethnicity and generation and class-status are all responsible for ending the onslaught of violence perpetrated against women, queer men, trans and non-binary individuals and groups, and children. Abuse is intersectional, as is the task of responding to it. I came into this awareness as I spent over fifty weeks in group therapy sessions for perpetrators of intimate partner violence.

Each week, I would join men of various racial and ethnic backgrounds as we took accountability for our behaviors toward others, beginning with intimate partners, then families, then colleagues, and then strangers. Each participant was required to literally "count" the abuses we had perpetrated across the previous week, as well as describe how we had been feeling in those moments, and then share this information with the group. Then, the group leaders would determine which stories of abuse offered the greatest teachable material or which of us required the most pressing acute intervention. The group would be forced to provide feedback to each of the men claiming abuses. Abusers were doing the work of preventing abuses. I learned a great deal in these sessions, a lot of which came to be included as portions of this book.

Abuse, whether we are talking about racism, sexism, or domestic violence, is learned. It is learned in and across culture. In the same way that in an anti-black racist society, all of us are taught something of the diminished value of black people, in a sexist society all of us across race are taught to devalue women. As men in this group, we shared these interlocking series of oppressions as if part of a brotherhood. We had learned from our families, our school and sports systems, the military, religions, and entertainments industries who mattered, who didn't, and how we were allowed to treat one another. In general, all the men in the room used the social structures we all knew intimately to determine who would receive our abuses. We perceived our individual values differently based on race and income and other factors like education, but we shared in feeling like the women around us were less valuable than we were. Sexism is so deeply held by many of us that even in sharing our stories of abusing our wives, girlfriends, mothers, and daughters, often we men were left with a genuine sense of camaraderie—rarely felt across race.

Most of the abuses listed each week were connected to situations where we felt harmed or victimized by women in our lives. Yelling, pushing, kicking, cursing, belittling, name-calling, reckless driving, other threats, gaslighting, withholding affection, demanding sex, withholding sex, and so many other abuses were almost always occurring as reactive behavior. Sheer, unbridled reaction to a perceived harm, and to a lesser extent but more insidiously, out of a desire to teach a lesson or to punish the woman we felt had harmed us. We felt aggrieved that we did not have adequate access to the "right" women or to mechanisms for controlling the ones we did have access to, and so we would lash out. Unable to control them, we would explode. In nearly every case of abuse, the men felt like the women were harming us (whether this was true or not, we would come to learn, is beside the point—most often, it wasn't true, anyway). We felt deeply entitled, arrogant, and our actions betrayed our stated beliefs about women; most of us professed to consider women as our equals, but we did not act like it. We followed a codependent pattern of perceiving them threats to our well-being but also status-symbols working as a replacement for our own (in)ability to love ourselves. Regardless of what we had done to others, we almost always *felt like* the real victims.

Complicating, but explaining much of the circumstances, it turned out that all of us in the group really were victims, in a very visceral, literal sense. For some of us, this included the actions of our intimate partners. But for most of us, our actual victimhood came from past physical abuse, emotional abuse, and sexual abuse experienced as children. At every meeting, I was confronted with the self-help adage: Hurting people hurt people. The men in this group tended to come from alcoholic and drug-addicted homes, poverty-stricken, and generationally dysfunctional family situations. In a word, my own story. All of us were victims before we abused others. To varying degrees, our parents had neglected us and abandoned us. Very *literally*, most of us had not been taught to "act right" by our parents. Whether we are talking about my own deadbeat-turned-dead alcoholic father or if we are considering a kid that grows up watching a parent participate in gang activity, or whether a child is forced to endure reckless behavior from a parent who parties all the time and has various sexual partners in and out of the home, across race and class, we had all been victims who became perpetrators. Afraid to admit or unable to process the real victimization we experienced as children, we grew up to repress, project, and otherwise defend against the harm that had been done to us. In our denial, we came to blame others for our own difficulties loving ourselves.

***

Rehabilitation of and response to the abuses we had perpetrated requires a delicate balance of behavioral and psychical intervention. This roughly equates to addressing the harm we have caused others, and the harm once done to us. It requires immediate attention to the twin priorities of 1) stopping our abusive behavior and 2) addressing the psychological issues preventing more healthy emotional regulation. Much of this book has already sought to address the second of these priorities, in a manner applicable to a variety of interpersonal and social circumstances. The rest of this chapter focuses attention on behavioral intervention.

Stopping abusive behavior begins with recognizing that abuse follows a predictable circular pattern. Lenore E. Walker developed a social cycle theory in the late 1970s to describe the patterns associated with domestic abuse. In any given cycle of abuse, whether interpersonal or between entire groups of people, there is a build-up of emotional energy that ultimately explodes through the surface. This could be expressed as punishing or controlling demands or as raising our voice, or some other sort of punitive reaction. Knowing this pattern allows people to know what is in store in the future and it offers possibilities to disrupt the pattern.

Suppose a conversation escalates to the point of yelling. Yelling is its own abuse. But the yelling gives way to name-calling and belittling. This yelling, name-calling, and belittling can be understood as an explosion of abuses (three distinct abuses in this example). When the explosion ends, the couple or community then experiences a period of distance. The spatial and temporal quantity of distance is usually proportionate to the severity of the explosion. In a relatively minor shouting match, the distance could be as simple and short-lived as going downstairs for half an hour. In severe cases of domestic violence, the distance could include restraining orders, outright arrests, and prison time. Regardless of how long the period lasts, it usually gives way to what is called a "honeymoon" or make-up phase. This make-up phase is characterized by things feeling good and decent, where each party is prioritizing one another's needs and expectations. This honeymoon phase is often marked by promises and an overly emotional attachment to one another. Essentially, across the entire cycle of abuse, the couple or the community is on an emotional rollercoaster. The honeymoon phase is the fun part of the ride.

Over time, the honeymoon phase feels less and less "honeymoon-ish" due to both external and internal pressures felt by each member of the relationship or community. Another explosion is all but guaranteed, as these pressures build. Internal pressures may build during an acute argument, but usually the tension has been building for a series of days, weeks, months, and even years. Throughout any given week, internal and external pressures add to our overall tension, and we start to feel like an ever-expanding balloon of chaos. Various external pressures faced by individuals in the relationship could include, but are in no way limited to, dealing with rude people, facing money problems, job stressors, traffic, or in some cases, social issues related to other past abuses (such as an angry girlfriend while married, etc.). Race and gender-based murders and assaults can result from "external" pressures felt by perpetrators having nothing to do with who becomes the actual victims of explosions. This last point speaks to the "toxic" nature of abuse. Its consequences often compound on other, earlier consequences. Internal pressures are mostly related to emotional regulation and emotional processing. It is here where so often, underlying codependency negatively impacts white men's abilities to emotionally regulate ourselves in the face of these internal pressures. These pressures can include feeling sad, resentful, lonely, jealous, tired, hungry, angry, prideful, and even hateful (or hated). As men, we are conditioned to ignore or deny many of these feelings, making it more difficult to release these internal pressures in a healthy fashion (through dialogue, exercise, etc.).

As men, we have been taught that it is wrong to feel certain feelings. In this regard, our male conditioning is equivalent to being taught that it is wrong to breathe. So often, our cycles of abuse continue because we have been taught to ignore many of our feelings. We have also been taught that the only healthy emotions men are to display are either sexual desire or anger. Many of us end up walking through the world only able to express ourselves emotionally through sex or violence. Many of us neither attempt emotional regulation nor do we have practice or know how to do this processing work unless it is unhealthily expressed through abusive violence and sexual objectification and exploitation of women and non-binary conforming people. The overall inability to process emotions turns many of us into ticking time bombs. Eventually, every bomb detonates if it is not diffused.

After the explosion, the couple or community will usually create distance—physical, geographic, emotional—yet again. After the distance, comes the make-up. The couple or community is back in the honeymoon phase. Usually this includes apologies and promises.

The cycle repeats itself over and over again. However, each iteration of the cycle intensifies the toxic effects of abuse. As our behavior improves during each honeymoon phase, our partners begin to expect the renewed or health(ier) behavior. Raised expectations inevitably lead to emotional letdowns and the emotional distance created with each cycle grows more and more severe. To the extent couples or communities are participating in cycles of abuse, the eventual breakdown of the relationship or the community is all but ensured.

So how do we stop the cycle of abuse when it is happening, and how do we work to end the cycle completely?

Stress management is one key to stopping the cycle. Stress is not always uniform for all people or groups. Financial stress is different than family stress, etc. And, adequate stress management also involves emotional awareness, the need to stay "checked in" with ourselves about how we are feeling, and what stressors and other circumstances are producing stress in our lives.

Cultivating a "bottom line" for oneself is another important strategy: For instance, telling yourself or partner "No matter what, I will not do ... " This bottom line will be different for each person and each relationship. For some of us, this might mean committing to do no physical violence. For others of us, this might mean committing to no name calling or cursing. For others still, this might be as seemingly mundane as committing to engaging in no mean-spirited sarcasm or diminishing of the other person's perspective (i.e., gaslighting). Yet, for others still, this might mean committing to not threatening to leave during an argument. Each person's, each couple's, and each community's bottom lines will be different. What is important is to spend time planning out and reviewing these bottom lines *before* the pressure builds again into an eruption of violence. Sometimes, the distance created during the cycle of abuse is difficult to accept. Often, agreeing to and sticking to bottom lines can exacerbate the distance. This distance might feel like the relationship is in danger of ending. However, taking time for oneself during the distance phase is perfectly appropriate. It is often prudent for each party to tell the other what each's distance will "look like" while it is happening. That way, they understand what is happening, and are less likely to feel abandonment.

Though a bit counterintuitive, another strategy for responding to the cycle of abuse includes no longer making promises—whether they would be "empty" or otherwise—during honeymoon phases. Making promises may seem like a way to profess love or devotion or responsibility toward another person, but such promises end up adding to the pressure experienced by the one making the promise. Getting out of the habit of making empty promises frees people up to simply apologize—articulating what we are precisely sorry for—and rather than promise not to do it again, simply take a few moments to breathe deeply and feel the feelings happening in that moment. Empty promises often come as an effort to respond to the lingering pain of the last abuse or explosion. In fact, many promises actually respond to internal emotional pressures by externalizing them, ultimately increasing the pressures by a factor of two (or more), rather than helping to process the initial feelings. Those initial feelings will be there regardless. It is better to simply feel them honesty and in intersubjective communication with our partners in those moments.

Especially important for breaking cycles of abuse is to focus on the form and not the content of our engagement with partners and community members. Most emotional explosions are rooted in real-life stressors like financial and other difficulties. In moments of heightened stress, it feels like the solution to escalating tension between two people or groups would involve addressing the root stressor. "If financial difficulties are serving as key external pressures, then only solving the financial difficulties would end the stress and therefore, the tension between the two parties." This is how it *feels*. If two parents are fighting over their teenage daughter wanting to go on her first date, it often feels like the tension would be mitigated by addressing the circumstance of the daughter's potential date. Yet, during my time in these sessions, my therapists emphasized that cycles of abuse stop when we focus our attention on how we are engaging with our partners, wives, and other family and friends. The cycle only repeats itself when we focus on controlling others, which is most likely to occur when we prioritize the content of the dispute. Internal and external pressures will be with us always, but when we focus our attention on our acute behaviors during stressful situations, we can begin to act and potentially think differently, and our relationships with others will improve.

Perhaps, the best expression of the proper "form" of relating in any relationship is through the sharing of feelings with our partners. How stressed are we? How much pressure are we feeling? Are we willing to share these feelings with our partners, friends, neighbors, and civic leaders? The more often we share our feelings—whether in calm times or stressful ones—the more likely it is that the cycle of abuse is going to halt. Even if our partners or neighbors are still mistrustful and angry at us, stopping the cycle of abuse involves our willingness to continue taking their hits and grounding ourselves in emotional processing that includes them. We have been engaging them in a "battle" for a long time. It will take time for them to trust that we have really put down our weapons. Their trust in us comes through our honesty with them. Simply put, it boils down to telling our partners how we feel.

An extended illustration may be helpful. Suppose an intimate partner begins communicating with an old boyfriend. This is almost sure to bring up feelings of insecurity and jealousy. It isn't wrong to feel insecure or jealous. We may be embarrassed that we feel that way. But it isn't wrong to feel those feelings. Importantly, however, jealousy is one of those feelings that *feel like* it is the other person's fault. "Well, I'm jealous because you talked to your old boyfriend, and I accidentally saw the email message where you told him that you used to love him and still care about him." This sort of situation will naturally hurt, no matter who we are. But through a focus on the form of our engagement, we can compartmentalize how we feel from whether it was appropriate for our intimate partner to speak with the former boyfriend. Some social interactions— even healthy ones—will inevitably hurt us. Certain reasonable interactions or involvements between people we love and other people will make us feel bad from time to time. This will be all the truer for anyone who struggles with codependency. Checking in with our partners during these feelings is one healthy way to process them. If I am jealous when my wife talks to a former boyfriend, I can tell her that I am jealous about the situation. Sharing the feelings, however, is not meant to change my wife's behavior or interaction with the former boyfriend. This is a point lots of men get wrong. Taking the opportunity to share the feelings should not be instrumentalized in effort to stop the behavior that caused the emotional discomfort. Doing so would amount to emotional manipulation, which erodes the possibilities of intersubjective communication because it positions our feelings ahead of her or their feelings and needs. Essentially, this is how babies act. Babies can get away with it because, well, they're babies. Grown men should not act like babies. When a baby shares its feelings, we as parents or adults adjust our behavior to address the baby's needs. Over time, healthy childhood development involves teaching babies, then toddlers, then children, then teenagers to address more and more of their own needs, and to emotionally regulate themselves in balance with their awareness of the same processes happening within all of us. As adult men in adult relationships, when we share our feelings with our partners, we do so because sharing feelings is one of the best ways to process those feelings. We feel them until they are gone. And often, talking about *how we feel* helps them to go away faster. Then, we repeat the process when they happen again. At no point should we respond to our negative feelings by trying to shape the behavior of our partners. Suppose I am jealous at my wife's email to her former boyfriend. I mention it to her when it is appropriate to do so, emphasizing that *"I feel jealous when or because ... "* This does not deny the connection between my feelings and her behavior, but it helps promote taking fuller responsibility for my feelings. "I feel jealous when you communicate with your old boyfriend" can potentially turn into "I feel jealous when you communicate with your old boyfriend *because* it triggers something in me connected to my childhood." Maybe, my jealousy is simply an underlying fear that she will abandon me. At the root of the feeling, however, is not actually her behavior but my needs, desires, and expectations programmed during childhood. Sharing my initial feeling of jealously, in this way, isn't received as an accusation by my wife that she's done something "wrong," and she is less likely to respond defensively. Rather, she ends up better equipped to fulfill my needs, because processing the initial pain allowed me to reach a deeper level of myself, and to share it with her. Ironically, jealousy about her interactions with the old boyfriend would then allow for an opportunity for greater intimacy between the two of us. Being honest about how I was not feeling special—and doing so in a way that did not make her behavior the problem—adds strength to the foundation of the relationship. This whole intimate experience would not have been possible, however, if instead of sharing how I felt, I told her she should not communicate with him. If I responded to my initial feeling of jealousy by trying to control her, it would only hurt her and it would leave both of us then in the position to not be able to help the other partner process their respective emotions.

A caveat to this point of open emotional communication is boundary maintenance. Boundaries are one useful way of working to prevent abuses down the road. They offer guideposts for the people in the relationship, constituting rules of engagement. They mark out the figurative playing field of any relationship. When the boundaries are respected, then a couple or a group can be said to be "in a relationship." When the boundaries are not respected, and players move on and off the field of play, then the relationship is not really a relationship at all. At best, it is a dysfunctional, unhealthy, and abusive relationship. Boundary maintenance is difficult and demanding, in part, because deciding to impose and respect boundaries opens us to the possibility of facing consequences when those boundaries are breached. Consequences and boundaries go together. Consequences usually exist on the front and back of boundaries. That is, every stated boundary is an opportunity and an invitation to communicate the nature of the relationship. Often, the establishing of a boundary by one individual will be met by the other with a statement of their own boundary or a suggestion for a compromise on the initial proposed boundary. The consequences of establishing boundaries are that they fundamentally impact the nature of the relationships they outline. This is one reason why so many codependent people are so bad at stating our boundaries. In our overwhelming fear of abandonment, most of us would rather take on the boundaries and goals of other people, in an ill-fated effort to never have them leave us. To be sure, establishing boundaries can lead to people leaving us. But more often and more importantly, boundaries provide the groundwork for healthy communication and relationships, ensuring that relationships do not so easily succumb to the cycle of abuse.

***

Taking responsibility for the "form" of our behavior rather than the supposed content of a life circumstance is like the shift that took place in western philosophy from essentialism and idealism to phenomenology and existentialism. At the turn of the twentieth century, a philosopher named Edmund Husserl decided to pivot away from a centuries-old debate within western philosophy concerning the foundation of truth. Across much of the history of western philosophy, philosophers were divided about how to provide a foundation for trusting the information we think we have. On one side of the debate were the idealists, who consider truth to be available and real, existing in some hypothesized place where the perfect version of any object or situation exists—called the Logos. These folks hold that we all—and all objects—have an essential quality. Truth exists in the form of that essence. Empiricists, on the other hand, hold that truth is found through experience, alone. Husserl came along and said both of these groups of folks were thinking about the whole issue the wrong way. The idealists were in error because there wasn't enough evidence to support their claims that all people and objects had essential qualities. The empiricists were in error because despite all their talk of focusing on experiences, they still treated most objects and people in the world as if they had essential qualities. Husserl came along and offered a new option in the form of, well, *form*. For so long, this philosophical debate had focused on the content of truth—what is it and how do we find it. Husserl said this focus on content was a problem. Instead, he suggested we start to look at the form that any social interaction or experience takes. No longer would we assume to know the essential qualities of one another or of external objects out in the world. We would start by trying to account for how those people and objects interacted with us and each other in the world. No good intentions. No assumptions about motives. We would focus on the form of our experiences with everything around us. This basic shift we call the advent of phenomenology, the study of phenomena (on their own terms as they are experienced).

A comparable shift in focus away from the content of social circumstances and toward the form of our engagement with others might offer strategies for white men eager to take responsibility for our broader social situation. Starting in our own homes, such a shift could also be practiced and applied to different levels of scale in the social world. Rather than assume our best intentions or our inner essence as a good person, we would focus on our acute behaviors toward other people. Are we acting entitled? Are we acting like a know-it-all? Are we acting closed-off to new ideas? Are we raising our voice? Are we acting stubbornly? Are we practicing empathy? Are we practicing assertive communication skills? As intimate partners, are we giving too much attention to how we really love and care for our wives and family members? What's great about making this phenomenological move is that nobody is telling you or me or us that we are bad people. Whether we are good or bad people is beside the point of whether we abuse those around us. We tend to think of abusers as "bad people." But in fact, there is not a specific type of person who is an abuser and who we can label as "bad." Most men deeply love their families and friends, but many struggle with consistently showing love to them because of our emotional dysregulation. By focusing on the form of our behavior, we take our egos out of the way of our response. Rather than ask "Am I an abuser, a racist, or a devil?" we shift toward asking "Do we want to commit an abuse or not?" We cannot control what others think about us, but we can begin to control ourselves. Focusing on the form of our communication and relating with other people becomes a moment of empowerment, genuine empowerment. We move from feeling helpless to focusing on specific things we *can* control like our behavior. We can't control whether our boss decides to fire us on a random Thursday morning. We can't control whether our lover cheats on us with that same boss, either. But we can control how we act with and toward our bosses and our lovers. In like manner, we cannot dictate what black or brown people feel about each other or about us as white men. We can fashion ourselves as the most tried-and-true personal responsibility libertarian and that will not mean we are safe from the harsh criticism or negative feelings of black and brown folks. We can spend our whole lives trying to be fantastic antiracist allies and doing grassroots organizing for the most progressive political candidates, but this work does not mean we are safe from the harsh criticism or negative feelings of black and brown folks. To the extent we are making these sorts of big picture identity decisions based on our hypothetical reception by other people, we are wasting our energy.

Making a phenomenological shift in our thinking and behavior at this level of social issues forces a radical truth-telling about how we move through the world as white men. In so many ways, we move with various levels of privilege that we don't want to admit. And lots of folks severely criticize us when we deny these privileges. Why do we deny them? Usually, this denial is because our lives are difficult and complicated, too, and so the idea of privilege sounds like other folks are telling us that our lives are somehow easy. Any ordinary white man knows this isn't true—our lives aren't easy. But a phenomenological shift will help us to see that privilege isn't about the denial of an easy life. Privilege is the capacity to deny life's hardships and live to tell the tale. Privilege is acting like we have our shit together even when we don't—especially when we don't. When we deny our privilege as white men, we are doing the same complicated philosophical jumping jacks that marked classical western philosophy. In those moments, we are responding to our emotional pressure by addressing the content of that pressure. Such effort is always self-defeating, because our better selves are made in those moments when we focus on the form of our intersubjective exchange with others. The content of our stories does matter! Husserl didn't say we needed to stop reading all the great philosophers of the western canon. He simply suggested we pivot. Focusing on the form of our behavior rather than the content of our intentions helps us to see that denying privilege is rooted in the same sense of white masculine entitlement that tells us we are supposed to have all the answers and solve all the world's problems. It is organized by the similar psychological mechanisms that make us feel the need to control others. We do love our wives and partners. We do care about them. But an underlying lack of love and care for ourselves means that we often hide our feelings, and we downplay our need for help. And our family, whether thought about in terms of daughters and sons and wives or our broader black and brown family in society, end up paying the price of our unrelenting expectation that we have all our shit worked out. Privilege is not having an easy life. Privilege is being in a situation where we act as if life is easier than it really is. Saying "I'm not going to listen to you" is an abuse at home. It constitutes neglect and abandonment, both abuses often associated with emotionally shutting down. But when we say it to whole groups, we chock it up to politics. Saying "Just let them talk" and then zoning out when they speak—whether that's my ex-wife or the President of the NAACP, we are committing neglect and minimization alongside whatever other acute abuses. When a person or group or a social situation forces us into a confrontation with that most fundamental truth—that we are just as in need of them as they may be of us—so often, we white men explode. In these and other ways, the denial of privilege and other sorts of abuses run hand in hand. We, like Achilles, seek to deny our most basic, most intimate connection to one another.

Ultimately, honest communication is the most important means of curbing the cycle of abuse. As white men, we must learn to account for ourselves more accurately in the world, to take responsibility for the space we take up in the universe. How we do this begins with emotional awareness. So much of what we do when we fight is acting out how we feel because we can't or aren't willing to discuss how we feel. We might not actually know, rationally, how we feel. And so, we explode, and we fight. Through these abusive behaviors we're able to hurtfully and counterproductively address our unmet need to process emotions. Having explored here certain behavioral interventions that promote an end to cycles of violence, the next chapter focuses specifically on the work of cultivating emotional intelligence.

12 EMOTIONAL INTELLIGENCE

In 2018's *White Fragility: Why It's So Hard for White People to Talk about Racism*, author Robin DiAngelo lists certain common "emotional reactions that white people have" when confronted with challenges to our (racial) assumptions and behaviors.[1] The feelings include being "singled out, attacked, silenced, shamed, guilty, accused, insulted, judged, angry, scared, and outraged."[2] She also describes several behaviors white people often exhibit alongside of these feelings. These behaviors include "crying, physically leaving, emotionally withdrawing, arguing, denying, focusing on intentions, seeking absolution, and avoiding."[3] Responding to these tendencies, DiAngelo charges that

> White people do need to feel grief about the brutality of white supremacy and our role in it. In fact, our numbness to the racial injustice that occurs daily is key to holding it in place. But our grief must lead to sustained and transformative action. Because our emotions are indicators of our internal frameworks, they can serve as entry points into the deeper self-awareness that leads to this action. Examining what is at the root of our emotions (shame for not knowing, guilt for hurting someone, hurt feelings because we think we must have been misunderstood) will enable us to address these frameworks. We also need to examine our responses toward other people's emotions and how they may reinscribe race and gender hierarchies.[4]

DiAngelo is not wrong in her analysis, nor in her admonition that we as white people do the work of "examining what is at the root of our emotions." However, she may be confusing her audiences. These white responses may be rightly labeled "fragile," but DiAngelo characterizes both these feelings and the behaviors as problems, when feelings as such, are never problems. They offer information that we use in either healthy or unhealthy ways. Perhaps, DiAngelo may be ignoring the potential difficulties white people—especially white men—genuinely have in emotional regulation. She frames these emotional responses as microaggressive colonizing experiences for people of color, where white women (and men) dominate race-based discourses through emotional manipulation. This *may be* how some black and brown folks experience these moments of interracial contact. However, this awareness does not lend itself to addressing *why* white people, to use DiAngelo's words, are so "fragile." Ostensibly, DiAngelo treats black and brown concerns as the norms for her argument. In this way, DiAngelo's text thoughtfully validates those black and brown perspectives. But what of the white audience most in need of correcting our behavioral responses to our feelings? Perhaps, these white emotions and behaviors are not rooted in racism and sexism but *result in* racism and sexism. Ironically, perhaps, part of addressing white racism and sexism requires addressing the emotions of these white folks, and locating their points of origin. Instead, DiAngelo minimizes and dismisses these feelings through the marketable concept of "fragility."

These white responses *are* emotional manipulation. The emotions and behaviors described here by DiAngelo are rooted in codependence. As codependent, we have been conditioned to control others through emotional manipulation, coercion, or violence. Many of us preoccupy ourselves with other people's problems as a way of avoiding our own difficulties with emotional regulation. Then, when confronted with the consequences of our codependency, we turn to various denial mechanisms and emotional explosions. As men, many of us have been conditioned to objectify women as a means of denying our own feelings. Often, when we show emotions as men, our manhood is questioned, and we are misidentified as women or as having characteristics generally associated with women. This teaches us that men are not supposed to know or to express our emotions and it teaches that women are inferior to men. In these ways, men are taught to be emotionally dysregulated. Our male conditioning is such that we self-police when we start to show too many emotions. On top of this general policing, we are also taught to objectify women as a kind of release valve for our emotional dysregulation. For instance, suppose a man asks a woman out, and she rejects the invitation. This will lead to feelings of abandonment and isolation and shame and any number of negative feelings in the man that men are not supposed to express. The isolation is intensified because supposing we have a friend group or peer group who would prevent us from feeling isolated, we still aren't allowed to share our real feelings with that group. Instead, we transmute our negative feelings into objectifications of women—whether it's the initial woman who rejected us or not does not matter much to our egos. Rather than tell our friends how we feel lonely and abandoned because of the situation, we instead talk about her body or call her a bitch. This objectification works to keep us from feeling isolated and alone. It works so effectively that it often forges a sense of shared identity among men. Objectification of women is historically a major component of male bonding, that is, "boys will be boys," "locker room talk," etc. The whole process of male emotional dysregulation creates a funnel, leading to two basic and prominent emotions that we are allowed to feel as men: anger and sexual desire. That's it. We feel the same range of feelings as everyone else, but we must hide all but these two. Nearly all men have experiences where other men have told us that if we're not "getting pussy," then we're not being or acting like a "real man." Nearly all of us have experiences where we are expected to retaliate or be aggressive in any number of situations where we or others perceive ourselves to have been harmed. When all we're allowed to be is either angry or horny, it prevents us from creating and maintaining healthy relationships with the rest of the world around us.

We are not "fragile" because we are "white" and "racist" or "male" and "sexist" but because as *white* and as *men*, many of us do not know how to regulate our emotions. Across many generations, this has led to a crisis of codependency impacting many white men, wherein we literally do not act in healthy ways toward self or others because we do not know how to act. Calling us "fragile" does not teach anyone how to respond to white men's emotional dysregulation. The concept of fragility, for many people, has enabled a call to action, but too few resources exist that address the root psychosocial cause of what DiAngelo calls "fragility." We need more—but not less—than critiques of our character. Such critique, when leveled against communities with codependent self-esteem issues, only produces more recalcitrance among some and escapism among others within that community. We either deny the charge or point the finger at other white men.

Thinking of white men as Adult Children may offer more help than these necessary, but limited critiques. The literature of Adult Children of Alcoholics describes recovery (from codependency) in terms of "becoming actors, not reactors" to the world. As Adult Children, white men have lived life "suspended between need and fear—unable to choose between fight or flight—[we] agonize in the middle and resolve the tension by explosive bursts of rebellion, or by silently enduring despair."[5] The grief and mourning described by DiAngelo as necessary for white people to experience occur alongside the "return of feelings" as part of ACA recovery. Having moved out of isolation, "sharing the burden of grief others feel gives us the courage and strength to face our own bereavement. The pain of mourning and grief is balanced by being able, once again, to fully love and care for someone and to freely experience joy in life."[6] What DiAngelo describes as a kind of colonizing moment is also a choice-point for white people, generally, and white men, especially. If our initial feelings are ignored or invalidated, white men are more likely to choose isolation. If the feelings are validated, white men will feel more inclined to continue in exploring our feelings with others. Doing such intersubjective communication work with others amounts to a shift in who we are, at the most fundamental level. At the point of choosing to share our feelings in group settings, we become more than white men (for many of us, this is a new experience). Suggesting that white people who share their feelings during race discussions are guilty of emotional manipulation undermines the growth point for white folks, especially men, who have trouble expressing our feelings in the first place. These moments of interracial dialogue are not necessarily colonizing or occluding efforts, but they speak to many of the ways white men are emotionally dysregulated. It is not the responsibility of black and brown folks to do this emotional labor for white people, but it will be necessary for white folks to process our emotions. Rather than shut down such processing with the charge of "fragility," ACA programming offers potential opportunities for white women and men to share our feelings with others, transforming ourselves in the process. Practically, this transformation occurs when we begin to speak the truth of our emotional state, generally, not merely when discussing social issues. Emotions, in this way, are the ciphers unlocking our honest relationship with the rest of the world. They provide sensory feedback for us and help to orient us in the river of life.

***

Emotional intelligence begins with understanding all feelings are important. Feelings tell us about our needs. They are not "problems" to be solved, avoided, or used as ammunition against our characters, but they steer us in the direction of taking care of ourselves. Making the shift described here really begins and ends with interpersonal emotional regulation. Two important components of emotional regulation are emotional awareness and emotional expression. Emotional awareness involves knowledge of the emotions we experience, and emotional expression involves how we respond to and make use of those emotions. Together, they help us with emotional regulation, meaning here the use of emotions for the promotion of psychological and social health. As white men, are we aware of the sensory input we are receiving *as our feelings*? Do we know how we feel? "Checking In" with our emotions is necessary not only in moments of crisis or confrontation, but in as many ordinary moments as possible, as well. Whether we are responding to white masculinity, alcoholism, codependency, or monotheism, the goal of recovery would be to remain constantly checked in with how we are feeling, taking an inventory of our feelings, and going easy on ourselves in moments when we find ourselves no longer checked in with our present moment. Am I anxious right now? Do I hold resentment about something that happened yesterday? Am I afraid of my daughter beginning to date? Have I eaten recently? Have I consumed drugs or alcohol recently? These and countless other questions are necessary to ask and answer as we float through the river of life.

Mindfulness techniques offer a shorthand strategy for beginning the process of emotional regulation. Slowing down, focusing on breathing, and paying specific attention to what is happening in the present moment aids in "Checking In" with ourselves. Meditation is an increasingly popular means of promoting mindfulness in our lives. Celebrated scholar of religion Alan Watts once suggested that it was "absolutely urgent that we do not allow our preoccupation with symbols to distract our awareness from the real world."[7] Whether we think of these symbols as our social, political, or religious identities, they distract us from awareness of ourselves. We are never *not* them, but we are also always potentially more than them. So many of us in the west think and behave based on symbolic meanings rather than actual meanings such as feelings and the like. "Meditation," for Watts, involves centering ourselves "in the eternal now, and can be maintained not only sitting in the lotus-posture but also in going about one's ordinary affairs."[8] The goal of meditation is varied, but in general, involves the promotion of a sense of unity of self with the universe, and the cessation of both thoughts and feelings. But before this point—if such a goal is possible at all—is the promotion of ideas and feelings as part of ourselves and our experience in the universe. Upon beginning a meditation practice, it is often extremely difficult to quiet the mind and body. Instead of growing frustrated, one common suggestion from mindfulness leaders is for the person meditating to recognize the thought or the feeling, and let it pass, before returning to "center." Another strategy is to take a specific body inventory or body "scan" starting at the top of the head and working down the body slowly, asking consciously about any feelings or sensations occurring at different places on the body. This promotes awareness of what is happening within ourselves. Moving beyond meditation, another mindfulness strategy promoted in ACA involves staying consciously "Checked In" with our Inner Child, asking them at least once a day how they are feeling. The strategy of talking to oneself as if distinct from oneself feels a bit hokey at first, but I have been amazed at how productive it is in helping me determine how I am feeling in the moment. I am constantly amazed at just how *little* I know about how I am feeling. Mindful exercises of the sort described here aid in emotional regulation. Mindfulness becomes an important component of healthy selfhood, in that it provides more opportunities to check in with ourselves about how we are feeling, and it gives us time and space to both process those feelings and cultivate strategies for responding to those feeling.

Another important way to increase our emotional awareness is adding to our lexicon of emotions. We must learn how to name our emotions. It can become something of a parlor game to men who are new to emotional awareness. Quite literally, many of us may not have names for some of the emotions we begin to recognize. In most cases, we have heard of the emotions, and we may have felt them many times, but we have been so disconnected from our own emotions, we don't have a frame of reference for them. ACA literature finds that "Many adult children are unsure of their feelings or cannot distinguish feelings" and that "Most adult children are terrified of feelings and believe they cannot withstand them."[9] The same holds true of many abusive men, generally, and white men, specifically. Gary Cooper, the strong silent type, serves as the model for many of us—quiet, reserved, industrious, emotionally unflappable. Generation after generation of this model of white masculinity has made it extremely difficult for contemporary white men to know how we feel.

For instance, many white men have a very shallow sense of what shame feels like. Shame is the feeling that we are unworthy to be around the people near us or to be in the situation we are in. That feeling of being unworthy then translates into behaviors that are overly concerned about the emotional well-being of those around us. We minimize our own emotional awareness—because it hurts—and we focus our attention on others. It also often produces reckless behavior that risks actually alienating us from a community, thereby validating the feeling of shame. This shame dynamic is at work in many white men, leading to an ironic condition of public shamelessness. This is why so many white men in the public eye seem incorrigible and impervious to criticism from others and from so many all-too-public moral failures. White politicians have made a reputation for themselves in part based on their apparent shamelessness. Despite everything morally questionable that some of them may do, no amount of criticism or public scorn seems to draw out remorse or critical reflection from them. These public figures validate the denial of shame rampant in so many of us as white men—hence, their popularity.

Early in my career, I wrote an essay called "On the Journey to White Shame" that asked the question: What will it take for white men to feel shame at our past behavior?[10] The piece was well-received by many colleagues and read in classrooms for a time. But the question remained unanswered for me for a long time, both in terms of my research on the subject as well as my personal relationship to the feeling of shame. I had difficulty defining shame, and even deep into my growth in emotional regulation, I struggled—and still do—to recognize moments when I feel shame. I've started to recognize it physically. In moments when I am feeling shame, I often store it in my eyes. It becomes very difficult to look people in the face during these moments. Imposter syndrome can be an expression of shame. It is for me. Sometimes, the shame comes from something that I may have done that my Superego thinks was morally problematic. But more often, it happens in moments when I am faced with intersubjective communication with people who make me nervous. In moments when I feel that I am competing with others, other men especially, it triggers feelings of being an imposter. Shame was taught to me at an early age. My father's alcoholism had him emotionally unavailable to me while my mother's preoccupation with his alcoholism had her emotionally unavailable to me. It wasn't that either of them did not love me. They did. And they would both constantly say so. But neither would avail themselves to my needs for emotional processing and therefore, my brain came to be wired to live in a near-constant state of shame. I was wired to feel like I did not belong and that my emotions did not matter.

Shame is also at work in larger social dynamics, such as anti-black racism and white masculine supremacy, historically. In her 1949 book *Killers of the Dream*, a memoir-styled account of the matrix of racism, sexism, and monotheism that killed possibilities for life flourishing in the American South during segregation, author Lillian Smith helps to expose how shame was taught to white children (to say nothing here of how it also plays out for black and brown children).[11] In the American South, the social expectation for white families was quite literally that the white parents would be emotionally unavailable to the white children until puberty. White fathers were expected to be physically and emotionally distant from their children, whether due to social or professional obligation. Equally, white women were expected to maintain an intense social agenda to the point that they were emotionally unavailable to their children. Established, "respectable" families would therefore have domestic help in the form of black maids and childcare workers. This dynamic existed during enslavement, continued through Segregation, and dies hard even today. "Mammy"—the stereotype of the black woman childcare worker—was the most significant adult figure in white children's lives up until puberty. Mammy would be responsible for teaching emotional regulation, as well as for explaining and mitigating the effects of the trauma white children felt from being abandoned by their parents. Adding to the insidiousness of the system of white supremacy, the black woman would essentially leave her own children and families, reinforcing the white cycle of abandonment on the black side of town. According to Smith, this social dynamic seriously impacted the ability of white kids to grow up into healthy, compassionate adults. Not only were they abandoned by their emotionally unavailable white parents, many of those same white parents as well as the larger white culture would use racism to denigrate the most important emotional connections that the white kids had ever known during their childhoods—mammy. The kids are not only abandoned but taught that the people who they value most at an emotional level are the least valuable people in the society.

Shame is such a difficult emotion because it is the emotion that makes us feel like we don't know how or deserve to act as agents in the world. Ironically, that's exactly what it causes us to do. Unable to name our shame feelings or our history of abandonment, we abandon ourselves. Our expressions of our *selves* end up merely reproducing what we find in society—giving it no unique quality of our own. We end up the white racist, emotionally unavailable man. Or we end up the white savior, still emotionally unavailable or narcissistically over-available man. We don't get to be engaged in a mutual process of participating with others to produce culture and society.

Shame is one example of many emotions that white men are poor at recognizing within ourselves. As we come into greater and ongoing clarity about how we are feeling in any given moment, we are empowered to make decisions about where we want to go. When we are unaware of how we are feeling, it causes us to simply mimic the responses we have seen from others. In moments of tension, then, we say and do things that reinforce our codependency. In terms of whiteness, we either drink up white supremacy becoming an addict to it, or we appropriate black experiences and priorities as our own, and in doing so, *still* fail to take care of our psychological health. We *react* in those moments, rather than *act* in terms that match how we feel or what we need. Opening ourselves up to the range of feelings that course through our bodies and spirits in any given moment helps begin the process of equitable, healthy intersubjective communication with others.

The effects and consequences of racism and patriarchy look an awful lot like the effects and consequences of growing up in an alcoholic or otherwise dysfunctional family. For white families, then and often now as well, distinguishing between the dysfunction arising from racism and sexism and the dysfunction arising from alcoholism or other addiction is impossible. Racism *is* an expression of emotional dysfunction, and it may be a symptom of it as well. Emotional dysfunction structures and is structured by—to borrow from the sociologist Pierre Bourdieu—racism, sexism, and many of these structural issues. Determining which of these features of white life is guilty of the harm is not nearly as important as is beginning the vital process of "Checking In" with ourselves emotionally. By choosing to focus on how we are feeling, and allowing those feelings to matter, many other aspects of our identity's formation fall into place, necessarily. White fragility, in this sense, isn't a problem so much as an opportunity. Surface-level emotional responses to charges of racism or sexism offer invitations for self-exploration of the many ways white people have used racism and sexism to hide deeper feelings of abandonment and neglect. Telling these family stories told by Smith and others is not about blaming our parents nor does it absolve us of responsibility for our stake in racism and sexism. Telling these stories involves taking responsibility for all the different elements of the vast river of culture that shapes who we are. I can never *not* be a white man, but in naming who I am and who I have been raised to be, I can begin to reimagine what a white man's self looks and sounds like. Growing in awareness of who we are and how we feel, we slowly find ourselves making decisions rather than reacting to circumstances. We learn to experience ourselves as part of society and culture, rather than feeling like it overwhelms us.

***

People rarely experience one emotion at a time. Usually, in any given moment of life, a person is feeling several emotions at once. When a person struggles with emotional regulation, this leads to constant confusion. And in fact, many men with emotional regulation problems mistake confusion for an emotion. Yet, confusion is not an emotion; confusion is a state of not knowing what emotions are being felt in any given moment. Working on our emotional regulation is a matter of growing more familiar with the myriad of emotions that we might feel, and in cultivating strategies to know when we are feeling which of these emotions. In an effort to cultivate greater emotional regulation, the ACA Workbook offers what it calls the "feelings sentence" as well as a word bank of emotions, potentially felt by Adult Children. Emotions listed in the word bank include: loved, joyful, ashamed, humorous, irritated, angry, embarrassed, trusted, betrayed, pleased, satisfied, ambivalent, hopeful, inspired, loving, frustrated, disappointed, grief, accepted, excited, grateful, confident, humiliated, guilty, serene, rested, shame, abandoned, pleasure, safe, tenacious, thoughtful, playful, fascinated, and enthralled.[12] The feelings sentence is as follows:

> I feel _____ when _____ because _____.[13]

This basic formula has become part of my personal emancipation from emotional dysregulation. While using the feelings sentence may initially feel sophomoric, I am constantly struck by both how many emotions I still struggle to be aware of within myself, and what the root causes of many of those emotions are. Taking greater control of my emotional regulation amounts to taking responsibility for myself. The process is ongoing and has not been easy. It is hard work, and risky, too. But according to ACA, the risk is "worth taking because the rewards are great. When we let others know about our feelings, we connect with people on a spiritual and equal level instead of a dependent and manipulative level."[14] We are emotional beings, and as such, the key to intersubjective communication and experience is knowing who we are in any given moment at an emotional level. To know thyself is to know how thyself feels.

The feeling sentence can be applied to a variety of different life circumstances and situations, including both interpersonal and societal. For instance, let's apply the feeling sentence to a scenario where I feel fear. As discussed in the previous chapter, I may feel scared when my partner communicates with a former lover when I am not present because she might rekindle feelings with him and leave me. In my case, and in many cases, these fears of abandonment are primarily related to early life events and have relatively little to do with the circumstances of my current relationship. Framing the feeling in terms of the formulaic sentence allows an opportunity to determine if I am blaming others for my feelings or recognizing that my fear in these moments involves reliving experiences of early childhood. At best, what happens when my partner communicates with a former lover when I am not present is that I am triggered into feeling fear and related feelings connected to the abandonment I felt as a child growing up in an alcoholic and codependent household where other people's needs came above my own. Coming into emotional awareness through the feeling sentence helps in freeing myself up from wanting to blame those around me for my feelings. The emotional awareness is increased by the sentence, allowing for an understanding also of just how often white men confuse anxiety about the future with fear. Again, for instance, at a societal level, I may feel scared when black people self-isolate away from white people because I imagine that they might be talking about me or plotting something that would cause harm to me. I feel scared when black lives matter activists talk about dismantling police departments because who would protect me from danger if the police did not exist. These two racialized examples illustrate the slippery slope many white men fall down when considering our emotional connection to certain social issues. As with the interpersonal example, there is nothing intrinsically connecting how we are feeling about other people or situations to the possible hypothetical scenarios we experience in the form of anxiety that is then misunderstood as fear. Recognizing this dynamic doesn't undermine how we feel but enables us to metabolize these feelings. It validates the feeling by allowing us to pause and recognize that we are feeling things about social groups in ways that we are taught should not be discussed openly or at all. For men, this learned silence around racialized or gendered emotions is very similar to how we are taught to deal with emotions in general. We are taught to not discuss race, gender, or religion issues in mixed company. In all these ways, we are "supposed" to act like Gary Cooper. But many of us do feel these feelings, and awareness of them is vital even if being honest about these feelings goes against conventional wisdom about not wanting to be perceived as racist or sexist or a sissy. In the case of many white households, we were raised to be racist and sexist, which is to say we were raised in environments where we blamed black and brown people and women for our problems as a way to avoid taking responsibility for our own problems, and we often also blamed them for their problems, too.[15] By recognizing and taking responsibility for our codependent emotional attachments to intimate partners and entire raced and gendered groups, we're in better position to process those emotions and free ourselves (and everyone) from our codependent emotional attachments.

13 STEP WORK

The January 6, 2021, assault on the US Capitol building recalled to my mind the white dysfunction I experienced as a child. It *looked* like childish behavior, but more importantly, the scene of grown white men and women expressing rage brought to mind moments in my childhood where I had felt aggrieved by adults but could not do anything but suppress my emotions. At certain points in my adolescence, those emotions billowed over in rebellious, destructive behaviors. The assault on the Capitol building reminded me of those feelings of powerlessness that took me to the brink of delinquency during my teenage years. And the behavior of the insurrectionists reminded me of my own dysregulated adult behavior that had occurred at times in my interpersonal relationships. As an adult, at times of extreme stress, resentment toward others and difficulties with emotional regulation seriously impacted my most important relationships. I was never suicidal or homicidal. However, I was severely emotionally dysregulated— deeply resentful and dangerous to the extent I so deeply connected my unaddressed emotional needs to other people's identities and situations. The white boys (and girls) storming Capitol Hill reminded me of myself.

Years prior to the assault on Congress, I found myself in the Twelve-Step Program of Adult Children of Alcoholics (ACA) and Other Family Dysfunction. As I have discussed in earlier chapters, the ACA program offers help for folks whose lives have been dominated by codependency and the effects of living with family and friends with emotional regulation issues and with alcoholism and addiction. At the center of this program are Twelve Steps, similar to traditional Alcoholics Anonymous, but augmented to reflect the specific issue of codependency. As my own "Step Work" progressed over the years, I came to imagine the program having something of value to offer the seemingly disparate topic of white masculinity.

Working to synthesize the changes taking place within me because of my "Step Work" alongside my professional research into the history of race and religion, I turned to codependency as an intellectual and clinical model for theorizing the root causes of racism, sexism, homophobia, and other modes of othering common among many white men, historically. Many white men are addicted to the objectification of and reliance on the rest of the world, and we also *act like* the rest of the world is dependent upon us. Psychological codependency offers a way of accounting for both the abysmal ethical and moral failures resulting from our behaviors over time as well as the mostly sincere claims that we are not doing these things "on purpose." We had tried to be angels but ended up devils in the eyes of others. Forever codependently preoccupied with God, we fashion our beliefs, practices, and moods based on the faulty assumption that we could be other than we are. We sought to be Gods ourselves or we sought to disparage God, similarly to how a spouse or child will center their entire lives around an alcoholic or addict in their family. Forever wanting recognition from the absentee alcoholic, addict, or God upon whom we wait, white men have created the hell that we and others around us experience. Whether the object of our codependency is an alcoholic or an addict (or some other soul we perceive to be helpless) is less significant than our mere belief that they are helpless. Our "hells" are made by blaming other people for our problems. Embodied by all the white folks on Capitol Hill dressed as shamans, veterans, law enforcement, bankers, Christians, and outright white supremacists who sent our elected officials scampering for safety, so many white men feel aggrieved, and we justify our reactions to moments of fear and uncertainty by blaming others.

In what I hope is received by readers as both a thought experiment as well as a practical intervention into white men's codependent behavior, this chapter offers a meditation on the efficacy of a Twelve-Step Program for responding to codependent white masculinity. I encourage readers to think critically and openly with me about this efficacy. Twelve-Step programs are *not* a panacea for social issues, nor do they have a perfect record for addressing alcoholism, addiction, and codependency. But for many people, myself included, they have enabled renewed and new relationships with family and friends. They enable many to experience levels of joy and gratitude with life previously unknown. I could not help but wish that the folks on Capitol Hill—both the politicians and the white folks who feel dispossessed—had the opportunity to experience a semblance of that joy and gratitude. What follows here is offered to them and those like us who deserve to feel joy and gratitude despite ourselves.

Clinical social worker Cristina Combs suggests that the Twelve-Steps of Alcoholics Anonymous (AA) can be augmented to "decenter whiteness" by centering it "differently, to expose and transform it."[1] She has developed "The 12 Steps of Recovery from White Conditioning," inspired and informed by the AA Twelve-Step Program. Step One is "We admitted that we had been socially conditioned by the ideology of white supremacy—that our minds were subject to racial biases, often unconsciously so."[2] The remaining Steps Combs developed are all focused on white supremacy, specifically. The ACA Twelve-Step Program is a bit different than both traditional AA and the augmented Steps developed by Combs, in that ACA seeks to address a root issue—generational dysfunction resulting from codependency. All the Programs are useful in their respective ways, but here I seek to consider the efficacy of the ACA Twelve Steps for a holistic intervention into the spiritual disease in the hearts of many white men that has prevented us from maintaining healthy relationships with ourselves and others. To the extent Combs' Program offers the possibility for behavioral disruption of white supremacy, it is an important tool at white folks' disposal. I am not offering a replacement or critique of Combs' efforts, just as ACA is not a critique or replacement for the original AA Twelve-Step Program. I am, however, convinced that at the root of so much misery caused and felt by white men is unresolved multigenerational trauma that can be metabolized through a creative embrace of the Twelve-Step Program of Adult Children of Alcoholics.

Here, I turn to the Twelve Steps of Adult Children of Alcoholics, which focus on "para-alcoholism," the codependency brought about by being raised in a dysfunctional alcoholic family setting. Para-alcoholism is a form of emotional dysregulation that mimics the dysregulation happening within an actual alcoholic or addict. Adult Children are taught to regulate our emotions from the standpoint of alcoholism, meaning we emotionally act like alcoholics even if some of us never actually drink. To this extent, the ACA Steps address a root generational disease of codependency that then expresses itself as alcoholism or codependency, or both. One need not have grown up in an actual alcoholic or addict home to benefit from these Steps. To the extent *White Devils, Black Gods* has argued that at the root of alcoholism, racism, and sexism is a religious codependency at work in the lives of millions of westerners across many generations, these Steps hold value for healing. In what follows, references to "alcoholism" can be reconsidered as "codependency."

***

1. We admitted we were powerless over the effects of alcoholism or other family dysfunction, that our lives had become unmanageable.[3]

White men are powerless over the impact of long-standing dysfunctional patterns in our families and communities on our lives. Because of this dysfunction, in many ways our lives have become unmanageable, exemplified by the variety of white folks who stormed Capitol Hill. Step One involves coming to terms with reality as it is, not as we may want it to be. We must let go and recognize our powerlessness in the face of the legacy we have inherited as white men. This flies in the face of much conventional wisdom concerning how to respond to toxic white masculinity. Whiteness and masculinity are usually thought of as powerful structural issues that require more than an interpersonal or individual psychological response. And these broadscale efforts must remain ongoing. Step One offers a pathway toward coming into greater relationship with people within and across race and gender, people we might have knowingly or unknowingly harmed, as well as people we might not have harmed, as well as people we have never wanted to harm. The first step is admitting that we are powerless over the effects of the many "isms" we participate in and benefit from as white men. I am not suggesting that the amount or severity of dysfunction is equally distributed across all white men, but recognizing we are powerless over the effects of our codependency is the first step toward finding ourselves in right relationship with ourselves and others.

Some folks may be upset by the idea of white men admitting we are powerless over the effects of toxic white masculinity. They might ask, "Doesn't response *require* claiming power *over* these effects of toxic white masculinity?" There is an important distinction to note between claiming *power over* something and *taking responsibility* for something. In some respects, the last 400 years of western history have been determined by white men who have perceived ourselves powerful enough to overcome all social problems we might face. Feeling power over other people and problems is an expression of white masculinity, historically. It is psychologically akin to the notion of "power over" discussed by German philosopher Friedrich Nietzsche and expressed historically as totalitarianism. However, to the extent this historical characterization is true, we are today able to both account for the collateral damage and outright harm we have done to others in our efforts to solve problems for ourselves and recognize that we are no longer in the position to try and solve current or future problems in a unilateral fashion. Today, we are powerless over the effects of our history and who we have been conditioned to be. Equally, we are powerless to control the responses of others to our past behavior. We are also powerless to control *their* association of us with other white men in history. Admitting we are powerless, rather than serving as a fatalistic admission of complicity or defeat, begins a process of taking responsibility for self and orienting ourselves toward others in such a way that our historical arrogance is placed in check. At this moment of Step One, we reenter the human family.

2. We came to believe that a power greater than ourselves could restore us to sanity.

This second step involves coming to terms with the natural order of the universe. This can play out in complicated ways depending on how we understand the "power greater than ourselves." In earlier work, I have argued that whiteness and masculinity operate as a god-structure. Functionally speaking, that is the work they do in society. They act like Gods, and for many white men, believing in and worshipping "God" reinforces the worship and belief in whiteness and masculinity. Step Two, for many of us, might be difficult to imagine submitting to the idea of whiteness or masculinity as a God. But Gods both gain and lose their power in our naming of them as such. Therefore, the naming of God by God as YHWY—I am that I am—is such a complicated theological idea. In Exodus 3, Moses asks the name he shall call the God of the ancestors of the Israelites. God replies that "I am that I am." In the Hebrew Bible, and in Judeo-Christian tradition, this tautology is remembered as the Tetragrammaton, YHWY, pronounced in English Yahweh. In the naming of this God, it provides a rubric for relating to that God by turning to the stuff of who God's believers have been, historically. Biblically, these are the "ancestors" of Israel—this God is the God of Abraham, Isaac, and Jacob. Thought of theologically for the contemporary west, this also sets in motion the structural relationship between whiteness, masculinity, and theism. As white men, our God has been white and male because it is the God of our ancestors. Hence, taking Step Two could seem counterproductive to confronting white masculinity.

Yet, in stating God's name it emboldens humans and allows for the deconstruction of that object of God. This is the theological reason why God is vague in stating God's name when asked. To know God's name is to know the power of God, which is another way of saying, to have the ability to let go of that God. This leads to a series of traditions where God's name is not to be spoken, for it contains power. ACA remains incredibly vague on the topic of who or what is this Higher Power. However, it describes well the effects of associating YHWY with this Higher Power. As YHWY enables the mirror image (or father figure image) we maintain between God and self, YHWY promotes dysfunctional codependency:

> In an attempt to heal our dysfunctional family from the past, many of us set ourselves up as a Higher Power in our current relationship. We played God by being all-knowing or being all-flexible to control or manipulate others. We wrongly believed we solved the problems from our birth family by keeping our own homes in order. We may have even eliminated alcohol or other dysfunction from our home. Our children, who often act out in addiction or aggression, give us a clue to our failing. We unintentionally passed on our family insanity or distorted thinking.[4]

Step Two does not promote nor guarantee escape from this toxic relationship to YHWY. Yet, it does not reinforce such a relationship, either, in that there is room to name the Higher Power on one's own terms. It makes use of the idea of a Higher Power to enable an ontological shift out of denial about who we have been. In coming to believe in the possibility of sanity, we organize our own egos toward the rest of the universe. Insofar as whiteness and masculinity have worked as a God to enliven a god-complex within ourselves, this second step offers the opportunity for reconciling ourselves to others. It short-circuits our codependent, monotheistic narcissism. Essentially, it ensures we begin to ask for help from others, because we finally arrive at the knowledge that we need help from others.

3. We made a decision to turn our will and our lives over to the care of God as we understand God.

Many people have been harmed by belief in YHWY. The God of Abraham, Isaac, and Jacob has been a perpetrator. These folks could not trust that God if our lives were in danger. YHWY has been that danger. The sacred books of YHWY are filled with murderers and martyrs. There is little room for ambiguity where YHWY is concerned. As argued earlier in this book, YHWY is the prototype for codependent white masculinity. This recognition does not prevent participation in Twelve-Step programs. It does, however, require creative thinking about what a Higher Power could look like. As I've discussed throughout this book, I came to understand my Higher Power as pure intersubjective exchange of energy, that is, intersubjective communication. The God I now turned my life over to I understood as pure experiential engagement with others. At some points, turning my will over to this God would feel uncomfortable. At other points, liberating. At all points, it removed my ability to blame God for my past harms, and it provided a model for ongoing health.

In Step Three, we learn that our worth is not predicated on what we can solve or accomplish, but on our relationships with others. Learning to love others as integral components of intersubjective exchange meant I decided and slowly learned how to love myself. God, being intersubjective communication, enables that love and those relationships. I am no longer an autonomous individual able to exert force over others, but my self is understood as an expression of my relationship with others, constantly reconfiguring itself and expressing itself in mutuality and reciprocity. Steps Two and Three do not involve the worship of a Higher Power. And certainly, there is no jealousy or accusations or demands placed on us by this Higher Power. Step Two and Three both started during my "theophany" with the God at Allah School in Mecca. At that moment, I made the decision to let go of my will to power and submit to the divinity of black men. These Steps enable coming to terms with our dependence on the natural movement of energy in the universe, and our mutual interdependence with others as we come to terms with that movement of energy in the universe.

Accepting God in our lives involves letting go of our everyday need to be in control of the dynamics at work in society, right now. We might hear people talk about this in terms of "our time has come" to step aside and let women of all cultural background and people of color and LGBTQ folks run with leadership. This is the sentiment presented in Jay-Z and Jay Electronica's "We Made It: Remix" that begins the book. This power-struggle plays out among our politicians on both sides of partisan divides, when stuffy old white people are seemingly unwilling to let go and share power and authority with others. Historically, our unwillingness to accept the features of social life that Step Three seeks to cultivate has created social and civic consequences that most white people blame on black and brown civic inclusion.

The degradation of infrastructure and public schools, changes in the natal family structure, and more, we blame on others, when our own ambivalence and inaction are ultimately responsible for any actual social decadence. As codependents, we blame others for our own failures to develop and grow as people. We blame our parents so we do not have to take responsibility for ourselves. No group of people can spend hundreds of years denigrating another group, and simply "decide" to be and act differently toward that group overnight. For instance, the Civil Rights Movement did not affect wholesale psychological change in white Americans. Rather, it sought to legislate full(er) black and brown and female participation in society. Assuming that the work done by activists during that time affected a change in white psyches on the order of what would be required for such a social shift is naive and speaks to our collective white denial. These Steps do not promise a quick cure, either, which is why ACA constantly reminds that these Steps must be worked as a cycle; they are not linear. They amount to principles to live by, rather than an acute course of treatment to be administered once.

4. We made a searching and blameless inventory of our parents because, in essence, we had become them.[5]

Step Four begins the most arduous work of the Twelve Steps. The work to didactically and clearly take account of who we are and who our parents are is ongoing and open-ended. Specifically, Step Four involves balancing "our knowledge of the effects of family abuse in our lives with our own troublesome behavior as adults."[6] This process is not about self-abasement but Knowledge of Self. Step Four emphasizes that this process is to be blameless, remembering that family dysfunction is passed down from one generation to the next. As we come to terms with this knowledge, we can free ourselves from blaming our parents, because they were only doing the best they could to deal with a dysfunctional disease that had been passed down to them, just as they passed it down to us. Much of Step Four involves taking an historical and sociological inventory of our families. Alongside of this work, it also involves beginning to come into awareness of our feelings. This process includes acknowledging which character defects common to codependent people are part of our adult personalities. Then, the step asks people to remember the earliest moments where we expressed those defects. The process is too robust to give full attention to here, but Step Four makes possible the recovery of the Inner Child through a radically honest assessment of our childhood family experiences. In the end, we come to see all the ways we have lived into the examples set by our parents. "In Essence, we had become them."

Does it not hold true for most of us that we had become our parents in terms of our outlooks on race and gender? Step Four can be augmented to give specific attention to race and gender and other salient social identities as they interacted with family dysfunction. How do race and gender shape the family circumstances of children? How do those experiences shape our dispositions and character traits as adults? In many of my classes, I have students complete a Social Strata Inventory, designed to promote their ability to understand the relationship between their families of origin and their social identities that include race, class, religion, gender, and sexuality. Developed by pioneering Womanist scholars of religion and systematized by social ethicist Stacey M. Floyd-Thomas, the inventory asks a series of eight questions, in four or more rounds. The questions are worth listing here:

1. What ethnicity and race are your grandparents? Was there a big difference between their cultures? [...] What were their expectations for you based on their ethnic culture?

2. What were the stated and unstated assumptions about race in your family? Was it ever talked about? [...] Do you know what your parents' racial climate was like when they were children? If not, why not, and how did that shape your own attitude about race?

3. What is the race of the majority of your friends? How do they and their parents perceive race? [...] Did the race of your friends change as you grew older? Did your view on race change? How and why did it change or remain the same?

4. How did your parents' ethnicity or race affect the structure of your family? Did it affect them and your family educationally, financially, or socially? If your parents were of a different race, how would your childhood have been different?

5. What has your racial climate been like? What kind of racist experiences have you personally encountered? [...] What do you like best about being your race? What do you hate most about it? Why?

6. If you had an absolute choice, without any external judgment, would you change your race or ethnicity? Why and what would you want to be? When you think of blacks, whites, Latinos, Asians, Indians, Middle Easterners, and Native Americans, what image do you have of them? What one word would you use to describe each group? Do you find it difficult to apply only one word? Why? Do you want to add a group to the list here? Who, and why?

7. In relation to race and ethnicity, what has been your most significant gain by being who you are? The most significant loss? In what ways do local groups (family, workforce, friends, religious groups, etc.) reinforce racial thinking? In what ways do they refute racial thinking?

8. How does answering this inventory focused on race make you feel? How does this exercise impact/change your understanding of one specific reading from class? What features of your own experiences substantiate arguments from class? What features of your own experiences refute arguments from class? (Name Thinkers/arguments, and explain).[7]

After answering these questions in terms of ethnicity and race, students are then required to answer them again in terms of gender. Once complete for gender, students answer the questions again for sexuality, then class, and finally religion, until they have moved through each of the social identities. Like Step Four of ACA, the Social Strata Inventory is usually exhausting, but also liberating. It empowers students to come into Knowledge of Self so that their experiences with self and others are not overdetermined by the experiences they unknowingly bring to social interactions. The inventory enables awareness of our family's impact on our thinking and doing and being where it concerns social identity.

Combining Step Four with the Social Strata Inventory unearths the different intersectional stories that shaped our character defects. If we are afraid of authority figures as adults, does the race of the authority figure matter? What story from our childhood might help explain the difference? If we were abandoned by our mother and developed attachment issues to women as a result, does the religion or the race of a woman impact expression of that character defect? Countless other questions could be asked, bringing us into acute awareness of the nexus of our pain and our harm, where we turned to pathological coping mechanisms in order to respond to the abandonment situations we faced as children. Not every child faces abandonment. There are many well-adjusted children who grow up to be well-adjusted adults. But by what criteria are we understanding health and "well-adjusted"? Wedding something of a Social Strata Inventory with the materials already available in Step Four would enable white men to begin asking these difficult questions.

5. We admitted to God, to ourselves, and to another human being the exact nature of our wrongs.

With Step Five, we challenge "the three main rules entrenched in our souls as a result of growing up in a dysfunctional home. The rules are: 'don't talk, don't trust, and don't feel.'"[8] What is true of shame and guilt within family units is also true of how we are conditioned to respond to racism and sexism. A cloud of shame hangs over all of us regarding these social issues, such that, when black and brown folks are victimized by racism, our response is often to suppress their feelings by minimizing or lashing out at them, or by repressing our own feelings toward them (often through isolation). When women are sexually assaulted, many men tell the women that they should not report the abuses because inevitably, they will be the ones most likely to face shame. And of course, the shame of participation in white supremacist activities has long meant a cloud of secrecy concealing the actual identities of participants in hate groups, hate crimes, and the like. Whether we are thinking about acute alcoholism or the response to racial unrest, many of us are taught to not trust what we see or what we feel or what our parents said.[9] And, experiences of abuse we faced or witnessed were "often minimized or blamed on another cause,"[10] which results in an overwhelming lack of trust that many of us hold within ourselves. The task of coming to trust oneself again begins with trusting someone else.

Once Step Four is complete, Step Five often takes place with a sponsor or another trusted person, who is willing to listen—without judgment—to what amounts to a person's life story. This process can take a series of hours, in many cases. It carries a ritualistic quality of learning how to share our lives with other people. So many who have faced childhood dysfunction struggle with social relationships. Step Five manifests healthy relationships by pulling us out of isolation. Importantly, this step is not merely about telling someone else about the harm done to us as children; it also requires willingness to see the connections between the harm done to us and the harm we've done to others. Through the radical honesty demanded from Step Five, we come to recognize the "exact nature" of our childhood abandonment.[11] For ACA, this usually involves recognizing that the harm we have done to others has ultimately harmed us.[12] In short, Step Five allows us to take ownership of the deeply intersubjective and mutual relationships we necessarily maintain with other people.

Step Five is also usually where participants begin to experience the grief that has been stored in our hearts, minds, and bodies since childhood. There is a great deal of grief to work through when confronting white masculinity, because it has been such a wholesale failure in organizing life healthily. It might have enabled a certain material advantage for white men, but that advantage has come at a high price. Once white men start on a healing process in these terms, the full weight of that price will expose itself. Grief will bubble to the surface. This is the work ushered in by figures like Lillian Smith, who sought to pull back the blanket of shame that kept segregation and sexism so tightly bound to religion in the American South. In unearthing grief, we come into a more honest, balanced relationship with ourselves and our place in the world.

6. We were entirely ready to have God remove all these defects of character.

Step Six involves discerning the distinction between survival traits learned as children and the character defects that they become for us as adults. As children, we learned certain survival traits—called the Laundry List traits that were discussed earlier in this book—that helped us to cope with our childhood abandonment. Things like fearing authority figures, reacting rather than acting, and judging ourselves harshly were coping strategies we developed in response to our missing or otherwise emotionally unavailable parents. Over time, these survival traits begin to produce defects of character in us as adults. Perfectionism, dishonesty, envy, feeling or acting self-centered, extreme judgment of ourselves and others, and isolating ourselves are all defects of character that, rather than protect us as adults, generally make our lives more *unmanageable*. The moment when our survival traits backfire is the point they produce these character defects.

Many Adult Children come to feel comfortable with these defects of character. But, in recovery, many of these same folks come to recognize the harm that these defects of character have produced in our adult lives. Many struggle to imagine a life where they are not overdetermined by these character defects. Step Six is about coming to terms with ourselves and learning to love ourselves enough that we're able to think and feel realistically about these defects of character. They may or may not have protected us as children, but as adults, we learn to "integrate" our survival traits into our self-image, while letting go of the character defects that they produced. The ACA workbook notes that "the key to becoming free of character defects while making peace with our survival traits involves a three-prong approach with willingness, prayer, and time."[13] Patience sees results over time, and prayer is the opportunity to align our will to the will of God, which in my case is intersubjective exchange with others. Through some sort of prayer, Adult Children come to realize that self-love determines our character traits as adults. Having not loved ourselves adequately enough for years, we treated ourselves harshly and treated others in kind; learning to love ourselves unconditionally sees the character defects lessen in our lives.

7. We humbly asked God to remove our shortcomings.

Step Seven requires accepting that "we cannot remove our shortcomings without the help of a Higher Power."[14] I do not believe in an agential God yet Step Seven calls on prayer as a strategy for healing. How could I pray with an expectation—an intercessory prayer—from a place of authenticity? When working Step Seven, I trust the process and allow that process to humble me. I let go of the need to control outcomes or understand how the steps work. My God is the movement of electrons between points of consciousness—pure, intersubjective communication. Relying on that awareness, perhaps it is the case that asking God to help us with our healing process amounts to a series of aphorisms asked of oneself. Perhaps, trusting in intersubjective communication amounts to the philosopher's alchemical stone, transforming us finally into our fully human selves. Not knowing how the transformation of healing works is humbling. But it does work. And as taught in Twelve-Step programs, humility "is the willingness to seek and do God's will with our best effort."[15] *Leaning in* to the discomfort of praying, Step Seven found me talking to God for the first time in fifteen or more years:

> God, I am now ready that you should remove from me all my defects of character, which block me from accepting your divine love and living with true humility toward others. Renew my strength so that I might help myself and others along this path of recovery. I humbly ask you to remove my defects of character. I humbly ask you to integrate my survival traits.[16]

What keeps so many of us in hell boils down to a lack of humility. Humility is what the devil never had to give because it requires recognition of the proper order in the universe, beginning with the naming of God as God. It is not necessary that your or my Higher Power be recognized as the "Highest" Power—that's what monotheism has always and still gets so wrong—but our Higher Power helps to orient ourselves toward our standing in the universe. In naming God as God, we orient ourselves toward ourselves.

> 8. Made a list of all persons we had harmed and became willing to make amends to them all.

Step Eight involves looking at our Step Four inventory and forgiving ourselves and our parents, followed by taking responsibility for all the situations where we have harmed other people. We are not *bad* people. But we have done hurtful things. Our actions have harmed others. Step Eight involves making an actual list that would account for those who have been harmed by our codependency. This would obviously include women and black and brown folks, to one degree or another. But more significantly, it involves looking at how these dynamics have harmed the people closest to us. To raise racists or sexists does harm to more than those we consider the "marginalized" or "oppressed" victims of racism and sexism. Jean-Paul Sartre wrote that "To do evil must in the long run harm everyone. Including the one who sets it in motion."[17] Step Eight asks us to do deeply intersectional work, coming to terms with the nature of our codependency and its many expressions in our relationships with others. This work involves recognizing the perpetrators of future harm—our loved ones and our children, especially—as victims of our own codependency. We have participated in cycles of abuse, and it here becomes possible to take ownership of our participation in those cycles. Unconditional love is made possible within ourselves at the point where we locate, name, and say out loud the names of the people we have harmed. This releases us from the guilt and shame we feel about those circumstances, and it sets in motion positive energy transmission with them and others. Receiving the unconditional love of our Higher Power is possible when we take responsibility for the huge impact of our small egos on those we have loved and lived with. Who, ultimately, is included on each person's Step Eight lists will be determined by unique circumstance.

> 9. Made direct amends to such people wherever possible, except when to do so would injure them or others.

Step Nine is an extension of Step Eight. Both involve letting go of the shame that fuels codependency. Step Eight is largely about reorienting oneself toward the possibility of renewed relationships with others. Step Nine attempts to make those renewed relationships concrete. This work usually begins with parents, but likely extends to intimate partners, current and former close friends, colleagues, and others. The Social Strata Inventory implemented as part of Step Four will help to organize and make sense of who Step Eight and Nine will involve. Step Nine is an opportunity to bring back into our lives the people who we left feeling abandoned, neglected, or otherwise harmed. And it offers resolution and acceptance for those relationships irrevocably harmed by our actions. White masculinity has prevented many white parents from loving their children unconditionally. White parents have no less love for their children than non-white parents. But white parents working from a codependency paradigm have not had access to unconditional love of the sort made possible by working these Steps. The Steps offer a healing modality of self-actualization. In the moment of our making amends to the people we have harmed, we actualize unconditional love as the transcendence of our pain received from and given to others.

> 10. We continued to take personal inventory and, and when we were wrong, promptly admitted it.

Step Ten involves maintaining active communication with others. This points us in two distinct directions. The first is inward, staying checked in with our Inner Child and growing in emotional intelligence. This amounts to remaining open and aware of how we are feeling each day and responsible for how we respond to how we feel. This work promotes emotional intelligence and trust.

At Step Ten, some of our old or ongoing relationships will have begun a rebuilding process. Other relationships may have ended or changed permanently. Still other relationships will be new, perhaps from recovery work or because recovery work has opened to us new relationship possibilities across a variety of spaces in our lives. In all these relationships, our ability to be present with the other person or group as well as our ability to build trust with them involves telling our whole truth to one another, what Gay and Kathlyn Hendricks refer to as the "microscopic truth."[18] Step Ten involves something of what the Hendricks describe as this "truth." Relationships are harmed when we withhold communication. The microscopic truth is "that which absolutely cannot be argued about … In a close relationship, the truth is most likely to be *a clear statement of feeling, of body sensation, or of what you actually did*" (italics in original).[19] Telling the "microscopic truth" through ongoing personal inventory and sharing with others is not about prioritizing the other person or group ahead of ourselves but is about cultivating an openness of self that will enable the flourishing of intersubjective communication.

Step Ten also involves taking immediate responsibility for those moments when our character defects cause us to do or say things during intersubjective communications that were not in service to our and others' highest and greatest good. Upon making amends with others, maintaining those relationships requires understanding that we will hurt other people and they will hurt us. Not often, we hope, but it will happen. Rather than succumb to shame and self-doubt during these moments, Step Ten has us practice taking immediate responsibility for the action. If the person is truly hurt, or seriously injured from the action, they may choose distance from us. That is okay. But we take responsibility for our wrongdoing for our own sake. As Tony A's version of the Step suggests, our ongoing personal inventory ultimately promotes self-love and self-approval.[20] When I have harmed someone else, or feel like I have, I check in with that person, and I check in with myself. When I have been harmed by someone else, or when I feel like I have, I check in with that person, and I check in with myself. Whether I am talking to myself or to another person, I try to maintain empathy and forgiveness for them, asking: What about their life situation or past experiences might be informing what they did and how they seem to be feeling? And, can I relate to their situation? Whether I am dealing with myself or another person, I try to remember that the self-help cliché "we are all doing the best we can" is popular because it is true. In moments when I have harmed someone else, I work to process how I feel about having harmed someone else and I ask: "What am I bringing to that relationship that caused me to act that way or think that thing?" Codependent people struggle with working to control other people, but none of us can control anyone but ourselves. In fact, we cannot even really control how we feel, only what we do. An exception to this rule is positive thinking, which does promote positive feelings. Importantly, though, for working Step Ten is recognizing that emotions *happen to us*. Whether we like them or not, even if we practice positive thinking, negative feelings will still encroach upon us against our will. Part of the work of admitting in a prompt fashion that we are wrong involves admitting to myself, first, the nature of the wrong committed. What feelings were happening within me during the time I committed the wrong? I then work within myself to process these feelings. I try to *learn from* my feelings rather than react to them. Then, as soon as possible, I try to have a conversation with the other person or group I may have harmed.

This sort of interpersonal work could certainly play out in broader sociological terms when we think about whiteness, masculinity, and religion in history. In so many ways, white men have yet to do the Step Ten work of apologizing for ongoing harms, much less ceasing the behaviors and thinking learned from our parents. What has come to be referred to as "call-out culture" or "cancel culture" offers an opportunity to think about atonement and forgiveness in sociological terms. The moral failure of one person ought not be grounds for total banishment of that person, but the ongoing topic of cancel culture is instructive of the need for making amends in the immediate moment of any given situation as well as the need for ongoing growth individually and within our communities of affinity and concern. To date, white men by and large remain ill-equipped to openly and honestly admit when we are wrong. Step Ten enables the courage to see our faults without succumbing to self-abasement and isolation.

11. We sought through prayer and meditation to improve our conscious contact with God, as we understand God, praying only for knowledge of God's will for us and the power to carry that out.

Step Eleven has been the fuel sustaining my Twelve-Step work. Based on Step Eleven, I started working on mindfulness exercises that I could implement in moments when I felt pressured or agitated. As I have worked these Steps, I have implemented and sustained many of these practices, including breath work, physical exercise, and more. It is not always easy to sustain these practices, but they have been life-affirming.

Particularly, Step Eleven has had an incredible impact on my life and well-being through the cultivation of a meditation practice. Today, I meditate almost every day, and many days, I meditate for at least one hour a day. I try to meditate in both individual and group settings. My journey inward, through prayer and meditation, is where I have been emboldened to seek out new relationships. Some of these new relationships have created such joy and gratitude that they have changed the nature of what I thought was possible in relationships. One key to the practice, and to Step Eleven, is to remain open to new experiences of intersubjective communication. Chasing curiosity and openness, I have practiced Zen meditation and Loving Kindness meditations, and I have meditated to communicate with aliens and other beings that may or may not actually exist in the multiverse. In these experiences with Step Eleven, I have learned that who we are and what we can potentially experience individually and together are multiplicative and not predicated on the pain we've experienced in our lives or the potential harm we have produced and sustained in the lives of others. Meditation has come to be a means through which I can achieve levels of intersubjective communication with other beings purely by turning inward. In this way, meditation and the Twelve Steps have exploded my sense of what a self truly is at its most fundamental level.

12. Having had a spiritual awakening as a result of these steps, we tried to carry this message to others who still suffer, and to practice these principles in all our affairs.

I never "worked" Step Twelve. Step Twelve happened to me in the form of a "spiritual awakening" resulting from working the eleven previous steps. This recognition took place as I furiously packed up my belongings from the house I once shared with my former wife. We were divorcing, and I was moving out. Yet, I was calm, serene even. I reflected on how far I was from who I was when I first began working these steps. My entire life had been impacted by working these steps, but I was at peace. My emotional situation in that moment reminded me of a passage from Tara Brach's book *Radical Acceptance* (2003), her words really capturing where I was before Step Work and where I was after having begun to live in step with these twelve principles:

> In our lives we often find ourselves in situations we can't control, circumstances in which none of our strategies work. Helpless and distraught, we frantically try to manage what is happening. Our child takes a downward turn in academics, and we issue one threat after another to get him in line. Someone says something hurtful to us, and we strike back quickly or retreat. We make a mistake at work, and we scramble to cover it up or go out of our way to make up for it. We head into emotionally charged confrontations nervously rehearsing and strategizing. The more we fear failure the more frenetically our bodies and minds work. We fill our days with continual movement: mental planning and worrying, habitual talking, fixing, scratching, adjusting, phoning, snacking, discarding, buying, looking in the mirror ... What if we were to intentionally stop our mental computations and our rushing around and, for a minute or two, simply pause and notice our inner experience?[21]

With my car packed and my dog feeling confused by all the boxes, all I wanted to do was get out of the house and get on the road. But without really thinking about what to do next, I simply paused. My weekly meditation group was about to meet. Meditation and checking in with the group were more important than leaving at that moment. I sat down on the floor of my living room for the last time, logged onto Zoom, and meditated for thirty minutes. During the meditation, it dawned on me that *that* moment had become an expression of the spiritual awakening I'd received as a result of making these Twelve Steps an active part of my life. After the meditation ended, I shared my spiritual experience with the group. Then, I hit the road.

***

White Devils, Black Gods has been an effort to integrate what I have learned from the last several years of working these steps with what I have learned from the wisdom of black esoteric traditions and black thought, in general. Coming to terms with who I have been at personal and political levels has aided in the transformation of my self-hatred into self-love. I still struggle with codependency. But increasingly, judgmentalness and isolation have become gratitude, trust, acceptance, asking for help, and friendship most of the time. Thanks to these Twelve Steps, I love myself for the first time in my adult life. Not for nothing, none of this would have happened for me had I not first submitted to the idea that the black man is God. All praise is due.

Looking around the United States and many parts of Europe, often I see angry white men. Still in charge in too many places, yet powerless to affect adequate social, civic, and interpersonal changes that would positively impact the lives of us all, I can't help but wish for them something of the recovery journey I've been on these last years. So many of us struggle to love ourselves. We struggle to understand why so many white men seem so recalcitrantly comfortable making decisions that negatively impact women, people of color, and the ecosystem. These two issues are related. The secret of understanding white men is not that we treat women and people of color differently than we treat ourselves. Rather, we treat them just like we treat ourselves—with hatred and codependent obsession. The difference between us and them, at the end of the day, may simply boil down to the fact that they demand more of themselves and of us than we have ever demanded of ourselves. Perhaps, with these steps, white men can begin to demand more of ourselves, too.

CONCLUSION: DISCERNMENT

The definition of discernment is the ability to judge well. The idea carries a particular Christian theological connotation, namely, that of obtaining spiritual guidance, the cultivation of wisdom (as right judgment), and application of that wisdom in service to ideas and practices that recognize one's rightful place in the universe. To discern is to draw conclusions that can be trusted, and to have a sense of how to make use of these conclusions considering the world's circumstances and one's place in the world. This conclusion is about discerning that our beliefs impact our capacity to be in community with other people. Our religious beliefs are shaped by the relationships we have with our parents as children as well as by the cultures from which we emerge. This conclusion is also about discerning how thinking about ourselves and our social differences—the overall "space" we have for inclusion of others unlike us within our worldviews and priorities—is also shaped by the quality of the relationships we had with our parents when we were children. Being abandoned by an alcoholic father or a codependent mother are related, but distinct forms of abandonment. Not all of us face these specific personal circumstances. Some of us face far worse. Others of us experience far more healthy home circumstances. However, being taught racism, sexism, homophobia, and misogyny as children is also a form of abandonment and neglect.

Right judgment is difficult for many of us with codependency-related issues. Often, codependents will judge ourselves and others harshly, whether deserved or not, and this judgment becomes a mechanism of isolation. In our judgments of others, we often isolate ourselves. This mode of judgment makes it harder to trust ourselves and others, because in not giving anyone the benefit of the doubt, we grow so distant from self and others that our capacities for right judgment (i.e., discernment) become diminished. We end up unable to trust our judgments, at all.

What might white masculine discernment look like, and how might it be possible? In what follows, I suggest that discernment might be possible through the spiritual principle of humility. Twelve-Step writer Veronica Valli suggests that "humility is the solution to self-obsession. It is a spiritual practice, and its definition is as follows: Humility is not thinking less of ourselves—it is thinking of ourselves less."[1] Humility is a spiritual practice of letting go of the feeling that the harms done to us by others reflect on our value *as individuals*. "What anyone else does, says, or doesn't do or say has nothing to do with us. Even our parents! Instead, their actions and words come through their own filters and limiting beliefs (just as ours do)."[2] Our ability to "judge well," to discern, hinges on humility. In humbling ourselves, we decrease the severity and frequency of our self-judgments, which also decreases the severity and frequency of our judgments of others. Through humility, our engagement with others comes to be marked not by critique and disappointment, but through mutual engagement, curiosity, and openness.

Few white men have done more to diagnose white masculine arrogance and isolation than the philosopher of religion Alan Watts. Across the twentieth century, Watts, along with Joseph Campbell, Paul Tillich, Jean-Paul Sartre, Gordon Kaufman, and many others, aided in diagnosing white western men's crisis of faith and indifference. Watts, however, actively introduced many white westerners to tools, prescriptions, and remedies for humility in the form of Eastern spiritual practices. At the root of Watts' analyses is the situation of failed religious efficacy confronting the white man's culture, and a comprehensive response that comes in the form of humbly letting go of the very notion that we, as white men, are separate individuals, at all. For Watts, a "mythology of objects" has seen to it that we white men regard ourselves as holding a "separate ego."[3] Watts suggests that

> Man so defined and so experienced is, of course, incapable of pleasure and contentment, let alone creative power. Hoaxed into the illusion of being an independent, responsible source of actions, he cannot understand why what he does never comes up to what he *should* do, for a society which has defined him as separate cannot persuade him to behave as if he really belonged. Thus he feels chronic guilt and makes the most heroic efforts to placate his conscience.[4]

Watts is describing the irascible alienation so long opined about by western philosophers and felt in the deepest recesses of many white men's cores. We are dirempted, disconnected from ourselves because we stay disconnected from others. We have effectively alienated ourselves and spent all our time working to save ourselves by attempting to save others or by blaming those same people when our efforts to save them fail or go unacknowledged. Astoundingly, however, Watts offers advice that some may resent hearing, in that we white men may not deserve it:

> No one can be moral—that is, no one can harmonize contained conflicts—without coming to a working arrangement between the angel in himself and the devil in himself, between his rose above and his manure below. The two

forces or tendencies are mutually interdependent, and the game is a working game just so long as the angel is winning, but does not win, and the devil is losing, but is never lost.[5]

Throughout *White Devils, Black Gods*, I have sketched out an image of what a white man's Knowledge of Self might look like given our characterization by others as having been devils. Here, Watts uses the idea of the devil to represent warring ideals within white masculinity, in general. The devil is an angel, after all. Watts encourages a recognition of both sides of ourselves. For some of us, we project the devil within onto outsiders and others; for others of us, we project the devil within onto other white men, seeking to escape the charge that we, too, have a devil within us. Watts speaks to this Manichean identity game at work among many white men, liberal or conservative, rich or poor, Christian, Jew, spiritual or secular. Watts cautions that

> In any foreseeable future there are going to be thousands and thousands of people who detest and abominate Negroes, communists, Russians, Chinese, Jews, Catholics, beatniks, homosexuals, and 'dope-fiends.' These hatreds are not going to be healed, but only inflamed, by insulting those who feel them, and the abusive labels with which we plaster them—squares, fascists, rightists, know-nothings—may well become the proud badges and symbols around which they will rally and consolidate themselves ...

The black esoteric charge that we are "white devils" is surely one additional inflammatory insult that could be included in this list of names we call white men who fear social difference. As this book has sought to demonstrate, the label "white devil" offers an opportunity for cultivating Knowledge of Self. When spoken by black and brown people, it carries the weight of ethical awareness. Yet, while all of us across various social identities have a shared obligation to dismantle systems and ideologies of oppression, our individual and group-based responses will not be identical. Each of us can learn from other points of view, but none of us is in the position to blindly accept all points of view. At the beginning of this book, I told the story of my decision to let go of unearned arrogance and imagine the truth in the claim that the black man is God. I wanted to know what that would mean for me. Initially, and immediately, it meant a confrontation with my status as a "white devil." I recognized that something about myself, my history, and my community came to be thought of by others as the embodiment of evil. Drawing this study to a close, I continue to believe in the truth of black divinity. I am grateful for this truth told to me and available to all white men as an expression of our Knowledge of Self. But there is judgment and then there is discernment. To call myself or any white man a devil, from my point of view, would be a poor, overly harsh, and naïve judgment made by an Adult Child. Discernment of my responsibility to the charge white men are devils involves recognizing that self-hatred cannot be responded to with self-hatred. From the mouth of black Gods, the myth of Yakub draws white men into self-awareness and potential intersubjective exchange. Spoken from our own mouths, it reinforces the low self-esteem and fragile egos that define the devil's lot. Watts continues,

> … Nor will it do to confront the opposition in public with polite and non-violent sit-ins and demonstrations, while boosting our collective ego by insulting them in private. If we want justice for minorities and cooled wars with our natural enemies, whether human or nonhuman, we must first come to terms with the minority and the enemy in ourselves and in our own hearts, for the rascal is there as much as anywhere in the 'external' world—especially when you realize that the world outside your skin is as much yourself as the world inside.[6]

The challenge for white men is not merely recognizing the divinity of black and brown men and/or the rest of the world, nor does discernment involve owning our status as devil and living into it, but in realizing that the division of the world into two ostensibly distinct parts is the first lie we ever heard, and the one we have repeated most often. We are here together—all of us. We are expressions of one another. Watts does not call for our throwing out the moral distinction we make between "me" and "them" altogether, but to realize it as part of the larger whole. As Watts suggests of the Hindu Vedanta, "nothing exists except God."[7] Watts concludes,

> There *seem* to be other things than God, but only because he is dreaming them up and making them his disguises to play hide-and-seek with himself. The universe of seemingly separate things is therefore real only for a while, not eternally real, for it comes and goes as the Self hides and seeks itself.[8]

We are neither Gods nor devils, but expressions of God or source or a cosmic consciousness that uses us to touch its creation. What any of us call ourselves or others is only significant to the extent those honorifics enable renewed and greater intersubjective exchange with each other and with the multiverse. This awareness is not a foundation for bloating one's already distorted individualistic sense of an ego, but "on seeing through the illusion of the ego, it is impossible to think of oneself as better than, or superior to, others for having done so. In every direction there is just the one Self playing its myriad games of hide-and-seek."[9]

***

At least as early as the 1940s, well-known public theologian and ethicist Reinhold Niebuhr had written what is referred to as the Serenity Prayer. Niebuhr, remembered for his doctrine of Christian Realism, understood the world to be a troubled place with both interpersonal and social problems all around us. White American Christianity, no less than western liberalism, demands we work to address these problems while recognizing that those efforts are always impossibly incomplete. White Christian liberal arrogance, witnessed in the form of assuming all problems could be solved, reinforced many of the problems, in the end. What was possible, Niebuhr maintained, was an internal about-face within believers wherein they could align their perceptions about what is and is not possible in the world. Part of Niebuhr's perspectives were distilled in his Serenity Prayer, usually recited as the following:

> God, grant me the serenity to accept the things I cannot change, the courage to change the things I can, and the wisdom to know the difference.[10]

This Serenity Prayer was adopted by Alcoholics Anonymous and has been a component of Twelve-Step fellowships for decades. It works by limiting expectations of outcomes and humbling ourselves toward a higher authority or fate. In Adult Children of Alcoholics (ACA), the prayer has been remixed to focus more squarely on the spiritual disease of codependency:

> God, grant me the serenity to accept the people I cannot change, the courage to change the one I can, and the wisdom to know that one is me.

This ACA version focuses on personal responsibility rather than broad-based ontological statements about the nature of reality, in general. We can only control ourselves, in the end. At some point in recent decades, a kind of critical rejoinder to the Serenity Prayer began to be attributed to black feminist activist and legal scholar Angela Davis. I could not find the original quote from Davis, but the reference bears repeating here, in that like the ACA version of the Serenity Prayer, it emphasizes personal agency. However, it also constitutes a powerful critique of the Twelve-Step model that the original Serenity Prayer has come to be associated with. Davis' version reads:

> I am no longer accepting the things I cannot change. I am changing the things I cannot accept.

These words critique the Serenity Prayer for its purported reinforcement of the status quo, a status quo that in the context of the United States has been historically white and male-dominated. My gut reaction to Davis's comment is to critique her critique and suggest that she might do well to recognize that the Serenity Prayer and the Twelve-Step programs more generally have for many, many people over the last decades enabled positive changes in their lives. That said, it is impossible to deny that Twelve-Step programs and fellowships are rooted in a history and heritage of white, Anglo-Saxon Protestant masculine heteropatriarchal, homophobic culture. Indeed, many Twelve-Step fellowships continue to be dominated by white straight men.

What I have offered in this book is informed by the Twelve-Step program of Adult Children of Alcoholics (ACA). The ACA program helps to provide a model for white men to come to terms with our intrinsic codependency. It also allows for white men to begin healing the internal psychological wounds that outwardly express themselves as racism, sexism, theism, atheism, alcoholism, and other forms of addiction, ideology, and codependency. Given the considerable weight I give to this program, it is important to maintain accountability by considering different opinions on such programs. Accountability involves clarifying the norms that govern our efforts to ensure our needs are met while also meeting the needs of others. None of us share all of the same needs, and therefore, neither do we share the same norms. Hence, we are forced—by virtue of the need for accountability—to submit ourselves into an intersubjective relationship across lines of social difference. Juxtaposing Niebuhr's and Davis's respective admonitions highlights the challenge of norm clarification.

Today, to whom do we owe allegiance and accountability? The norms that I have sought to cultivate, promote, and explicate in this book are norms that would govern the rehabilitation of white masculinity. At no point have I suggested that at the level of individual rehabilitation, this program is efficacious cross culturally or across gender. Rather, I suggest that this ACA program enables *for white men* the possibility for genuine cross cultural, intersubjective communication and exchange across lines of social difference. In the individual cultivation of Knowledge of Self that ultimately leads to self-love, white men are better equipped to build relationships and coalitions across these lines of social difference. The Twelve Steps offered by ACA are no panacea for resolving social issues, and I am taking no license or liberties in assuming that the Twelve-Step model might be applicable across social identities. To the extent this model emerges from within white masculine-dominated society, its ongoing efficacy for white men is a natural outcome considering the prevalence of codependency and addiction-related issues emerging from that community. Nevertheless, competing norms and needs require that we take seriously the potential harm the steps could carry with their application. However, to suggest that Twelve-Step programs are somehow guilty by virtue of their association with white men is to discount the creative human possibilities that unfold even amongst communities of oppressive people. These principles offer the possibility for an experience of spiritual transformation for white men, that neither racism nor sexism nor monotheism ever actually made possible. That these steps offer white men increased bandwidth for intersubjective exchange should not be taken as a promise of the realization of such exchange in all possible moments.

Connecting codependency to social issues has a complicated history. For instance, some have argued that white feminism is codependent on white patriarchy.[11] The connections here are easy enough to spot. Within the dynamic of whiteness, masculinity and femininity are in a codependent relationship, with the gender binary serving as the foundation for that relationship. But many criticisms have emerged, particularly among feminist voices of the 1980s and 1990s, in response to the perceived danger that psychological models of codependency might normalize otherwise politically and socially problematic behavior. Susan Faludi, for instance, argued that codependency discourses reinforced the notion of women as childlike (in many recovery models focused on the Inner Child).[12] According to Trysh Travis, some have "argued that recovery culture had appropriated the concerns of Second Wave feminism in order to gut its political analysis: 'Dysfunctional' replaces 'patriarchal'; 'toxic' replaces 'oppressive'; and so on … feminist critics of recovery's chief concern was with recovery's 'depoliticizing' effects, manifested in its suggestion to unhappy women that they should seek 'not to change society but simply to change themselves.'"[13] My framing of toxic white masculinity as an expression of a codependency disease is not meant to occlude the nuanced histories that emerge from the specific salient identities organized and subjugated by white men. Further, what I offer here is meant to be part of a more comprehensive response to toxic forms of white masculinity that includes policy, legal, structural, and other sorts of responses. Nevertheless, the turn to clinical self-help is meant to cultivate capacities among white men for self-acceptance. I recognize not everyone will find my argument worthwhile. One commentary from 1990, by Shana R. Blessing, describes an escape from Twelve-Step programs framed around the "new disease" known as "codependency."[14] Blessing offers an important critical rejoinder to anyone who would assume Twelve-Step programs offer a panacea to sociopolitical issues:

> I have since learned that I am living in a society that does not know how to take responsibility for itself, one that is not willing to examine the sociopolitical problems for which it is responsible. Rather than addressing fundamental social issues and working toward radical systemic changes, addiction theories help us to maintain the status quo by shifting emphasis from the cultural to individual causes and cures … in becoming victims of our habits, we have become walking myriads of disease. Disease conceptions have come to represent all our fears. We also have no hope for total cure, for even if we have not taken a drink for years, we still call ourselves alcoholics and the threat of a simple glass of liquid maintains its power over our lives as we continue to define our relationships to our old behaviors nor see our changing of behaviors as powerful choice. Personally, we shortchange ourselves.[15]

In these programs' reliance on submission to a higher power, some like Blessing will read models of recovery based on codependency as fatalistic. Again, norm clarification is key. While I would caution that powerlessness refers only to alcohol, drugs, and/or the dysfunction in one's life and is not a sweeping statement about total powerlessness, for communities who have lived their lives dealing with the effects of unhealthy codependent men who projected our weaknesses onto them, Twelve-Step fellowships may not be the most life-affirming spaces. Blessing considered the Twelve-Step program as a threat to her primary community of affinity and concern, writing that

> Politically, as a lesbian (and gay) community, we are annihilating ourselves ... We are so self-focused that our community is dying. We have become powerless, no longer believing we can effect change outside of ourselves ... I have since discovered that much of what I did during my time in 12-Step programs was replace one unhealthy family with another. I replaced one sorry set of rules for living with another.[16]

Coming from a community socially conditioned into self-hatred and destructive patterns (by her characterization, not mine), Blessing found similarly unhealthy people in Twelve-Step fellowships. To be sure, many in these fellowships have participated in homophobia, misogyny, and sexism, making Blessing's criticism completely understandable. In fact, some within the "recovery" networks Blessing participated in exposed her to systematic, religious, and interpersonal experiences of homophobia.

Holly Whitaker, in a *New York Times* opinion piece from 2019, charges Alcoholics Anonymous with reinforcing patriarchy. Admitting that she never participated in the program, she nevertheless opines that "it wasn't made with everyone in mind," in that the program "created in the 1930s by upper-middle-class white Protestant men" was "designed to break down white male privilege" by reminding them "that they were not God" and encouraging them "to humble themselves, to admit their weaknesses, to shut up and listen."[17] As Whitaker describes the program, it was solipsistically designed to address the existential and psychosocial concerns of white men. By her characterization, it does seek to make better white men. Nevertheless, Whitaker suggests that "today's women don't need to be broken down or told to be quiet. We need the opposite. I worry that any program that tells us to renounce power that we have never had poses the threat of making us sicker."[18]

Both Blessing and Whitaker seem to conflate the first step's charge to "admit we were powerless over alcohol or the effects of alcohol" and a broader assumed demand to admit to powerlessness in our lives, across the board. As explained by Valli, Step One "only means admitting powerlessness over alcohol ... it does not assert that we are without power, and nowhere does it ask that we renounce or 'give up' our power."[19] In some cases, recognizing and overcoming alcoholism and addiction has proved incredibly empowering. Alcoholics Anonymous historian

William White reminds that both Frederick Douglass and Malcolm X struggled with addiction, noting that the men linked their sobriety to a spiritual awakening and to their capacities to lead in the larger black freedom struggle.[20] Douglass "signed a temperance pledge in 1845 in the presence of Father Theobald Mathew (leader of the Irish temperance movement), and kept that pledge of sobriety for the remainder of his life."[21] While Douglass was instrumental in the black freedom movement, he was also actively involved in the "'colored temperance movement.'"[22] In the case of Malcolm X, sobriety was an integral component of his finding Knowledge of Self. Noting in his autobiography that he had constantly used and abused all sorts of drugs, Malcolm X was first "saved" through his introduction and conversion to the Nation of Islam.[23] Moreover, studies have shown that despite the potential of Twelve-Step fellowships to reinforce problematic social pathologies, they are more effective in promoting sobriety among marginalized groups than for those who seek sobriety without participation in a self-help group.[24] Admittedly, "sobriety" and "healthy" are not the same priority, but for many across gender and race, Twelve-Step programs have offered the opportunity for sobriety from alcohol, drugs, and other forms of emotional dysfunction like codependency. As Douglass and Malcolm X both bear witness, sobriety is often a step along a path of spiritual maturation.

So, are the steps for everyone?

The Twelve Steps have a definite history. White reminds that "the most significant alcohol problem for black people in America—in the North and the South, both slave and free—was the risk of what could happen to them when white people became intoxicated."[25] Similarly, White notes that "the history of alcohol problems among Native American tribes is not one of passive destruction, but one of active resistance. Addiction was an alien disease injected into Native cultures."[26] Eighteenth- and nineteenth-century cultural and spiritual revival movements among Native communities were often "sobriety-based." Ostensibly, white Europeans brought addiction and codependency with us to the New World shores and to Africa's West Coast. After centuries of experiencing intergenerational trauma in Europe, our dysfunction played out on the bodies and cultures of those we encountered. Addiction was one response to the inadequacy of our cultural resources for healing. As we destroyed the cultural resources of other communities, so too would many within these communities inevitably descend into addiction and other related psychosocial maladies. While racist depictions of drunk and high black, brown, and red folks would come to stoke fears among twentieth- and twenty-first century white folks, in step with many people of color across the last centuries, the founders of the Twelve-Step program seem to have understood alcoholism and addiction to be a *white* problem. Many of these early advocates of the program, like Bill W., the founder of AA and original author of the Twelve Steps of Alcoholics Anonymous, were coming from a particular Protestant, Christian, American, and white male perspective, for sure. A cynical read of this history of the steps could involve suggesting that the original white men who participated in AA were failed white men, and so the norms guiding "recovery" in the program came from the norms of white masculine success, more generally. Twelve-Step norms of behavior and health, perhaps, look like white masculine normativity and Protestant Capitalism. Such was the impact of white masculine culture on the development of the Twelve Steps. In a similar way to how Sigmund Freud's and Carl Jung's work are considered hopelessly antiquated by some today for the many ways that their ideas reinforce white masculine normativity, an argument could be made for the unbearable white masculinity of Twelve-Step programs. As I also have suggested of Freud, Jung, and other thinkers included in this book, it could be that the Twelve-Step program represents a white masculine wrestling with the intergenerational traumas we have experienced for centuries and centuries, and the racism and sexism found in fellowships today speak to the severity of the white masculine codependency problem. Christians go to church because they are sinners; not because they are without sin. The same logic holds true of Twelve-Step fellowships.

Just because the program emerges from within a white, heteropatriarchal Christian culture, that does not mean the program is bereft of value. It does mean that with our contemporary use of such a program, we ought to be honest about this history. Working any Twelve-Step program ought to involve active efforts to decolonize them. One example of this is happening lately through Twelve-Step programs deciding whether or not to allow for "closed" meetings based on different salient social identities. That is, ought a fellowship allow "men's only" or "black women's only" group meetings? Men's only meetings could risk reinforcing patriarchy and the exclusion of women, while *not* promoting black women's only groups could risk exposing black women to whiteness and patriarchal harm in "open" meetings. An honest historical accounting of many fellowships' relationship to oppression, thanks in part to the criticisms of Davis, Blessing, Whitaker, and others, reminds that many of them have long been *de facto* "closed" to only white men, anyway. Is it only when black and brown folks, women, and LGBTQ-identified folks are participating in these fellowships that the ethics of "closed" meetings becomes an issue?

Perhaps, it is worth recognizing the difference between a Twelve-Step *fellowship* and a Twelve-Step *program*. Valli makes this suggestion in a 2020 writing referring to them as

> two entirely separate entities. The fellowship is simply the people who attend meetings and consider themselves members. The program is the 12 steps, which are laid out in the basic text (commonly referred to as 'the Big Book') of Alcoholics Anonymous ... much of the misinformation about the program comes from the fellowship itself. There are many reasons why what is heard in meetings is so different from what the program actually teaches.[27]

Participants bring with them all of the broader trappings of culture, including the oppressive aspects of culture. The program, however, amounts to a set of spiritual principles articulated through particular "steps" that address an underlying spiritual disease. It is incumbent upon any would-be critics to discern the degree to which theological or spiritual principles are responsible for expressions of the *failure to live up to* those or similar principles. For example, churches aren't filled with angels; they're filled with sinners. In like manner, Twelve-Step fellowships consist of people who show up to meetings to gain clarity and advice on how to no longer drown under the weight of culture. Assuming that the principles they learn in these spaces are *why* they are drowning is as illogical as assuming the principles are somehow completely immune from the influence of culture.

These qualifications aside, there still seems to be an overwhelming problem of white masculine hegemony at work among many of these fellowships. In my personal experiences, ACA fellowships in the Philadelphia metropolitan area are overwhelmingly white and hosted in white neighborhoods. I have sought out alternatives, to which, I have not found any. AA and NA (Narcotics Anonymous) are both huge feeders for ACA fellowships. It could be that structural issues impact the amount of time potential black and brown participants have to commit to multiple distinct fellowships in any given week. White men, because of our privilege, may end up with the most free time and energy on our hands to reflect on our childhood trauma.

Two specific ways distinct fellowships reinforce racial and gendered disparities involve group conscience, and the unwillingness to provide critical feedback to other participants. The unwillingness to provide critical feedback is based on the desire to not trigger a shame response for any meeting participants. However, as racism and sexism and religious hegemony all shape the "shares" of individual fellowship members, a room full of mostly Christian, mostly white men will invariably do or say things that potentially alienate women, people of color, and nonreligious people. At this point, fellowships would do well to no longer organize themselves around the effort to shield participants from experiencing shame. Perhaps, instead, they might seek to equitably distribute shame when it is (inevitably) experienced. For instance, the choice could be made about who—the white man or the black woman, for a "real lived" example—would experience shame. Will ACA or the Twelve-Step fellowship prioritize the black woman's pain from the harm done by the white man's shameful racist or sexist comment or behavior? Or will the fellowship prioritize the white man's potential pain experienced when he is called out for reinforcing racist and/or sexist ideas in his share or engagement with other fellowship members? To the extent many fellowships try to be feedback-free during their meetings, they may be inadvertently reinforcing the very codependency the principles seek to overcome.

When reading some of the white and black feminist critiques of Twelve-Step programs, I cannot help but imagine that something of this dynamic has created an unwillingness or need to *not* distinguish the principles from the participants. Racism, sexism, elitism, and Judeo-Christian chauvinism within the fellowships impact the ability of each participant to make the most of the principles. The ongoing work white men must do on ourselves has gotten in the way of— yet again—the needs of others. In these ways, social critiques of Twelve-Step fellowships are necessary. However, they do not speak to the bankruptcy of the Twelve-Step model or program, but the need to double down on them through increased participation with decolonization (of them) in mind.

Furthermore, one of the most "Protestant" cultural expressions still at work within these fellowships is their reliance on lay leadership. Twelve-Step fellowships rely on very few paid or professionally trained leaders. In fact, many local fellowships empower people to sponsorship without any test of sponsorship capacity. They reinforce the faulty egalitarian notion that all people are equally capable of psychological, religious, or spiritual guidance. Fellowships follow a "priesthood of all believers" model of leadership, so to speak. This, combined with the fellowship members having no practice at providing constructive criticism to others, means these fellowships can promote situations where the fellowship's cultural trappings are taken for the fruit grown of the spiritual principles. Whether we think of the acute history of Twelve-Step fellowships or the history of American Protestantism, in both cases the *de facto* assumed racialized and gendered egalitarianism and concomitant reliance on laity make it easy for fellowship members to do harm to other members and to alienate would-be members.

Despite these legitimate critiques of the whiteness, patriarchy, and Christian normativity that infects Twelve-Step fellowships, correlation is not causation. The presence of these social maladies speaks to the ongoing need of Twelve-Step programs for white men, even if it is time for a reckoning about the efficacy of Twelve-Step fellowships for women and people of color. To wit, it will be important for anyone thinking about or making use of a Twelve-Step program to recognize the deep need for decolonizing these fellowships while maintaining awareness that Twelve-Step programs are helping white men to be more than white men, even if ironically, at times these white men fail to express themselves in meetings as anything more than white men.

***

Drawing this book to a close, I turn back to hip hop artist Jay-Z, but this time his track "Heaven," from his 2013 album *Magna Carta Holy Grail*. I put his "Heaven" in conversation with folk band The Everybodyfields and the song, "The Red Rose," from their 2004 album *Halfway There: Electricity & the South*. "Heaven" trades in black esoteric themes and imagines a future present world where black capacity overcomes the legacy of white male rule over the earth. "The Red Rose" is a lonesome Americana lament for the absence of an otherworldly God in the face of childhood neglect due to alcohol, and a somber recognition of the arrested emotional development that occurs within many of us when we first find God in the form of our parent. Effectively, the two songs represent the two Gods I grew up with, and mark out the ontological boundaries of many white men's relationships to God, historically.

Jay-Z's "Heaven" is a triumphal, hubristic celebration of black divinity: For students of religion and hip hop, "Heaven" exemplifies the wisdom of black esoteric traditions and the application of such wisdom in real time. Like much of Jay-Z's catalog, it is a *discerning* track. While I recognize that this song is not speaking to my experiences as a white man, it offers psychological and spiritual value to me insofar as it provides a kind of intersubjective experience with Jay-Z and those like him. Like the best of hip hop and popular culture, generally, the track offers an opportunity to express and experience part of the mutuality of self discussed by Watts. It does so, in part, through Jay-Z's religious references to black divinity. As with the track starting and inspiring this book, "We Made It: Remix" by Jay-Z and Jay Electronica, "Heaven" teaches listeners about the importance of having Knowledge of Self. "Arm, leg, leg, arm, head—this is God-body … Have mercy on this Judas … Y'all religion create division, like my Maybach partition … I confess, God in the flesh, live around the serpents, turn arenas into churches … these are not sixteens, these are verses from the Bible."[28] The value of such references to me as listener, as fan, and as subject to black divinity is that in Jay-Z rapping about his own orientation toward self—that is, *his* Knowledge of Self—he enables clarity in his listeners about our Knowledge of Self (regardless of our actual identities). In his talk of heaven, I gain clarity and humility regarding my Knowledge of Self, and my reliance on other selves for my Knowledge of Self.

Jay-Z's celebration of self as divine is part of the "hide-and-seek" game described by Watts. The language of "God"—as expressed in black esoteric traditions influencing Jay-Z's lyrics—enables for black men a rhetorical and symbolic means of taking their rightful recognition within this "game." Hip hop culture, specifically, and black cultural expression, generally, have offered opportunities to promote equity and intersubjective exchange cross-racially in ways white men have rejected and prevented for centuries. As a white man, I am more than the sum total of my consumption of black cultural products or black thought, while I am never less than this consumption. Yet, turning to black cultural resources is not enough to address the root causes of the white masculine desire to essentially cheat while playing the game of life. Much of this book developed as I mined "white" cultural resources for understanding and responding to our status as "devils." Would we have our own cultural resources for cultivating Knowledge of Self? Coming to understand that the moniker "devil" arises from a deeper codependent reliance on black Gods, I sought to include "white" voices such as Sigmund Freud, Jean-Paul Sartre, Carl Jung, and Alan Watts. Were I to rely exclusively on Jay-Z, black esoteric traditions, or women, I would simply be reinforcing my codependency. It is not Jay-Z's or hip hop's or black people's responsibility to teach white men about ourselves, even if the stories they will tell powerfully impact us as white men.

As I appreciate the art of someone like Jay-Z and revere many of the teachings of the Nation of Islam and the Nation of Gods and Earths, I also find Knowledge of Self in the music of Americana and folk artists like the Avett Brothers, Bob Dylan, John Prine, and so many others. One of my favorite folk acts over the last fifteen years has been the now-broken-up Knoxville, Tennessee duo, The Everybodyfields. Composed of singer-songwriters Sam Quinn and Jill Andrews (as well as other backing musicians), The Everybodyfields created a catalogue of lonesome Appalachian-inflected folk songs that vibrate at the same frequency as my soul. Their catalog gives voice to the pain of white dysfunction and the sorrow of trying to love others without ever really loving ourselves. Their track "The Red Rose" is even more relevant to my own white family history as it speaks to the tragedy of abandonment and neglect and self-hatred plaguing families like mine where alcoholism and religion comingle to all-but-ensure that white children are abandoned by our parents and our Gods, alike. In my case, a drunk father who left me twice—once for me to end up abused in church and the second, final time when he drank himself to death. God, a cosmic projection of my drunk father, was never there to save me from the sexual abuse and did not intervene to keep my real father from either drinking too much or dying too soon. In the place of this failed white God, I found Gods on the mic. In the tension between my love and reverence for black Gods whose outlook on life is complicated yet somehow affirming of joy and pleasure—seen through the prism of hip hop culture—and my anger toward a drunken, missing white God, I found Knowledge of Self.

"The Red Rose" expresses something of a theological reckoning of the sort I have engaged in my entire life. In effect, the white conflation of fatherhood with divinity, and those circumstances combining with alcoholism, addiction, and other codependency-related issues, leads many white men into patriarchal sexism, anti-black racism, homophobia, and alcoholic denial, and it also often leads white women into codependent obsession over their missing fathers, lovers, and God. Sung by Andrews, "The Red Rose" tells the story about "a bar in Alabama called the Red Rose," where she goes "when she's thirsty," having spent the last ten years in a relationship with a man who recently left her.[29] Subsequent verses find Andrews singing about Bibles falling from the skies and not thinking that God has any time for her. The chorus concludes that,

> I think God is a moonshiner/His skin is gold from the whiskey in his blood/I think in heaven there is a barroom/a place where men go to forget about their wives.[30]

In so much of my life I have reacted (rather than acted) in response to the tragic, sorrowful circumstances of my white father's failures by turning to black culture for escape and to be rescued, a kind of racialized atheism. My atheism had been an effort to escape from the white God who failed me, my father. Atheism was my alcohol, just as alcohol in "The Red Rose" is a means of denying and numbing the pain of abandonment. Atheism wasn't a panacea for the emotional pain and suffering that had been caused from intergenerational trauma resulting from the failures of white masculinity and the failures of alcohol to respond to a codependency problem that played out culturally and interpersonally within my family of origin and in my broader white community. Neither could I respond to generational and childhood white trauma by becoming a race-traitor or an "exceptional devil."[31] Escaping into the syncopated stylings of black Gods had been a clandestine attempt to have others heal my white wounds. In some respects, keeping company with black Gods makes sense; we have all been wounded by white men and missing mystery Gods. In other respects, expecting other victims to heal my trauma simply reinforced their trauma and turned me into a perpetrator. Through the Twelve-Steps, I have come to recognize that an overwhelming spiritual deficit was and is at work among white men that gets packaged as any number of issues, even including atheism. Contrary to what we might popularly hear from churchgoers, atheism is not an expression, necessarily, of a spiritual deficit or disease. But in my case, it was a symptom of that disease. In the failures of my father, I found failure and fault in the very idea of God. This unresolved grief inhibited my capacity to surrender to the limits set for me by the universe. My protest atheism prevented me from obtaining Knowledge of Self. That lack of Knowledge of Self led to most of the harm I have done to other people.

Something about the failure of our fathers and their fathers before them distorts the thinking and behavior of many white men. In this book, I have characterized this distorted thinking and acting as the spiritual disease of codependency. Growing up with an underdeveloped ego, we learn to blame others through racism, sexism, and homophobia, repress our feelings with drugs, alcohol, and other forms of addiction, or we grow up hating our fathers and seeking to escape from white masculinity through overidentification with black and brown culture that often turns into a savior complex (not to mention appropriation and exploitation of cultural resources not our birthright). When our salvific efforts go unrealized or unappreciated, we blame our mothers, wives, partners, girlfriends, sisters, and daughters. At a certain point, for me and many white men, loving black folks must come to mean letting go of our codependent reliance on them and learning to love ourselves. In letting go of my claim to black Gods, I make possible release of my father from the burden of his failures. His spirit can rest. Andrews's sorrowful sound brings up the question of forgiveness within the context of perpetrating harm toward self and others. Failure to forgive breeds guilt and shame, which erodes the health of the self. Many of us as white men are in desperate need of forgiving our fathers and their fathers, and our mothers who loved them more than they seemed to love us, and their mothers before them. They were, like most of us, really doing the best they could. Forgiveness enables the possibility for doing better, still. "The Red Rose" offers the possibility for forgiveness as we process who we've been as white men (and women) and imagine who we will be one day. To the black Gods, I give thanks and praise. To my father, I offer forgiveness.

Jay-Z's "Heaven" is an expression of agency. "Heaven," as described in "The Red Rose," is a "place where the men go to forget about their wives."[32] To the extent white men have so often in our history recognized other people as hell, the white man's heaven has been isolation from those we unjustly resent for our own failure to know ourselves. What will heaven and hell look like, for us, when we begin to prioritize intersubjective communication with others? Will we be able to discern heaven and hell upon our taking responsibility for our misguided effort to hide or deny or stave off the grief and otherwise emotional pain associated with our alienation from the rest of the human family? Will heaven be a place where we blame other people for our problems? Where we blame mothers and lovers and daughters, for the emotional dysregulation we face every day? If we choose to lean into our discomfort with intersubjective exchange, will we finally experience the heaven Jay-Z describes and embodies? Will we meet Jay-Z's heaven as an opportunity for an intersubjective exchange that might give life to new expressions of ourselves? This book has not sought to answer these questions so much as to offer an opportunity for white men to begin asking them. None of us can go back and right the wrongs of the past—not in terms of our interpersonal relationships nor in broader terms of responding adequately to all the trauma and pain resulting from patriarchy or white supremacy. Or, to the sordid, vicious monotheism that all these other "isms" are so deeply shaped by in our white western history. But to the extent we begin listening closely to the knowledge born of black Gods, we might make possible new opportunities for escaping the hell we've so long endured with others.

QUESTIONS FOR DISCUSSION

1. Should white men take responsibility for their characterization as devils? If so, why and what might that responsibility look like? If not, why not?

2. As discussed in Chapter 4, Michael Muhammad Knight develops the idea of an "exceptional devil" to refer to white people who seek to escape from their characterization as devils. When and how have you or someone you know acted like an "exceptional devil"?

3. Malcolm X called on well-intentioned white folks to do justice work in their own communities. What does this work look like? How does it involve Black and Brown people?

4. To what extent do our intentions matter when we consider the harm we cause others?

5. According to *White Devils, Black Gods*, alcoholism/substance abuse and structural issues (like racism and sexism) are related through the concept of religious codependency? Name several situations in your life or from someone you know where religious codependency was at work?

6. What is an Adult Child, and how does the concept help to understand white men historically and today?

7. How did race, gender, and religion shape your family circumstances as children? How do your childhood experiences impact your current beliefs and practices about race, gender, sexuality, and religion? How might those experiences continue to shape your character traits today? In what ways are you raising your children differently than your parents raised you? And, in what ways are you raising your children as you were raised by your parents?

8. What ideas are missing from *White Devils, Black Gods*? Where can those ideas be found? If they are not yet widely available, what can you do to make these ideas available to others?

NOTES

Introduction

1. The RZA, *The Tao of Wu*, Reprint edition (New York: Riverhead Books, 2010), 191.
2. Ras Kass, "Nature of the Threat," in *Soul on Ice* (Los Angeles, CA: Priority Records, 1996). The lyrics can be heard as either "their God" or "that God." In either case, the meaning, subject, and focus of the statement remain the same.
3. Thomas Keating, *Intimacy with God: An Introduction to Centering Prayer*, Third edition (New York, NY: Crossroad, 2009), 175.
4. Robin Wall Kimmerer, *Braiding Sweetgrass: Indigenous Wisdom, Scientific Knowledge, and the Teaching of Plants* (Minneapolis, MN: Milkweed editions, 2013), 305.
5. W.E.B. DuBois, *The Souls of Black Folk* (New York, NY: Dover Publications, 1903, 1994).
6. Ibid., 8.
7. W.E.B. DuBois, "The Souls of White Folk," in *Darkwater: Voices from within the Veil* (New York, NY: Cosimo, Inc., 2007), 19.
8. Ibid.
9. Kimmerer, 305.
10. Ibid., 304–5.
11. Ibid., 306.
12. Ibid.
13. Ibid., 304–5.
14. Judith Weisenfeld, *New World A-Coming: Black Religion and Racial Identity during the Great Migration* (New York: NYU Press, 2017).
15. See, for instance, Southern Poverty Law Center, "Radical Religion in Prison," accessed January 20, 2022, https://www.splcenter.org/fighting-hate/intelligence-report/2003/radical-religion-prison; and, Southern Poverty Law Center, "Nation of Islam," accessed January 20, 2022, https://www.splcenter.org/fighting-hate/extremist-files/group/nation-islam.
16. L. Timmen and M.D. Cermak, "Diagnostic Criteria for Codependency," *Journal of Psychoactive Drugs* 18, no. 1 (January 1, 1986): 15–20, https://doi.org/10.1080/02791072.1986.10524475, 16–17.
17. Dale S. Ryan and Jeff VanVonderen, "When Religion Goes Bad: Part 3—Religious Codependency," The National Association for Christian Recovery, February 16, 2013, https://www.nacr.org/center-for-spirituality-and-recovery/when-religion-goes-bad-part-3-religious-codependency.
18. This also implies that white people are likely not the only predominately monotheistic cultural group influenced by religious codependency, but white men remain the group I focus on in this text.

19 Jan Assmann, *Moses the Egyptian: The Memory of Egypt in Western Monotheism*, New edition (Cambridge, MA: Harvard University Press, 1998).
20 Peter Sloterdijk, *In the Shadow of Mount Sinai*, First edition (Cambridge, UK; Malden, MA: Polity, 2015), 468.
21 Michael Muhammad Knight, *Why I Am a Five Percenter*, Illustrated edition (New York: TarcherPerigee, 2011).
22 Master W. D. Fard Muhammad, *The Supreme Wisdom Lessons by Master Fard Muhammad to His Servant: The Most Honorable Elijah Muhammad for the Lost-Found Nation of Islam in North America*, ed. Suzanne Brawtley (Brawtley Press, 2014).
23 John L. Jackson Jr., *Harlemworld: Doing Race and Class in Contemporary Black America* (Chicago: The University of Chicago Press, 2003).
24 Ibid., 5.
25 Ibid., 6.
26 Ibid.
27 Resmaa Menakem, *My Grandmother's Hands: Racialized Trauma and the Pathway to Mending Our Hearts and Bodies*, Illustrated edition (Las Vegas, NV: Central Recovery Press, 2017), 7.
28 Ibid.
29 Ibid., 9.
30 Ibid.
31 Ibid., 10
32 Ibid.
33 Ibid., 11.
34 Ibid., 19.
35 Ibid., 211.
36 Menakem, 20.
37 Ibid.
38 Ibid.
39 Ibid.

Chapter 1

1 Jay-Z & Jay Electronica, "We Made It: Remix," accessed July 20, 2021, https://www.youtube.com/watch?v=iaLIzQJLBz0.
2 Mark Elibert, "A Timeline of JAY-Z and Drake's Competitive Relationship," *Billboard*, accessed February 5, 2019, https://www.billboard.com/articles/columns/hip-hop/8470558/jay-z-drake-relationship-timeline.
3 Paul Tillich, *The Courage to Be* (New Haven, CT: Yale University Press, 2000); see, also, Paul Tillich, *Theology of Culture*, ed. Robert C. Kimball (Oxford, UK: Oxford University Press), 1964.
4 Biko Gray, "The Traumatic Mysticism of Othered Others: Blackness, Islam, and Esotericism in the Five Percenters," *Correspondences* 7, no. 1 (2019): 201–37, 213.
5 Elijah Muhammad, *Message to the Blackman in America* (Litchfield Park, AZ: Secretarius Memps Publications, 2006), 16–17.
6 Malcolm X, *The Autobiography of Malcolm X: As Told to Alex Haley* (New York, NY: Ballantine Books, 1987), 162.

Chapter 2

1. "Catholic Church Child Sexual Abuse Scandal," *BBC News*, February 26, 2019, sec. World, https://www.bbc.com/news/world-44209971.
2. "20 Years, 700 Victims: Southern Baptist Sexual Abuse Spreads as Leaders Resist Reforms," *Houston Chronicle*, February 10, 2019, https://www.houstonchronicle.com/news/investigations/article/Southern-Baptist-sexual-abuse-spreads-as-leaders-13588038.php.
3. Delores Williams, in Rosemary Skinner Keller and Rosemary Radford Ruether, eds., *In Our Own Voices: Four Centuries of American Women's Religious Writing* (Louisville, KY: Westminster John Knox Press, 2000), 199.
4. Ibid.
5. Dietrich Bonhoeffer, *The Cost of Discipleship* (New York, NY: Simon and Schuster, 1959).
6. Anthony B. Pinn, *Why Lord?: Suffering and Evil in Black Theology* (London and New York: Continuum International Publishing Group, 1999).
7. Courdea – HISTORY, accessed March 7, 2019, https://www.menergy.org/about-us/history-2/.

Chapter 3

1. John Calvin, "Calvin's Commentaries, Vol. 3: Harmony of the Law, Part I: Exodus 3," accessed June 10, 2021, https://www.sacred-texts.com/chr/calvin/cc03/cc03006.htm.
2. Lord Jamar, "Supreme Mathematics (Born Mix)," in *The 5% Album* (New York: BabyGrande/Koch, 2006).
3. James H. Cone, *A Black Theology of Liberation*, 20th edition (Maryknoll, NY: Orbis Books, 1990), 63.
4. Ludwig Feuerbach, *The Essence of Christianity* (Buffalo, NY: Prometheus Books, 1989).
5. Jan Assmann, *Moses the Egyptian: The Memory of Egypt in Western Monotheism*, New edition (Cambridge, MA: Harvard University Press, 1998), 1.
6. Ibid.
7. Ibid.
8. Ibid., 3.
9. Ibid.
10. Ibid., 209.
11. Charles H. Long, *Significations: Signs, Symbols, and Images in the Interpretation of Religion*, 2nd edition (Aurora, CO: The Davies Group Publishers, 1999), 117.
12. Peter Sloterdijk, *In the Shadow of Mount Sinai*, 1st edition (Cambridge, UK; Malden, MA: Polity, 2015), 6.
13. Ibid., 38–9.
14. Long, 117, 208.
15. Cone, 58.
16. Long, 207.
17. Ibid., 207–8.

Chapter 4

1. Daniel Defoe, *The Political History of the Devil, as Well Ancient as Modern: In Two Parts; Part I. Containing a State of the Devil's Circumstances, and the Various Turns of His Affairs …; Part II. Containing His More Private Conduct, Down to the*

Present Times ... (London: Printed for T. Warner, 1726), http://archive.org/details/politicalhistory1726defo.
2   Ibid., 19.
3   Ibid., 18–19.
4   William Mason, *A Spiritual Treasury for the Children of God: Consisting of a Meditation for Each Morning in the Year, Upon Select Texts of Scripture: Humbly Intended to Establish the Faith, Promote the Comfort, and Influence the Practice of the Followers of the Lamb* (New York: Deare and Andrews, 1803), 95.
5   Hugh Murray, "Clapperton's Second Journey," in *The African Continent: A Narrative of Discovery and Adventure* (London: T. Nelson & Sons, 1853), 204.
6   Burt Garfield Loescher, *The History of Rogers' Rangers*, Volume 1, (San Mateo, CA: Burt Garfield Loescher, 1946), 311.
7   Supreme Understanding and C'BS Alife Allah, *The Science of Self: Man, God, and the Mathematical Language of Nature*, 3rd edition (Atlanta, GA: Supreme Design, LLC, 2012), 34.
8   "The Pathway of 'True Light,'" in Arthur Wilcockson, ed., Zion's Witness: Published Monthly, Exclusively for the Sect Which Is Everywhere Spoken Against – Acts. XXVIII. 22. (1866), 199.
9   Ibid.
10 James Greenwood, *Silas the Conjurer: His Travels and Perils* (Whitefish, MT: Kessinger Publishing, LLC, 2010), 229.
11 JNO. G. Williams, in D. H. Jacques, ed., *The Rural Carolinian, 1870, Vol. 1: An Illustrated Magazine, of Agriculture, Horticulture and the Arts* (London: Forgotten Books, 2017), 768.
12 *The Trained Nurse and Hospital Review* (Lakeside Publishing Company, 1900), 336.
13 *The Churchman*, Volume 85, Jan–June, (Churchman Company, 1902), 29.
14 Joseph Conrad, *The Nigger of the Narcissus: A Tale of the Forecastle* (Doubleday, Page, 1897), 191.
15 Edgar Rice Burroughs, *The Beasts of Tarzan* (New York, NY: Grosset & Dunlap, 1916), 169.
16 Edgar Rice Burroughs, *Jungle Tales of Tarzan* (New York, NY: Grosset & Dunlap, 1919), 168.
17 One such story is about a mission worker in the San Francisco Bay area named Donaldina Cameron. She is featured in "They Call Her 'The White Devil,'" in *American Magazine*, Volume 79, 1915, 60–1.
18 "120 Lessons – 1–20, 1–10, 1–14, 1–40, 1–36 (20+10+14+40+36=120)," accessed May 21, 2021, http://www.afrostyly.com/english/afro/diverse/120_lessons.htm.
19 Ibid.
20 Ibid.
21 Ibid.
22 Ibid.
23 Ibid.
24 Elijah Muhammad, *Message to the Blackman in America* (place of publication not identified: Secretarius Memps Publications, 2006), Chapter 54.
25 Ibid.
26 Elijah Muhammad, Chapter 55.
27 Ibid.
28 Ibid.
29 Ibid.
30 Ibid.
31 Michael Muhammad Knight, *Why I Am a Five Percenter*, Illustrated edition (New York: TarcherPerigee, 2011), 82.

32 Ibid., 91.
33 Ibid., 92.
34 Ibid., 92–3.
35 Malcolm X, quoted in Knight, 93.
36 Robyn Wiegman, "Whiteness Studies and the Paradox of Particularity," Boundary 2 26:3, accessed May 21, 2021, http://xroads.virginia.edu/~DRBR2/wiegman.html, 120.
37 Knight, 48.
38 Ibid., 95.

Chapter 5

1 Plato, *The Republic*, 360 BCE, 515c.
2 Elijah Muhammad, *Message to the Blackman in America* (Litchfield Park, AZ: Place of publication not identified: Secretarius Memps Publications, 2006), 116.
3 Nell Irvin Painter, *The History of White People*, Reprint edition (New York: W. W. Norton & Company, 2011).
4 Muhammad, 116–7.
5 Ibid., 117.
6 Big Head Scientist, "Big Head Scientist," accessed February 9, 2019, http://bigheadscientist.tumblr.com/post/131182353425/the-legend-of-general-monk-monk-it-took-yaqub-600.
7 Muhammad, 119–20.
8 Ibid.
9 Holy Quran, Sūrah Eighteen, line 22.
10 Muhammad, 104.
11 Plato.

Chapter 6

1 James Baldwin, "James Baldwin's 'Letter from a Region in My Mind,'" *The New Yorker*, November 10, 1962, accessed July 1, 2021, https://www.newyorker.com/magazine/1962/11/17/letter-from-a-region-in-my-mind.
2 Ibid.
3 Paul Ricoeur, *The Symbolism of Evil* (New York: Harper and Row Publishers, 1967), 19.
4 Ibid., 5.
5 Ibid., 8.
6 Ibid., 7.
7 Ibid., 145.
8 Ibid., 100.
9 Ibid., 101.
10 Ibid., 102.
11 Ibid., v.
12 Jean-Paul Sartre, *The Devil and the Good Lord, and Two Other Plays* (New York: Vintage Books/Random House, 1960), 2.
13 Ibid., 16.
14 Ibid., 10.
15 Ibid., 12.
16 Ibid., 60.

17 Ibid., 140.
18 Ibid., 141.
19 Ibid., 65.
20 Ibid., 137.
21 Ibid., 133.
22 Ibid., 138–9.

Chapter 7

1 FBI Documents include spellings of both "Jowars" and "Jowers."
2 Memorandum "Puddin" 10/11/65. FBI Field Office File 100-150520.
3 Ibid.
4 Barry Gottehrer, *The Mayor's Man*, First edition (Garden City, NY: Doubleday, 1975), 99.
5 File dated 1/17/66. FBI Field Office File 100-150520.
6 Memorandum "Changed: Clarence Smith Jowars, aka Clarence Edward Smith" 10/22/65. FBI Field Office File 100-150520.
7 Ibid.
8 Ibid.
9 File dated January 17, 1966. FBI Field Office File 100-150520.
10 Ibid.
11 File dated 11-12-65. FBI Field Office File 100-150520.
12 Michael Muhammad Knight, *Why I Am a Five Percenter*, Illustrated edition (New York: TarcherPerigee, 2011), 8.
13 FBI Field Office File 100-150520.
14 Gottehrer, 92.
15 Ibid., 99–100.
16 Ibid., 104.
17 Ibid., 119–20.
18 For more information on the FBI interest in Black and Africana religious traditions, see Sylvester A. Johnson and Steven Weitzman, eds., *The FBI and Religion: Faith and National Security before and after 9/11*, First edition (Oakland, CA: University of California Press, 2017).
19 Gottehrer, 220–1.
20 Christopher M. Driscoll, *White Lies: Race and Uncertainty in the Twilight of American Religion* (London, UK: Routledge, 2016).
21 Anna Freud and The Institute of Psychoanalysis, *The Ego and the Mechanisms of Defence* (London: Routledge, 1992), 4–5.
22 Ibid., 44.
23 Ibid., 34.
24 Ibid.
25 Ibid., 57.
26 Ibid., 109.
27 Ibid., 62–3.
28 Ibid., 175–6.
29 Sigmund Freud, *The Future of an Illusion* (Peterborough, CA: Broadview Press, 2012).
30 Sigmund Freud, *Moses and Monotheism*, First edition (United States: Vintage, 1955).
31 Freud, *The Future of an Illusion*, 92.
32 Deuteronomy 28: 2–6. Revised Standard Version.
33 Deuteronomy 28: 10.
34 Deuteronomy 28: 20.

35 Deuteronomy 28: 25–6.
36 Deuteronomy 28: 27–9.
37 Deuteronomy 28: 30–1.
38 Deuteronomy 28: 32.

Chapter 8

1. Elaine Pagels, *The Origin of Satan: How Christians Demonized Jews, Pagans, and Heretics*, Reprint edition (New York, NY: Vintage, 1996), 39.
2. Ibid., 39.
3. Ibid.
4. Ibid.
5. Ibid., 47.
6. "Bible Gateway Passage: Exodus 3—New International Version," *Bible Gateway*, accessed May 24, 2021, https://www.biblegateway.com/passage/?search=Exodus%203&version=NIV.
7. Pagels, 45.
8. Ibid., 47.
9. Ibid.
10. Ibid., 48.
11. Ibid., 49.
12. Ibid.
13. Ibid.
14. Ibid., 88.
15. "Nation of Islam," Southern Poverty Law Center, accessed May 24, 2021, https://www.splcenter.org/fighting-hate/extremist-files/group/nation-islam.
16. Pagels, xviii.
17. Ibid., xvii.
18. Adult Children of Alcoholics World Service Organization, *Twelve Steps of Adult Children Steps Workbook* (Torrance, CA: Adult Children of Alcoholics W, 2007), 6.
19. Robin DiAngelo, "White Fragility," *The International Journal of Critical Pedagogy* 3, no. 3 (May 16, 2011), http://libjournal.uncg.edu/ijcp/article/view/249.
20. Adult Children of Alcoholics, 9.
21. James Perkinson, *White Theology: Outing Supremacy in Modernity*, First edition (New York: Palgrave Macmillan, 2004).
22. L. Timmen Cermak, "Diagnostic Criteria for Codependency," *Journal of Psychoactive Drugs* 18, no. 1 (January 1, 1986): 15–20, https://doi.org/10.1080/02791072.1986.10524475.
23. Adult Children of Alcoholics, 5.
24. Cermak, 16.
25. Ibid., 16–17.
26. Ibid., 16.
27. American Psychiatric Association, and DSM-5 Task Force, *Diagnostic and Statistical Manual of Mental Disorders: DSM-5* (Arlington, VA: American Psychiatric Association, 2013), xxxiii.
28. Cermak, 15.
29. Ibid., 16.
30. W. E. B. DuBois, "The Souls of White Folk," in *Darkwater: Voices from within the Veil* (New York, NY: Cosimo, Inc., 2007).
31. Cermak, 16–17.

32 Ibid.
33 Ibid.
34 Christopher M. Driscoll, *White Lies: Race and Uncertainty in the Twilight of American Religion* (London: Routledge, 2016).
35 Marx Karl and Richard A. Davis, *Marx: Early Political Writings*, ed. Joseph J. O'Malley, Annotated edition (Cambridge; New York: Cambridge University Press, 1994), 243–4.
36 Ibid.
37 Ludwig Feuerbach, *The Essence of Christianity* (Buffalo, NY: Prometheus Books, 1989).

Chapter 9

1 Carl Jung, *Visions: Notes of the Seminar Given in 1930–1934*. Available via YouTube Academy of ideas, *Carl Jung, the Shadow, and the Dangers of Psychological Projection*, 2018, accessed May 20, 2021, https://www.youtube.com/watch?v=nI-Ko-d29X4.
2 Eduardo Bonilla-Silva, *Racism without Racists: Color-Blind Racism and the Persistence of Racial Inequality in America*, Third edition (Lanham: Rowman & Littlefield Publishers, 2009).
3 Paul C. Taylor, *Race: A Philosophical Introduction* (Hoboken, NJ: John Wiley & Sons, 2013).
4 Michael Kimmel, *Angry White Men: American Masculinity at the End of an Era* (New York, NY: PublicAffairs, 2017), xiv.
5 C. G. Jung, *The Undiscovered Self: With Symbols and the Interpretation of Dreams* (Princeton, NJ: Princeton University Press, 2012), 4–5.
6 Ibid., 25.
7 Michael Muhammad Knight, *Why I Am a Five Percenter*, Illustrated edition (New York: TarcherPerigee, 2011).
8 Jung, 36.
9 Ibid., 45.
10 C. G. Jung, *The Essential Jung*, ed. Anthony Storr (Princeton, NJ: Princeton University Press, 1999), 82.
11 Jung, *The Undiscovered Self*, 45.
12 Ibid.
13 Ibid., 3.
14 Ibid., 52.
15 Ibid., 46.
16 Ibid., 53.
17 Ibid.
18 Ibid., 54.
19 Ibid., 52.
20 Ibid., 53.
21 "Meadows, Tlaib Cool Down after Fiery Exchange over Racism at Cohen Hearing," *NPR.org*, accessed March 1, 2019, https://www.npr.org/2019/02/28/699009651/meadows-tlaib-cool-down-after-fiery-exchange-over-racism-at-cohen-hearing.
22 Robin DiAngelo, "White Fragility," *International Journal of Critical Pedagogy* 3, no. 3 (2011): 54–70, 54.
23 Sylvester A. Johnson and Steven Weitzman, eds., *The FBI and Religion: Faith and National Security before and after 9/11* (Berkeley, CA: University of California Press, 2017).

24 Andrew Reid Fuller, *Psychology and Religion: Eight Points of View* (Lanham, MD: Rowman & Littlefield, 1994), 88.
25 Ibid., 89.
26 Jung, *The Essential Jung*, 347.

Chapter 10

1 *The Pied Piper of Hamelin, and Related Legends from Other Towns*, trans and ed., D. L. Ashliman, 1999-2020, accessed May 28, 2021, http://www.pitt.edu/~dash/hameln.html#sinclair.
2 Darlene Lancer, *Conquering Shame and Codependency: 8 Steps to Freeing the True You* (Center City, MN: Hazelden Publishing, 2014), 1-2.
3 Adult Children of Alcoholics World Service Organization, *Twelve Steps of Adult Children Steps Workbook* (Torrance, CA: Adult Children of Alcoholics World Service Organization, 2007), 5.
4 Ibid.
5 Adult Children of Alcoholics World Service Organization, *Adult Children: Alcoholic / Dysfunctional Families*, First edition (Torrance, CA: Adult Children of Alcoholics World Service Organization, 2006), x–xi.
6 *Twelve Steps of Adult Children Steps Workbook*, 6-7.
7 Ibid.
8 Ibid.
9 Jean-Paul Sartre, *No Exit and Three Other Plays* (New York, NY: Vintage, 1989).
10 *Twelve Steps of Adult Children Steps Workbook*, 62.
11 Alice Walker, "Uncle Remus, No Friend of Mine," *The Georgia Review* 66, no. 3 (2012): 635-7.
12 Ibid., 636-7.
13 Ibid., 637.
14 Lancer, xiv.
15 Lancer, 3.
16 Lord Jamar, "Supreme Mathematics (Born Mix)," *The 5% Album* (BabyGrande/Koch, 2006).
17 Michael Muhammad Knight, *Why I Am a Five Percenter*, Illustrated edition (New York: TarcherPerigee, 2011), 125.
18 Ibid.
19 Ibid., 140.
20 Ibid., 146.
21 Ibid.

Chapter 11

1 Peter Sloterdijk, *Rage and Time: A Psychopolitical Investigation*, trans. Mario Wenning, Reprint edition (New York: Columbia University Press, 2012), 1.
2 Homer, *The Iliad*, trans. Robert Fagles (London: Penguin Books, 1990), page 77, line 9.
3 Carol Anderson, *White Rage*, Reprint edition (New York: Bloomsbury Adult, 2017), 3-4.
4 Michael Kimmell, *Angry White Men: American Masculinity at the End of an Era* (New York: PublicAffairs, 2017), 133-4.
5 Ibid., 9.

6   See, for instance, Tony Merriman and Vicky Cameron, "Risk-Taking: Behind the Warrior Gene Story," *The New Zealand Medical Journal* 120.1250 (February 1, 2007): 59–62.
7   Michael Bradley, *The Iceman Inheritance: Prehistoric Sources of Western Man's Racism, Sexism and Aggression*, Reprint edition (New York, NY: Kayode Publications, 1991), 61.
8   Ibid., 174.
9   Robert Kegan, *The Evolving Self: Problem and Process in Human Development*, Reprint edition (Cambridge; London: Harvard University Press, 1982).
10 Ibid., 7–8.

Chapter 12

1   Robin DiAngelo, *White Fragility: Why It's so Hard for White People to Talk about Racism*, Reprint edition (Boston: Beacon Press, 2018), 118.
2   Ibid., 119.
3   Ibid.
4   Ibid., 137–8.
5   Adult Children of Alcoholics/Dysfunctional Families World Service Organization, *Newcomer Pamphlet* (Lakewood, CA: Adult Children of Alcoholics/Dysfunctional Families World Service Organization, 2014), 8.
6   Ibid., 9.
7   Alan Watts, *Alan Watts—In the Academy: Essays and Lectures*, ed. Peter J. Columbus and Donadrian L. Rice, SUNY Series in Transpersonal and Humanistic Psychology (Albany, NY: SUNY Press, 2017), 248.
8   Ibid.
9   Adult Children of Alcoholics World Service Organization, *Twelve Steps of Adult Children Steps Workbook* (Torrance, CA: Adult Children of Alcoholics World Service Organization, 2007), 102.
10 Christopher M. Driscoll, "MRBlog: On the Journey to White Shame," December 8, 2014, accessed July 15, 2021. https://marginalia.lareviewofbooks.org/mrblog-journey-white-shame-christopher-driscoll/.
11 Lillian Smith, *Killers of the Dream* (New York: W. W. Norton & Company, 1994).
12 *Twelve Steps of Adult Children Steps Workbook,* 103.
13 Ibid.
14 Ibid.
15 Kristina DuRocher, *Raising Racists: The Socialization of White Children in the Jim Crow South* (Lexington, KY: University Press of Kentucky, 2011).

Chapter 13

1   Cristina Combs, "Part I: Recovery from White Conditioning: Building Anti-Racist Practice and Community," *Center for Practice Transformation* (blog), accessed June 4, 2021, https://practicetransformation.umn.edu/webinars/part-i-recovery-from-white-conditioning-building-anti-racist-practice-and-community/.
2   Ibid., 26.
3   "Steps," *Adult Children of Alcoholics & Dysfunctional Families* (blog), accessed July 27, 2021, https://adultchildren.org/literature/steps/.
4   Adult Children of Alcoholics World Service Organization, *Twelve Steps of Adult Children Steps Workbook* (Torrance, CA: Adult Children of Alcoholics World Service Organization, 2007), 47.

5   Here, I refer to Tony A's augmented Step Four rather than the formal ACA Step Four. For more information on Tony A's Steps, see John Theede, *Tony A Talks New Steps for ACA*, 2017, accessed June 1, 2021, https://www.youtube.com/watch?v=LnwoilL0q9E.
6   Ibid., 73–4.
7   Stacey M. Floyd-Thomas, *Mining the Motherlode: Methods in Womanist Ethics* (Cleveland, OH: Pilgrim Press, 2006), 100–3.
8   *Twelve Steps of Adult Children Steps Workbook*, 107.
9   Ibid., 7.
10 Ibid., 107.
11 Tony A's version of this step focuses attention on childhood abandonment. See, Theede.
12 *Twelve Steps of Adult Children Steps Workbook*, 110.
13 Ibid., 119.
14 Ibid., 126.
15 Ibid., 128.
16 Ibid., 126.
17 Jean-Paul Sartre, *The Devil and the Good Lord, and Two Other Plays* (New York: Vintage Books/Random House, 1960), 46.
18 Gay Hendricks and Kathlyn Hendricks, *Conscious Loving: The Journey to Co-Commitment*, Reprint edition (New York: Bantam, 1992), 112–13.
19 Ibid.
20 See, Theede.
21 Tara Brach, *Radical Acceptance: Embracing Your Life with the Heart of a Buddha*, Reprint edition (New York; Toronto: Bantam, 2004), 50–1.

Conclusion

1   Veronica Valli, "The Misinformation about Alcoholics Anonymous and Sobriety by Veronica Valli—Veronica Valli," January 12, 2020, https://www.veronicavalli.com/blog/2020/1/12/the-misinformation-about-alcoholics-anonymous-and-sobriety-1.
2   Ibid.
3   Alan Watts, *The Book: On the Taboo against Knowing Who You Are*, Reissue edition (New York: Vintage Books, 1989), 109–10.
4   Ibid., 110.
5   Ibid., 132–3.
6   Ibid., 133–4.
7   Ibid., 19.
8   Ibid.
9   Ibid., 21.
10 Fred R. Shapiro, "Who Wrote the Serenity Prayer?," *The Chronicle of Higher Education*, April 28, 2014, https://www.chronicle.com/article/who-wrote-the-serenity-prayer/.
11 Dawn Marie D. McIntosh, Dreama G. Moon and Thomas K. Nakayama, *Interrogating the Communicative Power of Whiteness* (New York: Routledge, 2018).
12 Trysh Travis, *The Language of the Heart: A Cultural History of the Recovery Movement from Alcoholics Anonymous to Oprah Winfrey* (Chapel Hill, NC: University of North Carolina Press, 2010), http://ebookcentral.proquest.com/lib/lehighlibrary-ebooks/detail.action?docID=475211, 188–9.
13 Ibid., 188–9.

14 Shana R. Blessing, "12 Steps Down: The Road from Recovery," *Off Our Backs* 20, no. 4 (1990): 19.
15 Ibid.
16 Ibid.
17 Holly Whitaker, "Opinion | The Patriarchy of Alcoholics Anonymous," *The New York Times*, December 28, 2019, sec. Opinion, https://www.nytimes.com/2019/12/27/opinion/alcoholics-anonymous-women.html.
18 Ibid.
19 Valli, "The Misinformation about Alcoholics."
20 William L. White, Sanders, Mark and Tanya Sanders, "Addiction in the African American Community: The Recovery Legacies of Frederick Douglass and Malcolm X," *Counselor* 7, no. 5 (2006): 53–8.
21 Ibid.
22 Ibid.
23 Ibid.
24 Keith Humphreys, Brian E. Mavis, and Bertram E. Stöffelmayr, "Chapter 7. Are Twelve-Step Programs Appropriate for Disenfranchised Groups? Evidence from a Study of Posttreatment Mutual Help Involvement," *Prevention in Human Services* 11, no. 1 (January 1, 1994): 165–79, https://doi.org/10.1080/10852359409511201.
25 William L. White and Mark Sanders, "Addiction and Recovery among African Americans before 1900," *Counselor* 3, no. 6 (2002): 64–6.
26 William L. White, "Introduction," in *The Red Road to Wellbriety* (Colorado Springs, CO: White Bison, n.d.).
27 Valli.
28 Jay-Z., *Magna Carta … Holy Grail* (New York, NY: RocNation, Universal, 2013), accessed June 4, 2021, https://www.amazon.com/Magna-Carta-Holy-Grail-Explicit/dp/B00DMRNMRQ.
29 The Everybodyfields, "The Red Rose," in *Halfway There: Electricity of the South* (Concord, NC: Ramseur Records/Red, 2004).
30 Ibid.
31 Michael Muhammad Knight, *Why I Am a Five Percenter*, Illustrated edition (New York: TarcherPerigee, 2011).
32 Ibid.

BIBLIOGRAPHY

Academy of Ideas. *Carl Jung, the Shadow, and the Dangers of Psychological Projection*, 2018. Accessed July 28, 2021. https://www.youtube.com/watch?v=nI-Ko-d29X4.
Adorno, Theodor W. *Negative Dialectics*. Translated by E. B. Ashton. London: Routledge, 1990.
Adult Children of Alcoholics & Dysfunctional Families Website. "Steps." Accessed July 27, 2021. https://adultchildren.org/literature/steps/.
Adult Children of Alcoholics World Service Organization. *Adult Children: Alcoholic/Dysfunctional Families*. First Edition. Lakewood, CA: Adult Children of Alcoholics World Service Organization, 2006.
Adult Children of Alcoholics World Service Organization. *Newcomer Pamphlet*. Lakewood, CA: Adult Children of Alcoholics World Service Organization, 2014.
Adult Children of Alcoholics World Service Organization. *Twelve Steps of Adult Children Steps Workbook*. Torrance, CA: Adult Children of Alcoholics World Service Organization, 2007.
Altizer, Thomas J. J. *The Descent into Hell: A Study of the Radical Reversal of the Christian Consciousness*. First Edition. Philadelphia, PA: Lippincott, 1970.
Anderson, Carol. *White Rage*. Reprint Edition. New York: Bloomsbury Adult, 2017.
Assmann, Jan. *Moses the Egyptian: The Memory of Egypt in Western Monotheism*. New Edition. Cambridge, MA: Harvard University Press, 1998.
Baldwin, James. "Letter from a Region in My Mind." *The New Yorker*. November 10, 1962. Accessed July 1, 2021. https://www.newyorker.com/magazine/1962/11/17/letter-from-a-region-in-my-mind.
BBC.com. "Sex Abuse and the Catholic Church." August 20, 2018, sec. World. https://www.bbc.com/news/world-44209971.
Bible Gateway. "Bible Gateway Passage: Exodus 3 - New International Version." Accessed May 24, 2021. https://www.biblegateway.com/passage/?search=Exodus%203&version=NIV.
Bible Gateway. "Bible Gateway Passage: James 2 - Revised Standard Version." Accessed March 8, 2019. https://www.biblegateway.com/passage/?search=James±2&version=RSV.
Bible Gateway. "Bible Gateway Passage: John 1 - New International Version." Accessed May 22, 2021. https://www.biblegateway.com/passage/?search=John%201&version=NIV.
Big Head Scientist. "Big Head Scientist." Accessed February 9, 2019. http://bigheadscientist.tumblr.com/post/131182353425/the-legend-of-general-monk-monk-it-took-yaqub-600.
Blessing, Shana R. "12 Steps Down: The Road from Recovery." *Off Our Backs* 20, no. 4 (1990): 19.
Bonhoeffer, Dietrich. *The Cost of Discipleship*. New York, NY: Simon and Schuster, 1959.

Brach, Tara. *Radical Acceptance: Embracing Your Life with the Heart of a Buddha*. Reprint Edition. New York; Toronto: Bantam, 2004.

Bradley, Michael. *The Iceman Inheritance: Prehistoric Sources of Western Man's Racism, Sexism and Aggression*. Reprint Edition. New York, NY: Kayode Publications, 1991.

Burroughs, Edgar Rice. *The Beasts of Tarzan*. Grosset & Dunlap, 1916.

Burroughs, Edgar Rice. *Jungle Tales of Tarzan*. New York, NY: Grosset & Dunlap, 1919.

Calvin, John. "Calvin's Commentaries, Vol. 3: Harmony of the Law, Part I: Exodus 3." Accessed June 10, 2021. https://www.sacred-texts.com/chr/calvin/cc03/cc03006.htm.

"Catholic Church Child Sexual Abuse Scandal." *BBC News*. February 26, 2019, sec. World. Accessed June 5, 2021. https://www.bbc.com/news/world-44209971.

The Churchman. Volume 85, Jan–June. Churchman Company, 1902.

Combs, Cristina. "Part I: Recovery from White Conditioning: Building Anti-Racist Practice and Community." *Center for Practice Transformation* (blog). Accessed June 4, 2021. https://practicetransformation.umn.edu/webinars/part-i-recovery-from-white-conditioning-building-anti-racist-practice-and-community/.

Cone, James H. *A Black Theology of Liberation*. Twentieth Anniversary Edition. Maryknoll, NY: Orbis Books, 1990.

Conrad, Joseph. *The Nigger of the Narcissus: A Tale of the Forecastle*. New York, NY: Doubleday, Page, 1919.

Courdea – HISTORY. Accessed March 7, 2019. https://www.menergy.org/about-us/history-2/.

Defoe, Daniel. *The Political History of the Devil, as Well Ancient as Modern: In Two Parts; Part I. Containing a State of the Devil's Circumstances, and the Various Turns of His Affairs ... ; Part II. Containing His More Private Conduct, down to the Present Times ...* London: Printed for T. Warner, 1726. http://archive.org/details/politicalhistory1726defo.

DiAngelo, Robin. "White Fragility." *The International Journal of Critical Pedagogy* 3, no. 3 (May 16, 2011), http://libjournal.uncg.edu/ijcp/article/view/249.

DiAngelo, Robin. *White Fragility: Why It's So Hard for White People to Talk about Racism*. Reprint Edition. Boston: Beacon Press, 2018.

Driscoll, Christopher M. "MRBlog: On the Journey to White Shame." December 8, 2014. https://marginalia.lareviewofbooks.org/mrblog-journey-white-shame-christopher-driscoll/.

Driscoll, Christopher M. *White Lies: Race and Uncertainty in the Twilight of American Religion*. London: Routledge, 2016.

DuBois, W.E.B. *The Souls of Black Folk*. New York, NY: Dover Publications, 1903.

DuBois, W.E.B. *Darkwater: Voices from within the Veil*. New York, NY: Cosimo, Inc., 2007.

DuRocher, Kristina. *Raising Racists: The Socialization of White Children in the Jim Crow South*. Lexington, KY: University Press of Kentucky, 2011.

Elibert, Mark. "A Timeline of JAY-Z and Drake's Competitive Relationship." *Billboard*. Accessed February 5, 2019. https://www.billboard.com/articles/columns/hip-hop/8470558/jay-z-drake-relationship-timeline.

The Everybodyfields. "The Red Rose." In *Halfway There: Electricity of the South*. Ramseur Records/Red, 2004.

Fabian, Johannes. *Time and the Other: How Anthropology Makes Its Object*. New York, NY: Columbia University Press, 2002.

Feuerbach, Ludwig. *The Essence of Christianity*. Buffalo, NY: Prometheus Books, 1989.

Floyd-Thomas, Stacey M. *Mining the Motherlode: Methods in Womanist Ethics*. Cleveland, OH: Pilgrim Press, 2006.

Freud, Anna. *The Ego and the Mechanisms of Defence*. London: Routledge, 1992.

Freud, Sigmund. *Moses and Monotheism*. First Edition. United States: Vintage, 1955.

Freud, Sigmund. *The Future of an Illusion*. Peterborough, CA: Broadview Press, 2012.

Gottehrer, Barry. *The Mayor's Man*. First Edition. Garden City, NY: Doubleday, 1975.

Gray, Biko. "The Traumatic Mysticism of Othered Others: Blackness, Islam, and Esotericism in the Five Percenters." *Correspondences* 7, no. 1 (2019): 201–37.
Greenwood, James. *Silas the Conjurer: His Travels and Perils.* Whitefish, MT: Kessinger Publishing, LLC, 2010.
Hendricks, Gay, and Kathlyn Hendricks. *Conscious Loving: The Journey to Co-Commitment.* Reprint Edition. New York: Bantam, 1992.
Homer. *The Iliad.* Translated by Robert Fagles. London: Penguin Books, 1990.
Humphreys, Keith, Brian E. Mavis, and Bertram E. Stöffelmayr. "Chapter 7. Are Twelve-Step Programs Appropriate for Disenfranchised Groups? Evidence from a Study of Posttreatment Mutual Help Involvement." *Prevention in Human Services* 11, no. 1 (January 1, 1994): 165–79. https://doi.org/10.1080/10852359409511201.
Jackson, Jr., John L. *Harlemworld: Doing Race and Class in Contemporary Black America.* Chicago: The University of Chicago Press, 2003.
Jay-Z, *Magna Carta … Holy Grail.* RocNation, 2013. Accessed June 4, 2021. https://www.amazon.com/Magna-Carta-Holy-Grail-Explicit/dp/B00DMRNMRQ.
Jay-Z & Jay Electronica. "We Made It: Remix." Accessed July 20, 2021. https://www.youtube.com/watch?v=iaLIzQJLBz0.
John Theede. *Tony A Talk New Steps for ACA*, 2017. Accessed July 28, 2021. https://www.youtube.com/watch?v=LnwoilL0q9E.
Johnson, Sylvester A., and Steven Weitzman, eds. *The FBI and Religion: Faith and National Security before and after 9/11.* First Edition. Oakland, CA: University of California Press, 2017.
Jung, C. G. *The Essential Jung.* Edited by Anthony Storr. Princeton, NJ: Princeton University Press, 1999.
Jung, C. G. *The Undiscovered Self: With Symbols and the Interpretation of Dreams.* Princeton University Press, 2012.
Keating, Thomas. *Intimacy with God: An Introduction to Centering Prayer.* Third Edition. New York, NY: Crossroad, 2009.
Kegan, Robert. *The Evolving Self: Problem and Process in Human Development.* Reprint Edition. Cambridge; London: Harvard University Press, 1982.
Keller, Rosemary Skinner, and Rosemary Radford Ruether. *In Our Own Voices: Four Centuries of American Women's Religious Writing.* Louisville, KY: Westminster John Knox Press, 2000.
Kimmel, Michael. *Angry White Men: American Masculinity at the End of an Era.* New York, NY: PublicAffairs, 2017.
Kimmerer, Robin Wall. *Braiding Sweetgrass: Indigenous Wisdom, Scientific Knowledge, and the Teaching of Plants.* Minneapolis, MN: Milkweed Editions, 2013.
Knight, Michael Muhammad. *Blue-Eyed Devil: A Road Odyssey through Islamic America.* Illustrated Edition. Brooklyn: Soft Skull, 2009.
Knight, Michael Muhammad. *Why I Am a Five Percenter.* Illustrated Edition. New York: TarcherPerigee, 2011.
Lancer, Darlene. *Conquering Shame and Codependency: 8 Steps to Freeing the True You.* Center City, MN: Hazelden Publishing, 2014.
Loescher, Burt Garfield. *The History of Rogers' Rangers.* San Mateo, CA,1946.
Long, Charles H. *Significations: Signs, Symbols, and Images in the Interpretation of Religion.* Second Edition. Aurora, CO: The Davies Group Publishers, 1999.
Lord Jamar. *Supreme Mathematics (Born Mix) The 5% Album.* New York, NY: BabyGrande/Koch, 2006.
Malcolm X. *The Autobiography of Malcolm X: As Told to Alex Haley.* New York, NY: Ballantine Books, 1987.
Mason, William. *A Spiritual Treasury for the Children of God: Consisting of a Meditation for Each Morning in the Year, Upon Select Texts of Scripture: Humbly Intended to*

Establish the Faith, Promote the Comfort, and Influence the Practice of the Followers of the Lamb. New York: Deare and Andrews, 1803.

McIntosh, Dawn Marie D., Dreama G. Moon, and Thomas K. Nakayama. *Interrogating the Communicative Power of Whiteness*. London: Routledge, 2018.

Menakem, Resmaa. *My Grandmother's Hands: Racialized Trauma and the Pathway to Mending Our Hearts and Bodies*. Illustrated Edition. Las Vegas, NV: Central Recovery Press, 2017.

Merriman, Tony, and Vicky Cameron. "Risk-Taking: Behind the Warrior Gene Story." *The New Zealand Medical Journal* 120 (February 1, 2007).

Muhammad, Elijah. *Message to the Blackman in America*. Litchfield Park, AZ: Secretarius Memps Publications, 2006.

Muhammad, Master Fard. *The Supreme Wisdom Lessons By Master Fard Muhammad to His Servant: The Most Honorable Elijah Muhammad for The Lost-Found Nation of Islam In North America*. Edited by Suzanne Brawtley. Brawtley Press, 2014.

Murray, Hugh. "Clapperton's Second Journey." In *The African Continent: A Narrative of Discovery and Adventure*. London: T. Nelson & Sons, 1853.

Nietzsche, Friedrich. *The Will to Power*. New York: Vintage, 1968.

NPR.org. "Meadows, Tlaib Cool Down after Fiery Exchange over Racism at Cohen Hearing." Accessed March 1, 2019. https://www.npr.org/2019/02/28/699009651/meadows-tlaib-cool-down-after-fiery-exchange-over-racism-at-cohen-hearing.

Pagels, Elaine. *The Origin of Satan: How Christians Demonized Jews, Pagans, and Heretics*. Reprint Edition. New York, NY: Vintage, 1996.

Painter, Nell Irvin. *The History of White People*. Reprint Edition. New York: W. W. Norton & Company, 2011.

Perkinson, James. *White Theology: Outing Supremacy in Modernity*. New York: Palgrave Macmillan, 2004.

"Pied Piper of Hameln." Accessed May 28, 2021. http://www.pitt.edu/~dash/hameln.html.

Pinn, Anthony B. *Why Lord?: Suffering and Evil in Black Theology*. London and New York: Continuum International Publishing Group, 1999.

Ras Kass. *Soul On Ice*. Los Angeles, CA: Priority Records, 1996.

Ricoeur, Paul. *The Symbolism of Evil*. New York: Harper and Row Publishers, 1967.

Ryan, Dale S., and Jeff VanVonderen. "When Religion Goes Bad: Part 3—Religious Codependency." The National Association for Christian Recovery, February 16, 2013. https://www.nacr.org/center-for-spirituality-and-recovery/when-religion-goes-bad-part-3-religious-codependency.

RZA. *The Tao of Wu*. Reprint Edition. New York: Riverhead Books, 2010.

Sartre, Jean-Paul. *Being And Nothingness: An Essay in Phenomenological Ontology*. Translated by Hazel Barnes. London; New York: Routledge, 2003.

Sartre, Jean-Paul. *The Devil and the Good Lord, and Two Other Plays*. New York: Vintage Books/Random House, 1960.

Sartre, Jean-Paul. *No Exit and Three Other Plays*. New York: Vintage, 1989.

Shapiro, Fred R. "Who Wrote the Serenity Prayer?" *The Chronicle of Higher Education*, April 28, 2014. Accessed June 3, 2021. https://www.chronicle.com/article/who-wrote-the-serenity-prayer/.

Sloterdijk, Peter. *Rage and Time: A Psychopolitical Investigation*. Translated by Mario Wenning. Reprint Edition. New York: Columbia University Press, 2012.

Sloterdijk, Peter. *In The Shadow of Mount Sinai*. First Edition. Cambridge, UK; Malden, MA: Polity, 2015.

Smith, Lillian. *Killers of the Dream*. New York, NY: W. W. Norton & Company, 1994.

Southern Poverty Law Center. "Nation of Islam." Accessed May 24, 2021. https://www.splcenter.org/fighting-hate/extremist-files/group/nation-islam.

Taylor, Paul C. *Race: A Philosophical Introduction*. Hoboken, NJ: John Wiley & Sons, 2013.
"They Call Her 'The White Devil.'" *American Magazine* 79 (1915): 60–1.
Tillich, Paul. *Theology of Culture*. Edited by Robert C. Kimball. First Edition. London: Oxford University Press, 1964.
The Trained Nurse and Hospital Review. Lakeside Publishing Company, 1900.
Travis, Trysh. *The Language of the Heart: A Cultural History of the Recovery Movement from Alcoholics Anonymous to Oprah Winfrey*. Chapel Hill, NC: University of North Carolina Press, 2010.
"20 Years, 700 Victims: Southern Baptist Sexual Abuse Spreads as Leaders Resist Reforms." *Houston Chronicle*. February 10, 2019. https://www.houstonchronicle.com/news/investigations/article/Southern-Baptist-sexual-abuse-spreads-as-leaders-13588038.php.
"120 Lessons - 1-20, 1-10, 1-14, 1-40, 1-36 (20+10+14+40+36=120)." Accessed May 21, 2021. http://www.afrostyly.com/english/afro/diverse/120_lessons.htm.
Understanding, Supreme, and C'BS Alife Allah. *The Science of Self*. Third Edition. Atlanta, GA: Supreme Design, LLC, 2012.
Valli, Veronica. "The Misinformation about Alcoholics Anonymous and Sobriety by Veronica Valli—Veronica Valli." January 12, 2020. Accessed May 15, 2021. https://www.veronicavalli.com/blog/2020/1/12/the-misinformation-about-alcoholics-anonymous-and-sobriety-1.
Walker, Alice. "Uncle Remus, No Friend of Mine." *The Georgia Review* 66, no. 3 (2012): 635–37.
Watts, Alan. *The Book: On the Taboo against Knowing Who You Are*. Reissue Edition. New York: Vintage Books, 1989.
Watts, Alan. *Alan Watts—In the Academy: Essays and Lectures*. Edited by Peter J. Columbus and Donadrian L. Rice. Albany, NY: SUNY Press, 2017.
Weisenfeld, Judith. *New World A-Coming: Black Religion and Racial Identity during the Great Migration*. New York: NYU Press, 2017.
Whitaker, Holly. "Opinion | The Patriarchy of Alcoholics Anonymous." *The New York Times*, December 28, 2019, sec. Opinion. https://www.nytimes.com/2019/12/27/opinion/alcoholics-anonymous-women.html.
White, William L. *"Introduction" in The Red Road to Wellbriety*. Colorado Springs, CO: White Bison, n.d.
White, William L. *Slaying the Dragon: The History of Addiction Treatment and Recovery in America*. Second Edition. Bloomington, IL: Chestnut Health Systems, 2014.
White, William L., and Mark Sanders. "Addiction and Recovery among African Americans before 1900." *Counselor* 3, no. 6 (2002): 64–6.
White, William L., Mark Sanders, and Tanya Sanders. "Addiction in the African American Community: The Recovery Legacies of Frederick Douglass and Malcolm X." *Counselor* 7, no. 5 (2006): 53–8.
Wiegman, Robyn. "Whiteness Studies and the Paradox of Particularity." *Boundary* 2, no. 26.3 (1990): 115–150. Accessed May 21, 2021. http://xroads.virginia.edu/~DRBR2/wiegman.html.
Wilcockson, Arthur, ed. "The Pathway of 'True Light.'" *Zion's Witness: Published Monthly, Exclusively for the Sect Which Is Everywhere Spoken Against* Acts XXVIII, no. 22 (1866).
Williams, JNO. G. *The Rural Carolinian, 1870, Vol. 1: An Illustrated Magazine, of Agriculture, Horticulture and the Arts*. Edited by D. H. Jacques. London: Forgotten Books, 2017.

INDEX

abuse/abuser/abusive behavior 39, 46, 78, 130, 135–43, 148–9, 167, 169. *See also* trauma; violence
   cycles of abuse 142–5, 147, 149, 172
   distance phase 143–4
   domestic 15, 35, 37, 140, 142
   emotional 95, 141
   intimate partner abuse 36, 131, 140–1, 145
   make-up/honeymoon phase 142–4
   sexual (*see* sexual abuse/trauma)
   share feelings 145–6
   substance 106, 195 (*see also* alcoholic/alcoholism)
   yelling 39, 141–2
accountability 140, 184
Adam and Eve 73
addiction 103, 108, 123, 129–30, 158, 161–2, 165, 184–7, 192–3
Adult Children 123, 125–7, 131, 153, 155, 158, 163, 171, 181
Adult Children of Alcoholics (ACA) recovery program 11, 37–8, 123–4, 126–7, 153–5, 159, 183–4
   ACA Workbook 158, 171
   Alcoholics Anonymous (AA) 125–6, 161–3, 183, 186–9
   Laundry List traits (14 Traits of an Adult Child) 124, 170
   Narcotics Anonymous (NA) 189
   Solution 125–6
   Tony A's version (of Step Program) 174, 206 n.5, 206 n.11
   Twelve-Step fellowship 183–4, 186–90
   Twelve-Step Program of 11, 37, 123, 125–6, 161–76, 183–90, 193
agriculture 48

Akkadian civilization 50
alcoholic/alcoholism 15, 30, 88, 103–4, 123–4, 126, 129–30, 154, 156, 158–9, 161–3, 169, 179, 184, 186–7, 192. *See also* para-alcoholics/para-alcoholism
alienation 34, 36, 180, 194
   vast alienation 129
Allah School in Mecca 42–3, 119–20, 166
allegory 5, 67–70, 72–6
   cultural allegory 74
ambiguity 39, 41, 78, 138–9, 166
Anderson, Carol 133–5, 137
Andrews, Jill 192–3
anger management 36, 38. *See also* stress management
Anglophone 60, 74
Anishinaabe peoples (Windigo myths) 5–6
antagonism 8, 12, 51–2, 118
anthropodicy 26
anthropology 47, 57, 78
anti-black racism 34, 56, 63, 70, 97, 111, 134, 140, 156, 192. *See also* race/racism/racist
antisemitic/antisemitism 52, 99–101, 108
anti-white 86–7, 101
anxiety 44, 46, 53, 60, 90–1, 95–6, 106, 138–9, 159–60
apophatic identity 106, 118
arrested emotional development 10, 38–9, 96, 123, 191
Asia/Asians 60
   Asiatic Black man 12, 61
Assmann, Jan 52
   Mosaic distinction 9, 50–1, 55

atheism 9, 33, 55–6, 184, 193. *See also* theism
  epistemological atheist 46
  moral 46
  racialized 193
St. Augustine 29
authentic/authenticity 75, 134
autoethnography 7, 12

Baldwin, James, "Letter from a Region in My Mind" 75
behavioral intervention 137, 142, 150
The Bible 25, 41, 53–4, 191–2. *See also* Hebrew Bible
biblical monotheism 9, 50–1. *See also* monotheism/monotheistic God
black culture 26, 66, 119, 128, 191–2
black devils 57–9. *See also* white devils
black esoteric traditions 2, 6–7, 11, 13, 17, 19–20, 47, 64, 66, 75, 88, 100, 115, 176, 181, 190–1
black freedom 69, 187
black Muslims/black Islam 20, 24, 27, 65
blackness 3–4, 8, 21, 23, 43, 46–7, 54, 69, 102, 119. *See also* whiteness
  ontological blackness 47, 56
black people 4, 12, 14, 19, 22, 27, 29–30, 34, 47, 53–4, 56–7, 60–2, 66, 69, 71, 85, 87–8, 101, 103–4, 111–13, 115, 120, 134, 136, 140, 147, 149, 152, 154, 160, 166–7, 169, 181–2, 187, 192. *See also* brown people; white people; yellow people
  black children 128–9, 157
  black pastors 35
  black woman 4, 38, 42, 106–7, 115, 117, 119, 130, 157, 188–9
  as reference to God 6, 12, 23–5, 44–5, 47, 49, 53–4, 56, 73, 120
  sacrificial murders of 45
Blessing, Shana R. 185–6, 188
Bonhoeffer, Dietrich 34
boundary maintenance 8, 146–7
Bourdieu, Pierre 158
Brach, Tara, *Radical Acceptance* 175–6
Bradley, Michael, *The Iceman Inheritance: Prehistoric Sources of Western Man's Racism, Sexism and Aggression* 136–7
brown people 12, 14, 25, 27, 47, 49, 54, 60, 88, 101, 104, 112, 115, 130–1, 134, 136, 147, 149, 152, 154, 157, 160, 166–7, 169, 182. *See also* black people; white people; yellow people
Burroughs, Edgar Rice, *Jungle Tales of Tarzan* 59–60

Caddo Parish (Bloody Caddo) 29
Calvin, John 42
Cameron, Donaldina 199 n.17
Cantor, Daniel 37–8
Caucasian (white man) 61–2, 70. *See also* white people
Cermak, Timmen L. 103, 106
  diagnostic criteria of codependent person 104–5
chauvinism 113, 190
childhood abandonment 103, 170, 206 n.11
Christian/Christianity 8–9, 72, 77–8, 81–2, 108, 181, 188. *See also* Islam; Judaism
  European Christian Reformation 78
  Western 55, 78, 101
  white 20, 31–2, 34–6, 45, 59, 101, 108–9, 183
  White American Christianity 32, 183
The Christian Church (Disciples of Christ) 29–30
church 29–30, 77–8, 82, 189
  black pastors 35
  racial separation 34
  sexual abuse/abuser in (*see* sexual abuse/trauma)
  white churches 29, 33–6, 38, 46, 54–6
The Churchman 59
civilizations 23, 49–50, 62, 72, 93. *See also* Akkadian civilization; Egypt/Egyptian civilization; Mesopotamian civilization; Sumerian civilization
Civil Rights Movement 167
Clapperton, Hugh 58
Clarence 13X (Father Allah) 6, 23–4, 43–4, 65
  arrest and release of 85–7
  diagnosed with schizophrenia 85–7, 91
  and FBI 87
  and Gottehrer 87–8, 92
  and Roberts 87–8
clean pain 16–17. *See also* dirty pain
clinical psychology 7, 12, 35, 107, 112

Cluster C Personality Disorder 105
codependency/codependents 2, 10–11, 32, 39, 45, 56, 66, 88, 95–7, 99, 101–8, 114–15, 123–5, 130, 134, 137–41, 143, 145, 147, 152–4, 157, 159–64, 167, 172, 174, 176, 183–8, 189, 191–3
    codependent dysfunction 97, 107, 125, 165
    codependent relationship 8, 10, 89, 185
    codependent reliance 45, 101, 105, 126, 132, 135, 191, 193
    emotional attachments 160
    with God 8
    and intergenerational transmission of trauma 15
    intrinsic 184
    parent 103, 123, 125, 179
    psychological 30, 102, 162
    racial 105
    religious 7–9, 13, 15, 17, 108–9, 163, 196 n.18
    shame-based 126
    and toxic masculinity 38
    well-intentioned 130
Cohen, Michael 117
Combs, Cristina 162–3
communication 147–9, 173
    emotional 146
    intersubjective (*see* intersubjective communication)
compassion 120, 127, 135–7
Cone, James 20, 46–7, 54, 56
confession 32, 77, 130
Conrad, Joseph, *The Nigger of the Narcissus: A Tale of the Forecastle* 59
Cooper, Gary 155, 160
cosmic order of the universe 18
covenant 9, 42, 52, 55
crisis of faith 10, 180
critical race theory 135
culture 9, 20–1, 24, 50–1, 56, 140, 158, 180, 189
    call-out/cancel 174
    cultural allegory 74
    cultural contact 4, 14–16
    cultural contingency 76
    cultural inheritance 74, 76, 82
    cultural resources 7, 187, 191, 193
    hip hop (*see* hip hop culture)
    popular 2, 7, 50, 68, 191
    western 10, 133

Davis, Angela 183–4, 188
defense mechanisms 7, 90–1
defilement/sin 76–7
Defoe, Daniel
    on devil 57–8
    The Political History of the Devil 57
    on race 58
    relationship between God and the Devil 57–8
demonarchy 33
dependent personality disorder 105
Deuteronomy 28 94–5, 97, 104
devil(s) 2, 5–7, 10, 12–13, 17, 21, 27, 31–2, 38–9, 61–4, 66, 70–1, 74–6, 79, 82, 89, 99, 102, 106, 112, 135, 162, 172, 181–2. *See also* evil; God
    black devils 57–9
    Defoe on 57–8
    exceptional devil 64–6, 112, 193
    racialized 58
    white 57–60, 65, 101, 105, 181 (*see also* white people, as (white) devils)
Diagnostic and Statistical Manual of Mental Disorders (*DSM-5*) 105
DiAngelo, Robin
    emotional reactions of white people 151
    white fragility 102–4, 117, 152–4, 158
    White Fragility: Why It's So Hard for White People to Talk about Racism 151
dingir (symbolic representation of God) 50
dirty pain 16–17. *See also* clean pain
discernment 179, 181–2
divine/divinity 10, 61, 73, 87–8, 119–20
    black divinity 45, 47, 56, 119, 166, 181–2, 191
domestic abuse 15, 35, 37, 140, 142. *See also* abuse/abuser/abusive behavior; violence
double-consciousness 3
Douglass, Frederick 64, 187
Drake 19, 21–2
Driscoll, Bobby 128–9, 131–2
DuBois, W. E. B. 3, 8, 10, 105
    blackness and whiteness 4
    double-consciousness 3

egalitarian/egalitarianism 65, 190
Egypt/Egyptian civilization 49–52, 55, 72, 99
    Amenhotep IV 50–1
    Lower/Upper Egypt 49
    Pharaohs 42, 47, 49, 53
Elibert, Mark 19
embodiment of evil 2, 27, 181
emotions 154–5, 158–9, 161. *See also* feelings
    Checking In with 154–5, 158, 173
    emotional awareness 143, 150, 154–6, 159
    emotional dysfunction 103, 123, 140, 158, 163–4, 187
    emotional dysregulation 39, 104, 131, 140, 147, 152–4, 159, 161, 163, 194
    emotional explosions 144, 152
    emotional expression 154
    emotional intelligence 135–6, 150, 154, 173
    emotional manipulation 145, 152–3
    emotional maturation 10–12, 17
    emotional pressure 144, 149
    emotional processing 143, 145, 156
    emotional regulation 8–9, 108, 111, 123, 126, 135, 143, 146, 152–8, 161
    emotional response 76, 140, 152, 158
    healthy 140, 142–3
    for men (anger and sexual desire) 153
    word bank of 158–9
empathy 126–7, 137, 174
energy 127, 147, 166, 172
    emotional energy 142
epigenetics 136–7. *See also* genetics
ethnicity 5, 65, 140, 169
ethnographic vitalism 12
euphemism 41, 57–8, 117
Europe/European 15, 25–6, 58, 62, 70–1, 77, 81, 100, 105, 114, 118, 176, 187
    European Christian Reformation 78
    European Jews 101
The Everybodyfields band 190, 192
    "The Red Rose" 190, 192–4
evil 2, 5, 24, 27, 51, 57, 60, 62, 70, 76–83, 95, 115–16, 138, 172, 181. *See also* goodness
exceptional devils 64–6, 112, 193
Exodus 100
    Exodus 2:21 73
    Exodus 3 165

Exodus 3:6 41, 55
Exodus 19 42
external pressure 142–5. *See also* internal pressure

fallen angel 61
Faludi, Susan 185
family dysfunction 30–2, 46, 103, 105, 122, 126–31, 158, 163, 167
Family Services of Philadelphia 36
Fardan, Dorothy Blake 65–6
Farrakhan, Louis 23, 65, 101
feelings 5, 8, 65, 90–1, 95, 103–5, 107, 112, 114, 124–6, 129–31, 133, 143, 145–7, 152–5, 158. *See also* emotions
    feelings sentence 158–9
    negative 91, 146, 148, 152, 174
femininity 185
Feuerbach, Ludwig 47, 53, 108
fight-or-flight mode 138–9, 153
Five Percenters/Five Percent movement. *See* Nation of Gods and Earths (NGE)
Floyd-Thomas, Stacey M. 168
forgiveness 174, 193–4
Freud, Anna 89–91
    defense mechanisms 90–1
Freud, Sigmund, 89, 126, 188, 191
    neurosis 57, 90–3
    on parts of psyche/mind (Id, Ego, and Superego) 90–1, 93, 95–7
    psychoanalysis 89
    on religion 89–94, 107
    universal neurosis 91, 107

Galatians 3:28 55
Garrison, William Lloyd 64
gender 32–3, 44, 46, 53, 56, 75, 88, 107, 130, 143, 160, 164, 167, 169, 184–5, 187, 189–90. *See also* race/racism/racist
Genesis 73
    Genesis 6 100
    Genesis 19 73
    Genesis 23:11 73
genetics 11–12, 14, 38–9, 62, 66, 103, 135–6. *See also* epigenetics
Glaucon 67–8
God 8, 10, 20, 22–3, 29, 31, 35, 41, 44, 61, 70, 78–9, 85–6, 89, 93–6, 100–1, 104, 106, 108–9, 118–20, 126–7,

130, 162, 164–6, 170–2, 175, 181–2, 191–2. *See also* devil(s); evil; God; Satan/Satanic
Allah 25
An 50
Anunnaki 50
archaeological records 47
Aten 50
Azrael 43, 65–6
black God 17–18, 20, 35, 47, 182, 191–4
black men as reference to 6, 12, 23–5, 44–5, 47, 49, 53–4, 56, 73, 120
codependency with 8
distance from God 76–7
excuse for bad behavior 2
god-idols 89
Godself 42, 99
grace 34
honorary 43
Judeo-Christian 29, 47, 54
monotheistic God (*see also* monotheism/monotheistic God)
mystery God 6, 10, 17, 21, 29, 33, 41, 46–7, 53–6, 107, 126, 193
oppressors' (God of slavery) 54
symbolic representation of 50
white God 34, 43, 47, 53, 65, 192–3
Yahweh (YHWY) 41, 50–6, 99, 120, 165–6
goodness 77–8, 80–2. *See also* evil
Gospels 55, 100
Gottehrer, Barry 87–8, 92
grafting process 11, 25, 62, 135
Gray, Biko Mandela 21
Greece/Greek 38, 73, 99–100, 118
Greenwood, James, *Silas the Conjurer: His Travels and Perils* 59
Gwai (ghost/devil) 60
Gweilo (white/foreign devil) 60

Harris, Joel Chandler 128
heal/healing process 2, 16, 125–6, 163, 170–1, 187
Hebrew Bible 41, 50, 73, 118, 165. *See also* The Bible
hegemony 189
Hellenistic dynasty 100
Hendricks (Gay and Kathyrn) 173
higher power, submission to 126–7, 165–6, 171–2

hip hop culture 6, 11, 21, 24, 27, 34–6, 44–5, 56, 66, 191–2. *See also* rap/rap songs
as religion 19–21, 36, 44
Homer, *The Iliad* 133
homophobia 130–1, 162, 179, 184, 186, 193
Hoover, J. Edgar 7, 85–8
human/human being 1–2, 4–5, 10, 14, 34, 53, 105, 115, 139
humanistic life philosophy 6, 24
humanity 2, 11, 17, 50–1
humility 11, 171–2, 179–80
recessive human traits 25
response to "No" 2–5, 10
special kind of human 6
suffering 35, 54
Hume, David 54
Husserl, Edmund 147, 149

idealism 68, 81, 147
imposter syndrome 156
indigenous people 5–6, 47, 60, 106. *See also* Anishinaabe peoples
individualism 118
intergenerational transmission 15, 93, 125–6
internal pressure 142–5. *See also* external pressure
interracial dialogue 66, 152, 154
intersectionality 7, 15, 44, 53, 56, 129–31, 140
intersubjective communication 88, 92, 119–20, 126–7, 144–5, 153, 156, 159, 166, 171, 173, 175, 194
intersubjective exchange 10, 17, 115, 119, 138–40, 149, 166, 171, 182, 184, 191, 194
intersubjective experiences 120, 125, 139–40, 191
intimate enemy. *See* Satan/Satanic
intimate partners (abuse) 36, 131, 140–1, 145, 148, 160, 173
Isaiah 14 100
Islam 9, 25, 64–5, 129. *See also* Christian/Christianity; Judaism
black Muslims/black Islam 20, 24, 27
Islamic Shahada 20
Israel 99–101
ancestors of 165
Israelites 41–2, 50–5, 94, 99–100, 165

Jackson, John L., Jr., *Harlemworld* 12–13
Jay Electronica 19–21, 26, 166, 191
Jay-Z 19–21, 26, 166, 190, 192
    "Heaven" 190–1, 194
Jews/Jewish 23, 42, 72, 99–101, 181
Johnson, Sylvester 119
Josephus' *The Antiquity of the Jews* 73
Judaism 9, 41
Judeo-Christian 101, 104, 165, 190
    (mystery) God 29, 47, 54, 93
Jung, Carl 112, 119–20, 188, 191
    ethnocentrism 114
    notion of shadow work/shadow 112–16
    revolutionary behavior 113
    The Undiscovered Self 113–14

Kaufman, Gordon 20, 180
Keating, Thomas 2, 10–11, 16
Kegan, Robert 138–9
Kimmel, Michael 111, 134–5, 137
Kimmerer, Robin Wall
    Braiding Sweetgrass: Indigenous Wisdom, Scientific Knowledge, and the Teachings of Plants 3
    The Windigo myths (cannibal monster) 5
King, Martin Luther, Jr. 34
Ku-Klux-Klan 29–30
Knight, Michael Muhammad 11, 66, 86, 129–30
    and Azrael (God) 65–6
    exceptional devil 64–5
Knowledge of Self 7, 10, 12, 23–7, 37–8, 44–5, 47, 52–3, 56, 60–2, 64, 66, 69, 73, 76, 82, 89, 106, 112, 114, 119, 127, 136, 167, 169, 181, 184, 187, 191–3

Lancer, Darlene 122, 129
liberalism 70, 114, 183
Lindsay, John 43, 87
Logos 147
Long, Charles 51–2, 55, 103
Lord Jamar 44, 129
Lost-Found Lessons (120 Lessons) 60–2
love 35, 108
    self-love 10–11
    unconditional 172–3
Loving Kindness meditation 175

Lower Egypt 49. *See also* Upper Egypt
Luther, Martin 57

Maccabees 99–100
Malcolm X 6–7, 22–3, 65–6, 86, 101, 187
Martin Luther Protestant Reformation 77
Marx, Karl, on religion 107–8
masculinity 19, 43, 89, 92, 102, 112, 116, 129, 134–5, 164–5, 185
    hypermasculinity 44
    toxic 14, 38
    white 2, 7, 11, 26–7, 38, 69, 102, 104, 107, 149, 154–5, 161–6, 170, 173, 181, 184–5, 188–9, 193
Mason, William, *A Spiritual Treasury for the Children of God* 58
Mathew, Theobald 187
Mecca 70–1
meditation 154–5, 162, 175–6
Melville, Hermann, *Moby Dick* 67
Menakem, Resmaa
    clean/dirty pain 16–17
    intergenerational transmission of trauma 15
    My Grandmother's Hands: Racialized Trauma and the Pathway to Mending Our Hearts and Bodies 13
    on racial trauma (trauma response) 13–15
    soul wounds 14–15
    white-body-supremacy 14–15
men's rights movement 134
Mesopotamian civilization 49–50
microscopic truth 173
Million Man March (1995) 22–3
mindfulness techniques 154–5, 175
misogyny 46, 97, 112, 130–1, 179, 186
misotheism 46, 53–4, 56, 108
Mohammed, Warith Deen 65
monotheism/monotheistic God 6, 8–9, 17, 46–7, 50, 52, 54–5, 76, 88–9, 94, 97, 100, 103–4, 115, 126, 131, 154, 156, 165, 172, 184, 194, 196 n.18. *See also* polytheism
    biblical 9, 50–1
Mosaic religion 17, 51
Moses 25, 41, 51, 72–3, 165
Muhammad, Elijah 23–4, 60–2, 70, 73–5, 86, 135, 137
    on Jewish rituals 72

Message to the Blackman in America 62, 70–2
   white *vs.* black personality traits 63
Muhammad, W. D. Fard 6, 19, 24, 60–2
murder 48, 61–2, 90, 94, 143, 166. *See also* violence
   sacrificial murders of black people 45
Muslims 24, 42, 61, 72, 85–6. *See also* black Muslims/black Islam; Christian/Christianity; Islam
mystery God 6, 10, 17, 21, 29, 33, 41, 46–7, 53–6, 107, 126, 193

narcissism 11, 103, 105, 165
Nation of Gods and Earths (NGE) 6–7, 10, 12, 20–1, 24–5, 36, 42–4, 47, 56, 63–5, 85–9, 101, 112, 115, 119–20, 129, 192
Nation of Islam (NOI) 6–7, 20–5, 47, 60, 65, 75, 86, 88, 100–1, 192
Native Americans 5, 59, 168, 187
natural order (of cosmos/universe) 10–11
Neanderthals 136
negative feedback 3–5, 8, 10
nervous system 138–9
New Testament 55. *See also* Old Testament
New World 117, 187
Niebuhr, Reinhold 184
   Serenity Prayer 182–3
Nietzsche, Friedrich 164

objectification 117, 143, 152, 162
Old Testament 99. *See also* New Testament
ontology 10, 65, 80–2, 116, 127, 140, 165, 183
   ontological blackness 47, 56
Original Man 12, 23, 61, 72–3
Orwell, George, *Animal Farm* 67
Others/other people 1–3, 5, 8, 10–12, 15–16, 37, 39, 47, 51, 97, 102, 106, 116. *See also* self

Pagels, Elaine 100–1
   The Origin of Satan 99
Palen, Lewis Stanton
   The White Devil of the Black Sea 60
   The White Devil's Mate 60
para-alcoholics/para-alcoholism 124–5, 130, 163. *See also* alcoholic/alcoholism

patriarchy 15, 33, 36, 88–9, 96–7, 103–4, 107, 112, 131–2, 158, 185–6, 188, 192
Patton, Lynne 117
Peasants' Revolt 77–9
Perkinson, James 103
Peterson, Jordan 114
phenomenology 77–8, 147–9
phrenology 136
Pied Piper of Hamelin 121, 123
Pinn, Anthony B. 20, 35
Plato, "Allegory of the Cave" 67–70, 72–3
polytheism 49, 51. *See also* monotheism/monotheistic God
Poor Righteous Teachers 24, 62
positive thinking 174
post-traumatic stress disorder 139
powerlessness 161, 163, 186
Protestant 190
   American Protestantism 190
   Protestant Capitalism 188
   Protestant Reformation 77–8
psychology 7, 9, 15, 39, 78, 92, 135–6. *See also* clinical psychology

Quran 72

race/racism/racist 8, 11, 13, 15, 23, 33, 35, 38, 43–4, 46, 53–4, 59, 62–5, 69–70, 75, 88, 97, 103, 107, 111–14, 117, 120, 128–32, 134, 137, 140–1, 152, 156–8, 160–4, 167–9, 172, 179, 184, 188–90, 193. *See also* gender
   anti-black 34, 56, 63, 70, 97, 111, 134, 140, 156, 192
   on Asians 60
   Defoe on 58
   Karens 14, 136
   Menakem on racial trauma 13–14
   racial anxiety 44, 60
   racial separation 34
   scientific 114, 136
   slave 50
radical contingency 76
Ramirez, Erika 21
rap/rap songs. *See also* hip hop culture
   rappers 6, 19–20, 35–6, 44 (*see also* specific rappers)
   and religion 19–21
Ras Kass 2–3, 10–11
   "Nature of the Threat" 196 n.2

rationality 68
reality 20, 51, 54, 58, 67–9, 72–3, 112, 116, 119, 137, 163, 183
reciprocity 3, 5, 166
Reconstruction period 29, 59, 128–9
redemptive suffering theology 31
rehabilitation 92, 107, 131, 142, 184
religion 15, 19–20, 22, 24, 29, 35, 45–6, 103, 114–15, 120, 126–7, 130, 160–1, 169. *See also specific religions*
    Freud on 89–94, 107
    hip hop as 19–21, 36, 44
    Marx on 107–8
    patriarchal/patriarchal monotheistic 9, 17, 96
    religious beliefs 47, 49, 55, 126–7, 179
    religious codependency 7–9, 13, 15, 17, 108–9, 163, 196 n.18
    religious dysfunction 97, 126–7
    religious formation 9–10
    religious hegemony 189
    religious language 76–7, 88
    religious persecution 15
    religious rituals 72
Renaissance 77
Ricoeur, Paul 76–7, 82
Roberts, Burt 87–8
Rogers, Robert 58
Ryan, Dale S. 8–9
RZA 2–3, 10–11, 16

salient identities 53, 89, 109, 131, 185
salvation 27, 34, 45, 55, 61, 66
1 Samuel: 24 73
Sartre, Jean-Paul 125, 172, 180, 191
    The Devil and the Good Lord 77–83
Satan/Satanic 11, 57, 99–102. *See also* devil(s); evil; God
    Pagels on 99, 101
savage 25, 59, 61–2, 71–4, 113
scientific racism 114, 136
Second Wave feminism 185
segregation 62, 69, 156–7, 170
self 9–10, 12, 15, 20, 37, 55, 111, 119, 139, 165, 182, 193. *See also* Others/other people
    to know thyself 38, 159
    self-confidence 111
    self-denial 8, 10, 124, 129
    self-esteem 8, 105, 108, 138, 153, 182

self-hatred 7, 11, 27, 38, 112, 176, 182, 186, 192
self-help 7, 141, 174, 185, 187
self-image 10–12, 37, 111, 171
self-knowledge 112–13, 115
self-love 10–11, 171, 174, 176
self-worth 11–12
Seven Sleepers 72–3
sexism 107, 112, 114, 129–31, 140–1, 152, 156, 158, 162–3, 169–70, 172, 179, 184, 186, 188–90, 193
sex/sexuality 30, 134, 143, 168–9
sexual abuse/trauma 15–16, 30–4, 36, 38, 45, 54, 108, 126, 192
    by Catholic Priests 30
    demonarchy 33
Shakur, Tupac 76
shame 31, 54, 62, 83, 95, 122, 125–6, 129–31, 156–7, 169–70, 172, 174, 189, 193
sin/sinner 31–2, 76–7, 188
slavery/enslavement 4, 8, 34, 41–2, 47, 50, 54–5, 59, 67, 69, 82, 97, 99, 118, 157, 187
Sloterdijk, Peter 133
    covenant 9
    In the Shadow of Mount Sinai 52
Smith, Clarence Edward. *See* Clarence 13X (Father Allah)
Smith, Lillian 158, 170
    Killers of the Dream 156–7
social interaction 9, 138–9, 145, 147, 169
Social Strata Inventory 168–9, 173
Socrates 67–8, 70, 73
Song of the South movie 128–9, 131
Sophocles, *Oedipus Rex* 92–3
soul wounds 14–16
The Southern Poverty Law Center 7, 100, 196 n.15
spirit/spirit world 5, 12, 107, 158
spiritual awakening 175–6, 187
spiritual practice 180
Storr, Anthony 119
stress management 143. *See also* anger management
Sumerian civilization 50
supreme God 6, 9
Sūrah Eighteen (Quran) 72
survival traits 46, 170–1

talk therapy 37, 92, 107
Taylor, Paul 111

tetragrammaton 41, 165
theism 107, 165, 184. *See also* atheism; monotheism/monotheistic God; polytheism
theodicy 26
theological anthropology 57, 78
theological language 10
theophany 41–2, 44–5, 119–20, 166
Tillich, Paul 20, 27, 180
    Systematic Theology 55
Tlaib, Rashida 117, 120
totalitarianism 164
transparency 51–3, 55
trauma 15, 107, 130, 139, 157. *See also* abuse/abuser/abusive behavior; violence
    childhood 189
    intergenerational 14, 188, 193
    Menakem on racial trauma (trauma response) 13–15
    multigenerational 163
    sexual (*see* sexual abuse/trauma)
    unprocessed 12, 14–16, 39
Travis, Trysh 185
tribes 48–9
    confederated 118
    Israelites 41–2, 50–5
    nomadic 48
    profane 48–9
    totems 48–9, 51–2, 118
    Yoruba 58
tricknology 25–6, 70
troglodytes 73–4
Trump, Donald 117
truth 26, 38, 45, 58, 67–9, 76, 147, 181
    fundamental 149
    microscopic 173
    radical 149
    uncertainty 103, 138, 162

The United States 6, 46, 59–60, 87, 101, 176, 183
    American Protestantism 190
    Harlem 6, 24, 43, 45, 75, 120
    Shreveport 29
    types of white men in 85
Upper Egypt 49. *See also* Lower Egypt
US Congressional Hearings (2019) 117

Valli, Veronica 179–80, 186, 188
VanVonderen, Jeff 8–9

violence 48, 52–3, 55, 97, 136, 140, 143, 150, 152. *See also* trauma
    anti-black 14, 134
    domestic abuse 15, 35, 37, 140, 142
    interpersonal 131
    physical 39, 144
    white-on-white 101
vitalism 12–13

Walker, Alice 128–9
    vast alienation 129
Walker, David, *Appeal to the Coloured Citizens of the World* 58
Walker, Lenore E. 142
Walt Disney 128
Watts, Alan 154, 180–2, 191
    Hindu Vedanta 182
    meditation 155
Webster, John, *The White Devil: Or, the Tragedy of Paulo Giordano Ursini, Duke of Brachiano* 57
"We Made It: Remix" (Jay Electronica and Jay-Z) 19–22, 26, 166, 191
Westerners 9, 50, 60, 105, 133, 163, 180
western philosophy 107, 147, 149
Whitaker, Holly 186, 188
white devils 57–60, 65, 101, 105, 181. *See also* black devils
white feminism 185
white fragility 102–4, 117, 152–4, 158
whiteness 4, 8, 11, 33, 46, 54–5, 64, 66, 69, 88–9, 92, 101–3, 107, 116, 118, 129–30, 132, 157, 163–5, 174, 185, 188. *See also* blackness
white people 2–5, 11–12, 34, 53, 62, 65–6, 69–70, 72–3, 76, 89, 101, 106, 111–12, 114–15, 119, 131–2, 135–7, 148–9, 153–4, 156, 163, 180–2, 184, 188–9, 194, 196 n.18. *See also* black people; brown people; yellow people
    behaviors 151–2
    childish codependency 2, 5, 11, 16
    as (white) devils 2, 4–7, 10–11, 13, 17, 25–7, 37–8, 61, 63–4, 66, 70, 75, 89, 115–16 (*see also* white devil)
    marauders 136
    origin of 25
    privilege of 38, 54, 102, 149
    psychological theory of 12, 15, 62–3
    and shame 156

spiritual transformation for 15
to treat other people as problems 5–6
Western white men 5, 7, 60, 92, 133, 180
white children 62, 128–9, 157, 192
white masculinity 2, 7, 11, 26–7, 38, 69, 102, 104, 107, 149, 154–5, 161–6, 170, 173, 181, 184–5, 188–9, 193
white supremacy 14–15, 34, 42, 65–6, 70, 101, 112, 128–30, 132, 156–7, 162–3, 169, 194
White, William 187
Wiegman, Robyn 66
Williams, Delores, demonarchy 33

Williams, JNO. G., *The Rural Carolinian, 1870, Vol. 1: An Illustrated Magazine, of Agriculture, Horticulture and the Arts* 59
womanism 33, 168

Yahweh (YHWY) God 41, 50–6, 99, 120, 165–6
Yakub (black scientist) 11–12, 21–2, 25–7, 64, 70–1, 101, 135
yellow people 24, 118. *See also* black people; brown people; white people

Zen meditation 175